C000255426

PRAISE FOR *ETHICAL DATA AN INFORMATION MANAGEMENT*

'Many data-driven businesses and innovative technology companies have a poor understanding of the ethical considerations that should underpin decisions to collect and process personal data. However, getting it wrong can result in huge customer dissatisfaction, damage to brand reputation, a decline in stock market ratings, and investigations by regulators across the world.

This book challenges data-driven companies to pause and ask themselves, "Just because we can collect and do something interesting with data, should we?" Importantly, the book provides a framework for answering this question. And a particular strength is that it works through ethical considerations by discussing real-life and hypothetical scenarios.

Ethical Data and Information Management is an invaluable resource for information management professionals (including data protection officers) and start-up tech companies seeking to model good practice. It is an excellent a supplement to texts that address the substantive principles of the General Data Protection Regulation (and related national legislation), as it will deepen the reader's understanding of, inter alia, the purpose limitation and data minimization principles, privacy by design, data protection impact assessments, and the accountability principle.' **Karen McCullagh, Lecturer, School of Law, University of East Anglia**

'This is a welcome and timely book given the increasingly clear need to make ethics as key a consideration as data protection and privacy law. Ethics are necessary to shape values that have huge societal impact. This book places data ethics at the core of a data-driven world that has enormous consequences not just for individuals but for communities and broader society and indeed, as recent events show, for democracy. *Ethical Data and Information Management* will be accessible to a broad range of individuals as a general primer in the area, or as a coursework text for students.' **Pat Walshe, Managing Director, Privacy Matters Ltd; former Director of Privacy, GSMA**

'This book could not have come along at a better time. Big data is the focus of a great deal of attention, much of it because of unethical uses. People working in the field need to learn about ethics, and learn quickly, and this book is an ideal way. It is both accessible and erudite, and uses practical examples to illustrate key points. Readers will also find it useful as a reference point and as a guide before setting out on a project. I thoroughly recommend it.' **Paul Bernal, author, _Internet Privacy Rights: Rights to protect autonomy_**

'With the news full of stories about people abusing their access to information for their own gain and in order to manipulate democratic institutions, it is time to take a hard look at the ethics of data and information management. This book is informed not only by a deep knowledge of data management practices – particularly with respect to information quality – but also by a broad knowledge of other subjects: ethical theories, the challenges of balancing between individual rights and social needs, the history of the misuse of information, the social implications of technological change, and the effort to legislate and regulate the use of information. Add to this mix the human element of imagination. O'Keefe and O Brien make connections that many of us would miss. They develop thoughtful and thought-provoking analysis of this critical aspect of information management. And they present it clearly in this readable and engaging book.' **Dr Laura Sebastian-Coleman, author, _Measuring Data Quality for Ongoing Improvement_**

Ethical Data and Information Management

Concepts, tools and methods

Katherine O'Keefe
Daragh O Brien

KoganPage

First published in Great Britain and the United States in 2018 by Kogan Page Limited

2nd Floor, 45 Gee Street	c/o Martin P Hill Consulting	4737/23 Ansari Road
London EC1V 3RS	122 W 27th St, 10th Floor	Daryaganj
United Kingdom	New York, NY 10001	New Delhi 110002
	USA	India

www.koganpage.com

© Katherine O'Keefe and Daragh O Brien, 2018

The right of Katherine O'Keefe and Daragh O Brien to be identified as the authors of this work has been asserted by them in accordance with the Copyright, Designs and Patents Act 1988.

ISBN   978 0 7494 8204 6
E-ISBN   978 0 7494 8205 3

British Library Cataloguing-in-Publication Data

A CIP record for this book is available from the British Library.

Library of Congress Cataloging-in-Publication Data

CIP data is available.

Library of Congress Control Number: 2018013614

Typeset by Integra Software Services Pvt. Ltd., Pondicherry
Print production managed by Jellyfish
Printed and bound by CPI Group (UK) Ltd, Croydon, CR0 4YY

In memory of Noel Coghlan – an ethical man who understood good filing.

In memory of Dan O'Keefe – a man of deep principles and wide learning.

To Donn... thanks for everything.
Katherine

For Sinéad and Róisín – every day, in every way, I love you both more and more.
Daragh

CONTENTS

And in conclusion... 310

ABOUT THE AUTHORS

Katherine O'Keefe

Katherine O'Keefe is a San Diegan living in Ireland and holds a PhD in Anglo-Irish literature. She joined Castlebridge in 2013 after a career in tutoring and lecturing in two of Ireland's leading universities. Since then she has developed a reputation nationally and internationally as an expert in data privacy and information ethics. She works with clients in Ireland and elsewhere in sectors as diverse as public-sector and not-for-profit organizations.

In addition to her role as a trainer and consultant with Castlebridge, Katherine lectures on information ethics and data privacy practice at the Law Society of Ireland Diploma Centre.

In 2016, Katherine was the runner-up in the Information and Records Management Society's Alison North Award for New Professionals. In 2017 she was awarded 'Best Newcomer' by DAMA International for her contributions to the development of the CDMP certification. Subsequently, Katherine has served on the Board of DAMA International.

Daragh O Brien

Daragh O Brien is one of Europe's leading information governance and data privacy consultants, with almost two decades of experience. Since 2009 he has been the CEO of Castlebridge, a specialist consulting and training company in the field, working with clients in a variety of sectors in Ireland and elsewhere. Prior to that he held senior roles in a leading telecommunications company over a 12-year period.

Daragh is a Fellow of the Irish Computer Society, and has served on the boards of a number of international industry organizations including DAMA International and IQ International. He is an advisor to Digital Rights Ireland. Daragh was also a lead contributor to the development of the Innovation Value Institute's IT-CMF framework, particularly in the areas of information quality and data governance.

He has worked with organizations such as the Law Society of Ireland's Diploma Centre, where he is Course Consultant, to develop professional certification courses in data privacy, data governance, and information ethics.

Daragh holds an interfaculty degree from University College Dublin's Schools of Law and Business, where he is a frequent guest lecturer.

ACKNOWLEDGEMENTS

We stand on the shoulders of giants and are grateful for the support and encouragement we have had in teasing out the ideas in this book. In particular, we would like to thank John Ladley, Danette McGilvray, John Zachman, Tom Redman, Michelle Dennedy and Pat Walshe, as well as our colleagues at DAMA International for their insights that have contributed to the foundations of this book and their support in the process it took to write it.

The book would not have appeared at all without the patience and support of Katherine Hartle, our intrepid editor.

Finally, this book, and all the other stuff we do, would not be possible without the patience and support of our families, friends and the team at Castlebridge.

LIST OF ABBREVIATIONS

The list below provides some of the acronyms and abbreviations we commonly use when discussing ethical information management:

DG	data governance
DMBOK	Data Management Body of Knowledge
DPIA	Data Privacy Impact Assessment (often used synonymously with PIA)
DQ	data quality
E2IM	ethical enterprise information management
EIA	Ethical Impact Assessment
EIM	enterprise information management
GDPR	General Data Protection Regulation (Regulation 2016/679/EU)
IA	information architecture
IoT	internet of things
IQ	information quality
PbD	Privacy by Design
PE	Privacy Engineering
PIA	Privacy Impact Assessment
TQM	total quality management

Introduction

Why write a book on information ethics?

What will we cover in this chapter?

In this chapter we introduce why information ethics is becoming a critical issue for business, society and for all of us as individuals. We think about topics such as:

- What are the implications of our data-gathering tools and technologies from an ethical perspective?

- What types of ethical dilemma might you face as your organization looks to become more 'data driven' and harness the various new and emerging sources of data and methods of data capture?

- Given that law makers and legislation increasingly lag behind the pace of technological innovation, is there value in taking a 'principles approach' to ethics for information management rather than waiting to be told what is the wrong thing to do?

- What is the importance of consciously assessing the trade-offs and balances that need to be struck in the adoption and development of new technologies and methods for putting information to use in organizations and society?

Introduction

We live in interesting times. The pace of innovation and development in various fields of information management and information technology continues to accelerate, with functionality and features common today that would not have appeared out of place in science-fiction movies of even a few years ago. We have been gathering and recording information in written and pictographic forms for around 5,000 years. Cuneiform texts from ancient Mesopotamia are among the oldest evidence of recorded history.

The advent of modern technologies means we are now recording, in a year, more information than we have recorded in all of the preceding history of humankind. The pace of logging, recording and cataloguing of information continues to accelerate as our technical capabilities evolve. The challenge we now face is whether our love affair with technology and technological innovation may have left us ill-prepared for the various ethical and moral issues that the uses of that technology increasingly throw up on a day-to-day basis.

The purpose of this book is to explore whether the fundamental ethical challenges we face are new variants of issues we have struggled with in all cultures for many thousands of years. While our technology capabilities advance at a phenomenal rate, the solutions needed to put ethical principles into practice might be found in the fundamental disciplines of information management and how we manage and lead our information organizations.

The tools of data gathering

It is worth remembering that the Apple iPhone is barely a decade old, but has triggered a revolution in hand-held computing that has placed the Apple-device ecosystem at the centre of a revolution in data collection through apps and device capabilities. Far from being a communications device, the smartphone has developed into a powerful personal computing platform, with increasingly powerful sensors either built into them directly or connecting to them via Bluetooth connections.

Google began as a search engine barely two decades ago, but has grown into a data management behemoth, developing everything from e-mail services to operating systems, to home automation systems. Again, this places Google at the centre of our lives and gives them an unrivalled capability to gather or generate data about us and our interactions with the world around us.

These companies are not alone. Facebook has created a phenomenally powerful tool for connecting with friends and family. This has been supplemented with their 2015 acquisition of WhatsApp, which gives them information about who is messaging who, helping to develop a very detailed map of your personal connections and interactions – even if your family members or friends are not using Facebook themselves.

Other innovative companies gather and use information in a variety of ways. Some piggyback on the existing technology platforms such as smartphones through the development of new software applications. These applications are not limited to trivial social networking applications. For example, there are smartphone applications using the sensors already built into the phones themselves to support agriculture (Pongnumkul, Chaovalit and Surasvadi, 2015). For example, smartphone apps have been created that use the camera on the phone to help measure the chlorophyll in plants. This is a good indirect indicator of the health of food crops such as rice.

Innovative methods for gathering and analysing data are emerging as researchers and companies develop or deploy new sensor technologies that transmit their data to online applications or smartphone applications. From the humble fitness tracker to wearable cameras to telematics devices in cars, to glasses frames capable of recording video and still images and uploading them to the internet – eg Google's Google Glass (Wikipedia, 2017) or Snapchat's Spectacles (Indentity Guard, 2017) – the modern information-gathering and information management ecosystem is increasingly complex and powerful.

The data generated or derived from mobile devices or other sensor technologies that we are using can increasingly be used for a range of things, from keeping semi-automated diaries of various aspects of our personal lives or health – known as 'Life Logging' (Lifestream Blog, 2011) or the 'Quantified Self' (Wikipedia, 2017) – to tracking traffic bottlenecks on motorways, or the number of people passing by a particular place on a city street. The deployment of powerful data-gathering capabilities is now substantially cheaper and less invasive than it would have been even a few years ago.

To put this in context, when Daragh was a student in the 1990s he helped a friend of his in the Faculty of Medicine with a term-paper experiment and had to wear a heart-rate monitor for a few days. The device was the size of three or four paperback books stacked on each other and had to be worn strapped to his chest day and night. The monitor had to be given to one of the local hospitals to be downloaded and analysed.

Today, as he writes this, he is wearing a wristband fitness tracker that sends data about his heart rate, movement and activity levels to his smartphone, integrating via an app on that device. Daragh is also using an app to track his sleep patterns, which uses the microphone on his phone to record his breathing patterns, and incorporates the heart-rate monitoring from his wrist-worn fitness tracker.

Rather than having to struggle with a bulky recording device, he uses two lightweight gadgets and some low-cost software running on his phone to record the same type of data his med-student friend was logging 20 years ago. Rather than having to wait a few hours or days for the data to be analysed and presented, when he wakes up Daragh can look at some graphical charts on his phone that tell him how well he has slept and what his heart rate is at any time of the day.

However, unlike 20 years ago, when the data on Daragh's heart-rate monitor was accessed only by the laboratory staff in the hospital and his med-student friend, today his data is exposed to a wide range of potential third parties: the app developers, the fitness tracker manufacturer, the sleep-tracking application developer, the manufacturer of his smartphone and its operating system.

The tools of data analytics

In parallel with the tools and technologies for gathering information, we have witnessed a substantial increase in the ability of organizations, and indeed individuals, to analyse data. The emergence of 'big data' and data management tools and technologies to support the analysis of large and varied data sets has given rise to the emergence of job descriptions such as 'Data Scientist' in organizations.

In 2012 'Data Scientist' was proclaimed as the sexiest job title of the 21st century by the *Harvard Business Review* (Davenport and Patil, 2012). Not unlike the smartphone, the term 'data science' has only been around for about 15 years (Cao, 2016). As a term, it is still evolving and includes a spectrum of technical disciplines over and above traditional statistical analysis or database querying.

Already, the field includes domains such as artificial intelligence (AI), natural language processing (the use of artificial intelligence to process text to figure out patterns or infer meaning), machine learning (the use of AI to figure out more complex problems based on a function that learns the parameters of the required outcome from the data available), and deep learning (the development of mathematical models that break complex analysis into simpler discrete blocks that can in turn be adjusted to better predict final outcomes from the AI process).

These tools, and the technology platforms they run on, are increasingly powerful. Just as the world of data management software has evolved in recent years to develop more powerful software tools and platforms for data analytics and visualization, hardware manufacturers are now beginning to develop processing chips for the next generation of smartphones, computers and internet of things (IoT) devices to allow complex AI functions to be deployed 'on device', rather than relying on servers in data centres or hosted in cloud-based environments.

The 'Quantified Self' movement is a good example of the development of our data-gathering and analytics capabilities over the past few years. Twenty years ago, if we were tracking our exercise routines, we would have used a range of independent technologies such as stopwatches and heart-rate monitors and would have recorded our progress and performance indicators in a physical notebook (because our computers were too big to bring to the gym or too heavy to bring on a run). We might have kept a food diary in the notebook as well. We might have manually tracked historic trends or used group activities to compare our progress against a representative sample of our peers.

Today, we wear lightweight fitness trackers that also track our location and movement, recording our exercise performance in terms of distance, effort and other performance indicators. We might log the food we are eating by taking photographs of our meals instead of writing in a notebook. Further logging of our activities and actions is automatically through our wearable technologies. We track our performance against peers through pooled data that is shared via our applications.

Increasingly, our software tools can infer the calorie and nutrient content of food we eat based on a machine-learning analysis of a photograph of our meals. AI and analytics can enable the automatic tailoring of our exercise regimes to our fitness levels, our ability and our progress. The same technologies can also predict health issues that might arise based on the data they ingest about us. Add to the mix more specialized additional technologies to read blood sugar, blood pressure, or other aspects of physical health, and our simple smartphone is the hub of a device that increasingly resembles the tricorder in *Star Trek*.

Of course, this data is useful and valuable. While the pencil-and-paper life loggers of old may not have sat recording the speeds they drove at when travelling from A to B, today's life loggers are using the incredible information-processing power of technologies that have relatively recently entered the consumer space to record increasingly granular details about themselves, which can then be made available to third parties such as insurance companies. Governments can use this data for planning health and social policy. Insurers can use it at a macro level to refine their risk models, and at a micro level to target and tailor the policies that they offer to us.

Marketers can use the data to identify whether we would be receptive to different methods of advertising for the products they are promoting, and when we would be most suggestible to be influenced by such marketing.

The tools of analysis, and the abundance of data sources that are now available to organizations (and to individuals), create an environment that is rich with potential and ripe with opportunity to develop insights into the world at a level of detail and at a level of cost that previous generations could only have dreamt about. However, with this potential we begin to see the re-emergence of a perception of data and analytics as a panacea for all ills, as if access to the right information will magically unlock the strategic vision for a government or organization, or trigger a miraculous improvement in physical well-being among fitness-tracking loggers of all of life's activities.

For example, the Samaritans in the United Kingdom do phenomenal work supporting people who are stressed and depressed and helping them find alternative methods to deal with their mental state. One of the methods they deployed in 2014 was 'Samaritans' Radar', an app that allowed you to put the Twitter handle of a friend or family member into it and it would then conduct sentiment and mood analysis on the person's tweets to help identify if they were in an up or down state of mind. All of this happened without the knowledge or consent of the selected individual whose posts were being analysed.

This is an innovative use of AI, machine learning and text analytics to help people know when they need to reach out to offer support to a friend, family member or colleague. However, the exact same tool, in the hands of a malicious actor or bully, could be used to target harassing messages at a vulnerable person more precisely and track the effectiveness of a harassment campaign. Furthermore, the UK Information Commissioner's Office expressed concerns that the application was, by its very nature, processing sensitive categories of personal data relating to the physical or mental health of individuals without their knowledge or consent (Orme, 2014). At the time, the National Association of Data Protection Officers in the UK also expressed concerns (Lee, 2014).

In this respect, we risk repeating the errors of previous generations when faced with the potential for technology to automate the processing of data. The Vietnam war was one of the first heavily analytics-driven wars in the era of modern computing. From the Secretary of Defence Robert McNamara down, there was an emphasis on and an obsession with quantitative analytics as a way of gauging the success or failure of operations.

From not recognizing the inability of computers of the time to measure intangible factors to not factoring in the quality of the input data, horrendous decisions impacting on the lives of people for many generations were made – because the data said it was the right decision.

A key missing link in our rationalization and analysis of technology is the motives of both the person creating the data and the person seeking to use the data. In the Vietnam war, McNamara and US military failed to consider the motivation of the chain of command to filter information upwards, giving the 'brass' the answers they wanted, not the insights they needed. McNamara should have been warned of this – when he was with Ford Motor Company he had implemented a rigorous metrics-driven approach to management that resulted in production staff simply dumping parts into the river so they could work around metrics-driven rules on when new car models could be introduced (Cukier and Mayer-Schönberger, 2013). Today, we give fake names and e-mail addresses to websites when registering for services, or take other steps to control how our data is accessed or used by others, such as using virtual private network (VPN) services or ad blockers when surfing the internet. The organizations we interact with analyse and use our data for their own purposes. The clarity and transparency of those purposes to us as individuals or consumers is often lacking. Or the processing may be essentially invisible to us, carried out below the surface of our interactions with companies, products, services or government agencies for aims and objectives that are unstated or unclear.

Of course, while we may not have learnt that information technology is not always the panacea for our problems, it has evolved to a point where the data gathered and processed by social media networks and other new technology platforms has the potential to influence people's moods (Arthur, 2014), the information that they are presented with (Pariser, 2011) and the decisions that they take (Samson, 2016). The emergence of psychographic targeting, a technology that requires the use of AI to analyse and filter vast amounts of data about people from social media, has led to what the Online Privacy Foundation has referred to as 'the weaponized, artificially intelligent, propaganda machine' (Revell, 2017). By gathering data in contexts where people are less likely to be misleading or provide inaccurate information or take other steps to mask or protect their data from being gathered or measured, and by combining data across multiple data sets and data points, it has apparently become possible to manipulate and undermine a democracy without firing a single shot (Neudert, 2017).

With great power comes great responsibility

The issues raised above highlight one of the key challenges we face as the potential and power of information management in our lives becomes more pervasive, and one of the key reasons that we decided to write this book. The pace of development of data-processing technology has been such in recent years that we have scarcely had a chance as a society to draw breath and consider the implications of the technologies we are developing and deploying. Innovations make it from the research lab to the consumer shelves in a fraction of the time a manufactured product might have in previous generations. Technologies that influence the mood, mental state or behaviour of people are capable of being deployed, in many cases, with minimal cost and negligible testing or oversight.

Of course, books take time to research and write. When we started on this process, there were very few publications of any kind in the area. A PhD candidate conducting research would have had a very short literature review in the context of information ethics. Beyond some key pioneering research, including work in academia by Luciano Floridi at Oxford University (Floridi, 2017) and in industry by Gartner Group (Buytendijk, 2015), and the under-recognized work of several other academic and industry researchers and practitioners, this was a niche area. We fully expect this to change rapidly over the coming years, but a critical challenge will be to translate the discussion of information ethics from abstract concepts to tangible methods and practices.

The emergence of a regulatory focus on information ethics from the European Data Protection Supervisor in late 2015 (European Data Protection Supervisor, 2015) is, to our view, a sea-change moment. From 2016 and 2017 there has been a growing stream of commentary in media, discussion in standards bodies, and debate among practitioners. Discussion has ranged from the security of IoT devices and whether it is ethical to go to market with an unsecure technology (Wadell, 2017), to the use of data to influence elections and behaviour (Helbing et al, 2017), to the ethical issues in AI.

At the heart of this evolution in focus on ethics in information management is the realization, however trite it may sound, that 'with great power comes great responsibility'. The origin of this quote is traced variously to Voltaire, the French Revolution, Winston Churchill or the pages of *Marvel* comics. But, regardless of the origin, the sentiment is clear – we cannot lightly introduce powerful technologies that have the potential to deliver significant benefits to individuals or to society but equally have the potential to inflict great harms. The complication we face in the Information Age is that a failure to implement technologies with the appropriate balances in place (eg easy-to-configure security in IoT devices, appropriate governance in analytics planning and execution) has the potential to affect many thousands, if not millions of people, directly or indirectly, before remedies can be put in place. The alleged manipulation of voters through social media during the UK Brexit referendum and the US presidential election is a telling example of this (Novi, 2017).

The core issues to be addressed, however, go far deeper than the superficial issues of technology implementations and require us to consider the question of what type of society we wish our technologies to enable, and what controls or constraints we might wish to apply to the applications of technologies and the development of such capabilities.

But we have been here before. Every generation has faced technological changes or drives for social improvement through new technologies or industries that have promised huge potential. From the printing press, to the development of the factory in the Industrial Revolution, to the development of new medicines or medical procedures, industry after industry has had to face ethical challenges. Often these have been addressed through regulatory measures. For example, Lord Shaftesbury and others pioneered the Factories Acts in the United Kingdom during the Industrial Revolution, which curtailed the use of child labour and set minimum standards for schooling for children working in factories (Wikipedia, 2017). In other cases, industry regulators or oversight bodies act, such as in the case of the Tuskegee syphilis experiments (Wikipedia, 2017) conducted in Alabama from 1932 to 1972, in which treatment for syphilis was intentionally withheld from African American sharecroppers in rural Alabama. This study, which we will look at in a later chapter of this book, resulted in the publication of the Belmont report that established ethical guidelines for biomedical and behavioural research.

As information management practitioners live through this Information Revolution, increasingly we find ourselves facing a variety of dilemmas and difficult decisions. These arise through the potential capabilities of the tools, technologies and data sets that are, at least in theory, available to us.

The data-driven dilemma

The 'data-driven dilemma' is the label that Daragh applies to the position that information management professionals and data analysts increasingly find themselves in, given the potential analytics capabilities of software tools and the increasing richness of the 'data exhaust' left behind by people as they use common tools and services such as mobile phones.

For example, imagine for a moment you are tasked with developing statistical reports to support government investment in tourism policy. The recommendations you make will have potentially significant impacts on the livelihoods of many tourist businesses in remote areas of the country. You know that mobile-phone operators have all the data you need regarding the movements of visitors to the country who have mobile phones from other operators in their home countries and are roaming on mobile networks in your country.

However, you will also capture data about business travellers and diplomats. People have no mechanism of opting out. The data will not only show you where each person has been travelling, but who was with them (or rather, what devices might ultimately be linked to a person). The available data is far beyond what you need for your stated analytics purpose. You will also identify at a very granular level of detail the holiday activities of travellers, including how long they spend at locations, and how quickly they get from point A to point B when travelling. You will also get data about people in your country and where they go (or where their devices go) on holidays.

This data is generated because of travellers using mobile-phone networks in your country. It allows your analysis to be done quickly and at almost negligible cost once you have the data, particularly when compared with the cost and error rates inherent in doing surveys of travellers. Should you move heaven and earth to get the mobile-phone network data? What are the other implications and risks associated with this processing that might give rise to ethical or legal issues? Should you seek forgiveness rather than permission?

All too often, particularly in the context of big data and analytics processes, we can be faced with a significant short-term win or benefit from the use of data in new or novel ways. Often there is a potential benefit to society arising from the processing. Sometimes that societal benefit is substantial. However, often the impact on individuals and the choices they might make or the freedoms they may otherwise enjoy can be disproportionate to the benefit to society. In these contexts, the data-driven dilemma is one of determining whether, even if we can do something fancy with data or data-related technologies, *should we*?

The innovator's dilemma

Linked to the data-driven dilemma is the dilemma we face where the pace of technological change is accelerating. The perception is that legislation is lagging further behind the pace of change. For example, the European Union's General Data Protection Regulation (GDPR) comes into force in 2018, a full 23 years after the original Data Protection Directive was enacted, and about as long again since the development of the world wide web by Sir Tim Berners-Lee.

Even within defined legal frameworks such as the GDPR, there is potentially a wide range of ethical choices to make within the formal parameters of what is legally acceptable. For example, the concept of 'legitimate interests of the data controller' as a basis for processing personal data of individuals under the GDPR requires decision makers in organizations to assess the balance between the competing rights and interests of the affected data subjects and the organization.

In this context, we increasingly find ourselves having to make evaluations of the ethics of a course of action or a proposed application of technology in information management. But traditional computer science degrees, business management or law degrees leave us significantly ill-prepared for this type of analysis. In addition, our standard business or technology innovation or implementation processes often do not always allow for the consideration time necessary to reflect on ethics as an explicit quality characteristic of our product or service development.

As innovation does not exist in a vacuum we must also consider the organization culture and governance frameworks we operate within and how they can support or undermine ethical considerations. Increasingly the articulation of these governance approaches and the rigour with which organizations embrace and apply ethics and ethical principles in their information management practices will become a source of competitive advantage, both when seeking customers but also for attracting and hiring employees (Jenkin, 2015).

Many organizations are attempting to innovate in this area through the introduction of ethics forums or taking part in public ethics discussion groups or conferences. Increasingly, organizations are turning to standards bodies such as the Institute of Electrical and Electronics Engineers Standards Association (IEEE) to define and develop standards for information ethics. But standards frameworks can only really advise or give guidance on what your data ethics should be, they can only provide guidance on the types of ethical decisions you should be taking. Likewise, an internal data ethics forum that is not linked to some form of operational governance will be unable to manifest any sustainable change in information management practices.

Societal value versus individual rights – the root of our own dilemmas

The common thread between both the data-driven dilemma and the innovator's dilemma is one of social value versus individual rights or agency. To paraphrase the EU's GDPR, the management and processing of information must be designed for the benefit of mankind. The challenge for the information management professional is to understand how to make the trade-offs between competing value and benefits to mankind arising from processing.

If processing is significantly invasive or harmful to the rights or freedoms of individuals, but delivers an equally significant social benefit, it may well be that there is a valid ethical trade-off to be made. If, however, the processing is invasive to the individual but of limited value to society then the trade-off is less compelling. Also, even in scenarios where the trade-off is skewed against the individual, organizations might be able to take some action to redress that balance through education, communication or other mechanisms.

Societal and social value needs to include or factor in the value to the individual as well. Something may not improve the greater good, but may be a benefit to individuals and support, or impinge on, their dignity or their ability to exercise other rights. For example, CCTV may have a social benefit in supporting the detection of crime. However, too much CCTV, or CCTV that overlooks private as well as public locations, can be highly invasive. It impacts the right to privacy of individuals on a mass scale, and could affect the choices people make about their movements (impacting freedom of movement) or who they meet where (impacting rights of assembly).

The type of trade-off we see in Figure 0.1 is at the heart of the balancing test required under EU data protection laws when organizations are seeking to rely on the fact that something is in their legitimate interests. It may be in the legitimate interest of the organization, but that interest

Figure 0.1 The value/invasiveness matrix

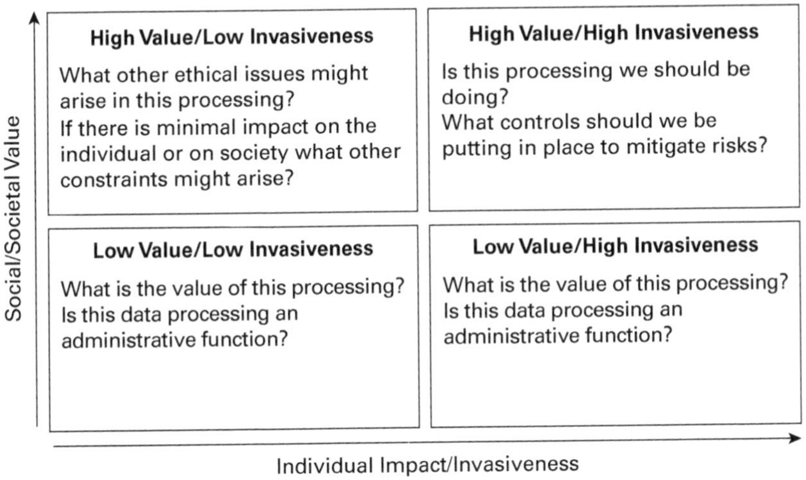

	High Value/Low Invasiveness	High Value/High Invasiveness
	What other ethical issues might arise in this processing? If there is minimal impact on the individual or on society what other constraints might arise?	Is this processing we should be doing? What controls should we be putting in place to mitigate risks?
	Low Value/Low Invasiveness	**Low Value/High Invasiveness**
	What is the value of this processing? Is this data processing an administrative function?	What is the value of this processing? Is this data processing an administrative function?

Social/Societal Value ↑

Individual Impact/Invasiveness →

needs to be balanced against the rights and interests of the individuals affected by the processing. It also arises in other countries in the context of Privacy Impact Assessments, where many countries now require consideration of the impact of data processing on the choices people might make about interacting with services, particularly services offered by government agencies.

This type of trade-off and balancing decision is also at the heart of many of the ethics frameworks that govern professions such as lawyers or doctors. For example, the lawyer's professional duty of confidentiality has high value to society, as without it people who need legal advice or representation might be afraid to seek it out (Law Society of Ireland, 2013; American Bar Association, 2017). Likewise, medical practitioners, psychologists or counsellors all operate under an ethical presumption of confidentiality. This has social value and minimizes the invasiveness or intrusion into the personal and private life of the patient or others (American Medical Association, 2016; Psychological Society of Ireland, 2010). However, these ethical duties can be overruled where there is a wider societal issue or where the disclosure is in the interests of the individual.

For example, many countries now require doctors, lawyers or psychologists to notify law enforcement where there are indications of child sexual abuse in a matter they are dealing with. The ethical juggling act that must be performed is unenviable – providing sufficient information to the authorities to investigate while protecting the confidence of their client or patient. Similarly, the disclosure of information for the purposes of seeking advice on a matter, or a consultation on a case where this is in the interests of the client or patient, also requires the balancing of the amount of information disclosed (invasiveness) with the benefit that is being sought for the individual (societal or individual value).

In mature professions that have struggled with ethics issues since their inception, and whose practitioners have made some horrific errors of ethical judgement over the years (we will read more about some of these later), the ethical questions continue to be a constant and pervasive challenge on a day-to-day basis. In information management we have been shielded, to an extent, from these complexities by the ethical codes and frameworks of the industries for whom we were implementing information management systems.

However, as technology for data gathering becomes more pervasive and enters our pockets, our classrooms, our living rooms and our bedrooms, as the volume of data we are recording about people and events continues to grow, and as the technical capabilities to analyse and process that data become both more accessible (low-cost analytics tools and cloud-based technologies) and more autonomous (machine learning and artificial intelligence), the need for a maturing of ethical practices in information management is more pressing than ever.

Introducing the rest of the book

The rest of this book is divided roughly into two thematic parts. The first part is principles-focused and gives a crash course in the basics of ethical principles and the types of ethical issues that modern information management professionals face. The second part focuses on tools and practices, looking at some of the existing good practices in information management and exploring how they can be applied to support ethical information management.

Our hope is that readers will develop an understanding of both what principles we need to be implementing as part of an ethical enterprise information management philosophy but will also become familiar with approaches to integrating ethical information management into their existing information management practices.

Chapter summary

In this chapter we started to set out the reasons why it is increasingly important for information management professionals to become more 'ethically aware' and what that might actually mean for our methods and practices for managing information. Key topics we addressed include:

- The issues, risks and potential benefits that are presented by our increasingly pervasive tools and technologies for data capture and data analysis, much of which has evolved rapidly over the last decade.

- The importance of responsibility of action in the context of these increasingly powerful data-processing technologies and the need for a maturing in our approach to identifying and addressing the ethical issues they give rise to.

- The potential for information management as a profession to learn from the successes and failures of other professional disciplines, such as medicine, in defining methods and practices for addressing their ethical challenges.

- The importance of consciously and deliberatively considering the ethical trade-offs that arise in the development of new technologies for data capture and processing, particularly as information management matures into a professional discipline in its own right and our technical capabilities begin more and more to drive innovation in other areas, rather than technology innovation being driven by the needs of disciplines with existing models of ethical governance.

Questions

Throughout the book we will end each chapter with some questions and thoughts for practitioners and students. These are intended to trigger introspective learning and may not have an answer. In this chapter, we start off easily:

1 Why is our approach to information ethics so flawed?

2 What kinds of data-processing activity are you or your organizations engaging in that raises ethical concerns or questions?

3 How would you know if proposed processing of data raised ethical concerns?

4 If something in your organization's approach to managing data raised an ethical concern for you, how would you express that and who would you express it to?

Further reading

In this section of each chapter we provide some hints for other related reading you might want to consider relevant to the chapter. This will be in addition to the references for each chapter. For this introductory chapter, we would suggest the following further reading:

Floridi, L (2014) *The Fourth Revolution: How the infosphere is reshaping human reality*, Oxford University Press, Oxford

Hasselbach, G and Tranberg, P (2017) *Data Ethics: The new competitive advantage*, PubliShare, Copenhagen

References

American Bar Association (2017) [accessed 1 August 2017] Client-Lawyer Relationship: Rule 1.6 Confidentiality of Information [Online] https://www.americanbar.org/groups/professional_responsibility/publications/model_rules_of_professional_conduct/rule_1_6_confidentiality_of_information.html

American Medical Association (2016) [accessed 1 August 2017] AMA Principles of Medical Ethics – Chapter 3 [Online] https://www.ama-assn.org/sites/default/files/media-browser/code-of-medical-ethics-chapter-3.pdf

Arthur, C (2014) [accessed 1 August 2017] Facebook Emotion Study Breached Ethical Guidelines, Researchers Say [Online] https://www.theguardian.com/technology/2014/jun/30/facebook-emotion-study-breached-ethical-guidelines-researchers-say

Buytendijk, F (2015) [accessed 1 August 2017] Think About Digital Ethics Within Continually Evolving Boundaries [Online] http://www.gartner.com/smarterwithgartner/think-about-digital-ethics-within-continually-evolving-boundaries/

Cao, L (2016) Data science and analytics: a new era, *International Journal of Data Science and Analytics*, **1** (1), pp 1–2

Cukier, K and Mayer-Schönberger, V (2013) [accessed 1 August 2017] The Dictatorship of Data [Online] https://www.technologyreview.com/s/514591/the-dictatorship-of-data/

Davenport, TH and Patil, D (2012) [accessed 1 August 2017] Data Scientist: The Sexiest Job of the 21st Century [Online] https://hbr.org/2012/10/data-scientist-the-sexiest-job-of-the-21st-century

European Data Protection Supervisor (2015) [accessed 1 August 2017] Towards A New Digital Ethics: Data, Dignity, and Technology [Online] https://edps.europa.eu/sites/edp/files/publication/15-09-11_data_ethics_en.pdf

Floridi, L (2017) [accessed 1 August 2017] Google Scholar – Luciano Floridi [Online] https://scholar.google.com/citations?user=jZdTOaoAAAAJ

Helbing, D et al (2017) [accessed 1 August 2017] Will Democracy Survive Big Data and Artificial Intelligence? [Online] https://www.scientificamerican.com/article/will-democracy-survive-big-data-and-artificial-intelligence/

Indentity Guard (2017) [accessed 1 August 2017] Wearing Snapchat Spectacles Could Be a Privacy Disaster [Online] https://www.identityguard.com/news-insights/wearing-snapchat-spectacles-privacy-disaster/

Jenkin, M (2015) [accessed 1 August 2017] Millennials Want To Work For Employers Committed To Values and Ethics [Online] https://www.theguardian.com/sustainable-business/2015/may/05/millennials-employment-employers-values-ethics-jobs

Law Society of Ireland (2013) *A Guide to Good Professional Conduct of Solicitors*, Law Society of Ireland, Dublin

Lee, D (2014) [accessed 1 August 2017] Samaritans Pulls 'Suicide Watch' Radar App [Online] http://www.bbc.com/news/technology-29962199

Lifestream Blog (2011) [accessed 1 August 2017] Lifestream Blog [Online] http://lifestreamblog.com/lifelogging/

Neudert, L-M (2017) [accessed 1 August 2017] Computational Propaganda in Germany: A Cautionary Tale [Online] http://comprop.oii.ox.ac.uk/wp-content/uploads/sites/89/2017/06/Comprop-Germany.pdf

Novi, S (2017) [accessed 1 August 2017] Cambridge Analytica: Psychological Manipulation for Brexit and Trump? [Online] https://politicsmeanspolitics.com/cambridge-analytica-psychological-manipulation-for-brexit-and-trump-2e73c2be5117

Orme, J (2014) [accessed 1 August 2017] Samaritans Pulls 'Suicide Watch' Radar App Over Privacy Concerns [Online] https://www.theguardian.com/society/2014/nov/07/samaritans-radar-app-suicide-watch-privacy-twitter-users

Pariser, E (2011) *The Filter Bubble: How the new personalized web is changing what we read and how we think*, Viking, London

Pongnumkul, S, Chaovalit, P and Surasvadi, N (2015) [accessed 1 August 2017] Applications of Smartphone-Based Sensors in Agriculture: A Systematic Review of Research, *Journal of Sensors* [Online] https://www.hindawi.com/journals/js/2015/195308/

Psychological Society of Ireland (2010) [accessed 1 August 2017] Code of Professional Ethics of the PSI [Online] http://www.psychologicalsociety.ie/find-a-psychologist/PSI%202011-12%20Code%20of%20Ethics.pdf

Revell, T (2017) [accessed 1 August 2017] How to Turn Facebook Into a Weaponised AI Propaganda Machine [Online] https://www.newscientist.com/article/2142072-how-to-turn-facebook-into-a-weaponised-ai-propaganda-machine/

Samson, A (2016) [accessed 1 August 2017] Big Data Is Nudging You [Online] https://www.psychologytoday.com/blog/consumed/201608/big-data-is-nudging-you

Wadell, K (2017) [accessed 1 August 2017] The Internet of Things Needs a Code of Ethics [Online] https://www.theatlantic.com/technology/archive/2017/05/internet-of-things-ethics/524802/

Wikipedia, 2017 [accessed 1 August 2017] Factories Acts [Online] https://en.wikipedia.org/wiki/Factory_Acts

Wikipedia, 2017 [accessed 1 August 2017] Google Glass [Online] https://en.wikipedia.org/wiki/Google_Glass

Wikipedia, 2017 [accessed 1 August 2017] Quantified Self [Online] https://en.wikipedia.org/wiki/Quantified_Self

Wikipedia, 2017 [accessed 1 August 2017] Tuskegee Syphilis Experiment [Online] https://en.wikipedia.org/wiki/Tuskegee_syphilis_experiment

Ethics in the context of information management

01

What will we cover in this chapter?

In this chapter you will:

- Develop an understanding of how ethics and technology have evolved in tandem since the earliest days of human thought.
- Explore why it is important for information management professionals to have a grounding in fundamental concepts of ethics, particularly in the context of modern information management capabilities.
- Be introduced to some of the ethical discussions around technology and the responsibilities of the technologist when developing or integrating technologies.
- Explore data privacy as an example of information ethics in action.
- Be introduced to some fundamental ethical questions that you can ask when planning or performing any information-processing activity.
- Develop an understanding of the emerging importance of information ethics in the context of the regulatory oversight of information management.

Ethics and the evolution of technology

As ethical issues relating to the application of information management technologies and practices are gaining more prominence in mainstream news and political discussion there are calls for the development of new ethical frameworks and approaches to help technologists deal with the complexity of the issues that are raised. However, the evolution of technology has gone hand in hand with the evolution of ethics since the earliest times. Much of that parallel evolution has centred on the discussion and debate of the ways in which evolving technologies might best be applied. However, while computer science and business management courses may teach modules on ethics, often these courses fail to provide the tools necessary for information management professionals to work from first principles and apply robust ethical concepts in the execution of our day-to-day roles. This can result in the 'law of unintended consequences' being invoked, with technologies or analytics capabilities being deployed in the real world without an appropriate analysis of the ethical implications or impacts of the processing activity in question.

Increasingly, the tools and technologies we have at our disposal as information management professionals have the potential to bring benefit or cause harm to people. All information that is processed, with very few exceptions, impacts on people in some way. Whether it is information that allows us to identify a person and make a determination about their eligibility for a loan, or information that trains an artificial intelligence system that provides sentencing recommendations to judges, or whether it is information about the performance of a car's engine in environmental impact tests, the outcomes that result from the processing of that data impact on people through an impact on privacy, a potential for bias in decision making, and an impact on governmental policies and climate change investments. With the incredible increase in computing power, data-gathering capabilities and machine-learning technologies, the potential for harm to be caused to individuals or to groups of society, either by accident or by intentional design, is significant.

As a result of this significant power and significant risk, it is more important than ever that information management professionals have an appropriate grounding in ethics so that decisions that are made in relation to the management and use of information are based on sound ethical principles. Furthermore, as the potential fields of application for information technologies and data capture and analytics technologies continues to expand, information management practitioners need to be better equipped to extrapolate ethical issues from first principles. Therefore, just as when you learn a programming language you usually start with some common core fundamentals such as variable definition and <If><Then><Else> logic, to start to get to grips with ethics in the context of information management you need to go back to some basic ethical concepts to give a common foundation from which to build your understanding.

Of course, none of this is new. Plato, writing in the *Phaedrus* in 370BC (Plato, 2009), recounted Socrates's view of the new information management technology that was emerging in Greece at that time – writing: 'This discovery of yours will create forgetfulness in the learners' souls, because they will not use their memories; they will trust to the external written characters and not remember of themselves.'

Socrates was describing here the impact on memory and the transfer of information in an oral tradition. His warning was that this new-fangled writing would create the illusion of memory but not the reality of recall and understanding. Later in this dialogue between Socrates and Plato, Socrates says that, with the advent of written characters, people 'will appear to be omniscient and will generally know nothing'.

Socrates's words could easily be adapted to any of the emergent technologies in information management and would still be as relevant and provocative of debate as they were when first recorded 2,500 years ago. At their heart is a fundamental truth that in any technology there are both benefits and risks. Consider for a moment what has happened to your memory for telephone numbers or other contact information since you got your first mobile phone.

Daragh got his first mobile phone in 1997 when he was still at university. It could hold about 30 names and numbers. Back then, Daragh could remember the phone number of every single person he knew. Even today, he can remember the contact numbers of people he knew pre-1997, even if he hasn't dialled the number in decades. Today, he has a modern smartphone that has hundreds of phone numbers in it. He struggles to remember newer numbers. In effect, he has outsourced a function of his memory to the device. He can still find the numbers and can indeed appear omniscient, but generally knows nothing. Does your experience match Daragh's? Does Socrates's point still have relevance today?

Four decades ago, Martin Heidegger argued that modern technology allowed us to have new relationships with the world that were not previously possible, which presented challenges as the evolution of technology means that objects in the real world are capable of being manipulated (Heidegger, 1977). Heidegger considered the ways of thinking that lie behind technology and saw technology as a means to an end, not an end in and of itself. But the advent of technologies changed the relationships between people and the other objects in nature that we interact with and, through the operation of technology, a new nature of a thing can be revealed. For example, the use of mining technology can turn a beautiful hillside into a tract of land that produces coal or iron ore. He also gives the example of technology being used to manipulate uranium to produce nuclear energy, but highlights that that process is an example of one that can have either a destructive or a beneficial use.

By way of another example, the technologies that are required to produce something as simple as a pair of kitchen scissors are, by and large, ethically neutral regarding the user of the scissors. The mining and metallurgical technologies that create the metal for the blades, the plastics moulding technologies that produce the handles, and the manufacturing technologies that assemble the scissors are not making a determination as to the dignity of the person who might wield the scissors. However, the determination of whether the pair of scissors is assembled as one to be used by a right-handed person, a left-handed person, or as an ambidextrous set of scissors, can have an impact on individuals in terms of the usability of the scissors. It is the combination of the technologies, and the decisions that are taken about what combinations of those technologies to make available, that can give rise to ethical questions about the relationships we have with technology. The thinking and considerations that are applied to the design and application of technology affect (in this case in a literal way) how objects in the real world are manipulated.[1]

Unfortunately, it is not just the aching arm of a left-handed paper cutter that might be manipulated by technology. The potential for people to be manipulated using technology is also a concern, and one that is increasingly topical given the growing concerns about the abuse of social media and associated technologies to influence people's moods, market products and services, and influence elections. While there are potentially significant benefits from the technologies in question, they create significant ethical questions about their impact on individual choice and agency.

In the same time frame as Heidegger, Bunge argued that the technologist must be held not only technically but also morally responsible for whatever he designs or executes: not only should his artefacts be optimally efficient but, far from being harmful, they should be beneficial, and not only in the short run but also in the long term (Bunge, 1977). This echoes the sentiment in Recital 4 of the EU General Data Protection Regulation, which says that 'the processing of personal data should be designed to serve mankind' (European Union, 2016). This, however, highlights one of the key points of difference between the European Union (EU) and the United States when the ethics of information are considered. In the US-centric mindset for data, it is considered the 'new oil', a raw material to be exploited. This engenders different approaches to the consideration of information-related risk. This US model of information innovation has, until relatively recently, been to the fore. This is changing, but the difference in ethical positions on the handling of data about or relating to people will likely continue to be a key battleground in which legal and regulatory remedies to balance ethical differences will continue to evolve.

In response to the rapid development of data gathering and analytics capabilities, there is an increasing call for a 'big data ethics'. But 'big data ethics' does not require a new ethics. Rather, it is a call for a framework in which we can ensure big data technologies are applied ethically. This is no different to the domain of computer ethics, which is itself simply a specific application of fundamental ethics principles. Indeed, one of the pioneers of computer ethics has argued that the field of computer ethics will disappear as the field of computing matures (Johnson, 1999). The challenge we face is that the pace of evolution and invention in computing, information management, data analytics, data science and artificial intelligence means we have not had the opportunity to mature consistently across all of these disciplines. As a result, the ethical issues we face are all too often framed as being novel or different, but are essentially iterations and variations on historic ethical themes. So, while we face calls for 'big data ethics', and computer ethics or information management ethics continue to be labels that have value, the answers (or at least the correct questions) can often be found in the fundamental principles of ethical philosophy. Furthermore, as we will see when we look at the ethical implications of the vehicle emissions scandal, these fundamental ethics need to be applied to all aspects of information management, not just the computer science or analytics functions.

The emergent technological abilities are in themselves inherently neutral, but care must be taken to define the nature of protection required to recognize and preserve human rights and the common good in the development and use of the technology, particularly in the way in which technologies might be combined. As such, an 'ethical framework' is a scaffolding to structure our understanding of already existing systems of ethical values and norms. It should consider socialized behavioural norms and biases, providing tools to determine right action, and identify possible ethical violations.

An ethical framework for information governance and information management will not invent new determinations of what is ethical, but rather will identify the applicability or application of ethical values already present to new developments in information processes and technologies.

The evolution of privacy and technology

One of the great risks identified in the application of modern information management capabilities and analytical tools is violation of the fundamental human right to privacy. However, this is not the first time that new developments and applications of technology have raised concerns about the preservation of the right to privacy in the face of the danger of its dissolution by use of technology.

Samuel D Warren and Louis D Brandeis founded their argument for a 'right to privacy' in the light of developments in business and technology. They referred to the basic principle in common law 'that the individual shall have full protection in person and in property', stating that 'it has been found necessary from time to time to define anew the exact nature and extent of such protection' (Warren and Brandeis, 1890) and arguing that changes in political, social and economic realities reveal the need for new legal recognition of human rights. They argued that, 'Recent inventions and business methods call attention to the next step which must be taken for the protection of the person, and for securing to the individual what Judge Cooley calls the right "to be let alone".'

Warren and Brandeis therefore conceptualized privacy as a basic fundamental right to the development of the human as an autonomous individual with thoughts and feelings. Essentially, they argued for the preservation of human dignity in two forms: individual autonomy and the development of personality, and the preservation of public face. In doing this, they presented two models for understanding privacy that reflect the different ways privacy rights are approached in the United States and in Europe. While in the United States case law regards privacy with a focus more on the idea of privacy as related to intellectual property or as a 'liberty right', Warren and Brandeis also clearly linked the 'right to privacy' to first and fourth amendment rights, with a clear emphasis on privacy rights as fundamental to the dignity of the individual. One can read this as an argument for privacy as a 'personality right'.

Bart van der Sloot has identified a clear link between the conceptualization of privacy rights in a European context to the German concept of

'Persönlichkeitsrecht', referring to Article 2, paragraph 1, of the German Constitution, which states that 'Everyone has the right to the free development of his personality insofar as he does not violate the rights of others or offend against the constitutional order or the moral code' (van der Sloot, 2015). In this, 'privacy' is not just a negative right to be 'left alone', but a positive right to be free to develop one's personality as an autonomous human.

Building on the concepts of privacy as a right related to human dignity as Warren and Brandeis framed it, Samuel I Benn defined privacy in the context of respect for the person as an autonomous individual or 'chooser'. Essentially, Benn framed the violation of privacy as a failure to respect personhood (Benn, 1971; Hudson and Husack, 1979). This human rights focus brings us back to first principles, with an understanding that privacy as a right upholds the treatment of a human as an autonomous individual, a 'chooser' who must be treated as an end, not just a means. The conceptualization of the individual as 'chooser' directly relates to the need to be able to actively and knowingly consent to the processing of one's information and the purposes for which it is processed.

In the wake of human rights violations perpetrated in the years leading up to, during and after the Second World War, European nations have adopted a strong fundamental rights approach to privacy, regarding privacy as a necessary right fundamental to the respect for human dignity. This fundamental rights-based focus is reflected both in the institution of an overarching data protection directive, and in Articles 7 and 8 of the European Convention on Human Rights, which has binding treaty power.

This rights-based understanding of privacy has a deep history in European philosophy and ethics, which are based in philosophical understandings of personhood and the individual, including Immanuel Kant's formulations of the categorical imperative.[2] In tracing back our understanding of privacy to first principles, we may uncover the foundations of an ethical framework for new developments in technology and actions.

This ethical approach ultimately finds expression in many of the fundamental principles of data privacy laws, which attempt to provide a legal framework to give effect to the ethical values of privacy as a defined right.

Other ethical dilemmas

Privacy, and the impact on individuals that can arise from the loss of that privacy, are the entry point for ethical discussions in information management, as the discussions in this context tend to be the longest running. The discussions are more complex now in the face of machine learning, big data, and the proliferation of technologies and tools for data gathering, processing, storage and distribution.

However, as we explore later in this book, there is a range of other topics and challenges arising from modern information management disciplines and capabilities that equally require a framework for analysis and assessment. These include the development of artificial intelligence capabilities, and the proliferation of data-gathering capabilities. What we lack in an information management discipline are formalized ways of assessing and evaluating these issues. However, by referring back to first principles rather than seeking to define a new ethical framework, we can apply a two-stage examination of the outcomes against first principles, balancing the outcomes against four ethical questions regarding the preservation or enhancement of human rights.

The first step of the test is to ask whether the outcome might contribute positively to 'the good', or positive preservation of human rights:

1 Does it preserve or enhance human dignity?

2 Does it preserve the autonomy of the human?

3 Is the processing necessary and proportionate?

4 Does it uphold the common good?

The second step of the test is to ask: does the outcome violate any of these four points?

This test seeks a positive outcome as a determiner of ethical action. Where the positive contribution to the social good is not the priority, it balances the priorities against the necessity of preserving human rights. An action with an outcome that violates these rights may be expected to come into conflict with the societal ethic that regards human rights as a fundamental priority.

As modern information management capabilities may process, combine or link, and make available, vast amounts of information, it is important to consider the outcomes resulting from data processing that are not the focus or intended outcome. This test will need to consider not just the intended outcome but other anticipated possible outcomes.

Example test of outcomes against first principles

A few brief example scenarios may show how real-world processes and outcomes might be tested against first principles. These are rough illustrations rather than in-depth analyses:

Scenario 1: health identifiers

A public-health-services body is planning to implement universal health identifiers for all individuals who use the health services. They foresee many benefits to the implementation, including increased accuracy in prescriptions, a 'single view of patient', and possible cost savings through increased efficiency.

Question 1: Does it preserve human dignity? Does it enhance human dignity? A properly implemented individual health identifier has the potential to preserve and enhance human dignity; accurate identification of patient and procedure required for patient can mean the difference between an oral exam and a rectal exam. Reducing the chances of procedural error in delivering medical treatment would not just preserve but enhance the dignity and well-being of the individual.

Of course, we must ensure we have a clear understanding of what we mean by human dignity to help us answer this question. In most moral, legal or ethical discussions, the concept of dignity is usually understood as being the right to be valued and respected as an individual and the ability to enjoy and benefit from fundamental rights. Philosophers such as Immanuel Kant also link dignity to concepts of autonomy and agency and the ability of people to choose their own actions.

Question 2: Does it preserve the autonomy of the human? The question of autonomy raises issues of free and informed consent, which are extremely important for ethical medical practice. The existence of a health identifier might not necessarily adversely affect the autonomy of the patient, but people may object to having their medical information combined in a way that provides an overarching view of what is often extremely sensitive information.

It will also be necessary to consider who is to be allowed access to patient information, and what controls are in place to ensure decision rights are restricted. Control measures will have to be in place to ensure that information management is centred on the individual and ensures their autonomy as active 'choosers' is preserved.

Great care will need to be taken to ensure that the design and implementation of the health identifier preserves the individuals' privacy and their rights to autonomous action as 'choosers'.

Question 3: Is it necessary and proportionate? If the organization wishes mandatory use of health identifiers across the board, this processing of personal data will have to be justified as necessary and proportionate.

Question 4: Does it uphold the common good? It could be argued that the identifier will increase accuracy in reporting and statistics, providing necessary information to identify which services are needed most and increasing the ability to provide needed services to the public.

This will have to be balanced against the privacy aspects and the proportionality and necessity of processing.

Scenario 2: applications of life-logging technology for Alzheimer's patients

An organization is developing advanced life-logging capabilities to aid people suffering from conditions affecting their memory and cognitive processes. Day-to-day actions and events are recorded to serve as a reviewable record of events, acting in essence as a prosthetic memory.

Question 1: Does it preserve human dignity? Does it enhance human dignity? As this application of technological advancements might possibly do a great deal to ease the distress of a person suffering from conditions such as Alzheimer's disease, it could very much enhance the dignity of the person.

Question 2: Does it preserve the autonomy of the human? The planned capabilities of the technology would help to preserve the autonomy of the device wearer. However, the life-logging technology would, by its nature, record the interactions of the device wearer with other people, capturing their personal data as well. Controls would need to be implemented, taking their autonomy into account, including the possibility of choosing not to have their data processed.

Question 3: Is it necessary and proportionate? In the context of the device wearer, the processing would likely be necessary and proportionate. However, the question of necessary and proportional processing also arises in the context of the other people the device wearer comes into contact with. Measures should be taken to ensure that processing of the personal information of these people is minimized, particularly if there are no measures in place to ensure free and informed consent.

Question 4: Does it uphold the common good? This application of technology is primarily focused on the enhancement of individuals' dignity, but it could also be argued that its availability would also be of more general benefit to communities as a whole. Family and friends of a person affected by

Alzheimer's disease might also benefit from its use. Developments in care to aid members of a community are likely to improve the community as a whole.

Scenario 3: use of analytics to create a granular profile for targeted messaging

An organization uses algorithmic analysis of the patterns of social media 'likes' to create granular profiles of anonymized users, identifying information such as age, gender, ethnicity, socioeconomic status and sexual orientation. These profiles are to be used to provide targeted messaging for marketing or political purposes to identified users who match the granular profile.

Question 1: Does it preserve human dignity? Does it enhance human dignity? These capabilities themselves may not necessarily violate human dignity. However, this depends on the message delivered. Controls would be required to ensure that the uses of this information-processing capability do not violate human dignity.

Question 2: Does it preserve the autonomy of the human? Although the initial data captured for processing is anonymized, the resulting outcome of the aggregation and analysis is essentially identification of individuals, processing sensitive personal information. This is done without the possibility of meaningful consent on the part of the individual. Autonomy is not preserved.

Question 3: Is it necessary and proportionate? It would be difficult to argue that this processing is necessary and proportionate. There may be a societal necessity to enable this type of targeted communication, but it must be balanced against the individual's right to be left alone. Controls would be necessary to justify and ensure the necessity and proportionality of the information processing.

Question 4: Does it uphold the common good? As with the question of human dignity, the technological capability is neutral. It would entirely depend on the use to which it was put.

Scenario 4: destruction of only physical copies of medical records from a redress scheme

A government agency has been running a redress scheme for survivors of certain medical abuses. The persons affected were required to submit their original hard-copy medical records for review as part of a defined statutory redress scheme. The scheme is coming to an end, and the director of the redress board has determined that all the records will be destroyed once their task is completed, on the basis that they are legally required under data privacy laws to destroy records once their purpose for having them has ended, despite the survivors having initially been told that records would be returned to them. The United Nations has invited some survivors to give testimony to a hearing on similar abuses globally. Other survivors wish to keep their records for reference in ongoing medical treatment.

Question 1: Does it preserve human dignity? Does it enhance human dignity? The obligation not to retain data for longer than is necessary is a legal duty in the country in question, but non-retention does not equate to destruction. Human dignity is not preserved or enhanced by the destruction of the records in question. Destruction may impair the ability of the individuals to obtain appropriate medical care.

Question 2: Does it preserve the autonomy of the human? The affected individuals wish to be able to present their story to the United Nations (UN) or to inform clinicians about their medical histories. Destruction of records deprives them of these choices.

Question 3: Is it necessary and proportionate? It is not a necessary step. The physical records could be returned to the survivors. Where the survivor could not be identified, it would be possible to anonymize files and submit them to a university archive or other repository for historical research purposes.

Question 4: Does it uphold the common good? No. There is no common good in question in this case.

The drive for effective ethics in information management

In announcing in 2015 the formation of an external ethics board for data protection issues, the European Data Protection Supervisor (EDPS) expressed the need to 'promote an ethical dimension in future technologies to retain the value of human dignity and prevent individuals being reduced to mere data subjects' (European Data Protection Supervisor, 2015). This statement revealed a concern that the understanding of the 'data subject' – as an individual human whose rights and dignity must be preserved – might be lost, which in turn directly reflects Kant's formulation that ethical action will treat the human as an individual as an end, not a means.

The EDPS opinion paper 'Towards a new digital ethics' places clear importance on the link between ethics and preserving the dignity of the human to enable 'empowered individuals' (European Data Protection Supervisor, 2015). That paper outlined four tiers of ethical considerations:

1 Future-oriented regulation of data processing and respect for the rights to privacy and to data protection.

2 Accountable data controllers who determine personal information processing.

3 Privacy-conscious engineering and design of data-processing products and services.

4 Empowered individuals.

In this, the EDPS calls for a 'big data ethics' (Figure 1.1) that looks to preserving human rights via a focus on privacy in the design and engineering

Figure 1.1   EDPS vision for big data ethics

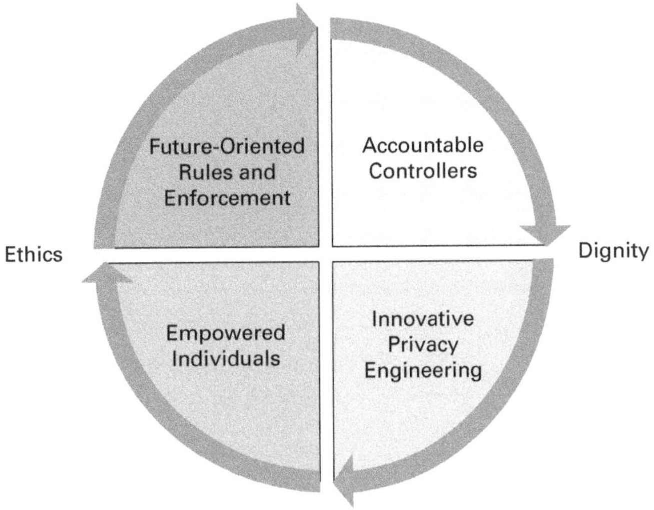

Ethics

Dignity

Future-Oriented Rules and Enforcement

Accountable Controllers

Empowered Individuals

Innovative Privacy Engineering

SOURCE   adapted from EDPS (2015)

of 'big data' projects, and an increased accountability for data controllers as key aspects of a future in which the individual human is seen as an end, not a means. Giovanni Buttarelli, the European Data Protection Supervisor, thus follows in the footsteps of Warren and Brandeis, recognizing that new technologies and modes of business call attention to the next steps that must be taken to preserve human rights, establishing a call for an ethical framework founded on a recognition of human rights and the fundamental concepts of human dignity and autonomy.

The opinion paper also follows the reasoning of Heidegger, in expressing concern about how the real-world objects, represented in the abstract by data, are manipulated in a way that is ethical. The emphasis on 'accountable controllers' and privacy-conscious engineering echoes Bunge's call for technologists to be morally responsible for the technologies they develop. The call to empower individuals is ultimately grounded in the Kantian view that people should not be the means to the end but the end themselves.

However, the practical application of an ethical framework in the context of modern information management will need to consider organizational values, processes and development of technology in the context of fundamental ethical principles such as human rights and dignity. This extends beyond an agreed-upon 'code of practice' into ensuring communication of values across an organization, and governance of processes and behaviour. Without an ethical 'tone' set from the top, and full integration of ethical values across an organization and into the planning and design phases of the life cycle, a code of practice may run the risk of ending up a dead and useless 'strategy' document that bears little relation to an organization's strategic practice, or 'tick box' compliance to a minimal standard that does not uphold ethical information management practices. These scenarios may result in unexpected adverse consequences.

The drive for effective ethics in information management has its roots in the substantial potential and significant risks that are increasingly an inherent part of our information-processing capabilities. In Chapter 7 we will explore the themes raised in the EDPS opinion paper in more detail as we set out a framework for ethical information management in the organization that can help provide a platform for addressing these fundamental ethical considerations.

Chapter summary

In this chapter we have begun the exploration of ethics in an information management context:

- We discussed why it is important for information management professionals to have a good grounding in ethical concepts, particularly in the modern information age.
- We introduced some of the ethical discussions around technology and the use of technology from Heidegger and Bunge, and highlighted how many of these concepts are echoed in data privacy laws in the EU.
- We discussed how the term 'information ethics' is one that should (ideally) go away so that we can focus on the fundamental question of ethics.
- We discussed data privacy as a high-profile example of applied information ethics, with core ethical concepts underpinning the definition of the right to privacy in both the United States and EU contexts.
- We introduced four basic ethical questions to pose when considering any information-processing activity and presented answers to them based on four real-world scenarios.
- We outlined the drive for ethics in information management that is emerging from the regulatory perspective, and examined the EDPS call for 'big data ethics' from the perspective of Kant and Heidegger.

Questions

1 Apply the four-question test to the processing of data by your favourite (or least favourite) social network. Is it acting ethically?

2 What barriers to ethical information management practices do you consider exist in your organization or in an organization with which you are familiar?

3 As a society, do we tend to rush to adopt new technologies without assessing the implications? Is Socrates's point still valid today?

4 Companies and public-sector organizations are often faced with an inherent conflict between goals and ethics. Discuss.

Notes

1 As a left-handed person, Daragh has battled for years with scissors that were biased against him and can attest to the impact on his interaction with things such as wrapping paper.

2 Immanuel Kant (1993) [1785] *Grounding for the Metaphysics of Morals*, trans. James W Ellington, 3rd edn, Hackett, London.

Further reading

In this chapter we have begun to introduce some foundational concepts of ethics and information ethics. Further reading that might be of interest includes:

Blackburn, S (2003) *Ethics: A very short introduction*, Oxford University Press, Oxford

Kleinman, P (2013) *Philosophy 101: From Plato and Socrates to ethics and metaphysics, an essential primer on the history of thought*, Adams Media

Waddington, DI (2005) A field guide to Heidegger: understanding 'the question concerning technology', *Educational Philosophy and Theory*, 37, pp 567–83

Young, PC (2004) Ethics and risk management: building a framework, *Risk Management: An International Journal*, 6 (3), 23–34

References

Benn, SI (1971) Privacy, freedom, and respect for persons, in *Privacy: Nomos XIII*, ed. J Pennock and J Chapman, pp 1–26, Atherton Press, New York

Bunge, M (1977, January 1) Towards a technoethics, *The Monist*, pp 96–107

European Data Protection Supervisor (2015, 1 September) [accessed 1 August 2017] EDPS to Setup an Ethics Board [Online] https://secure.edps.europa.eu/EDPSWEB/webdav/site/mySite/shared/Documents/EDPS/PressNews/Press/2015/EDPS-2015-07-EDPS_Data_Ethics_EN.pdf

European Data Protection Supervisor (2015, 11 September) [accessed 1 August 2017] Opinion 4/2015 – Towards a New Digital Ethics: Data, Dignity, and Technology [Online] https://secure.edps.europa.eu/EDPSWEB/webdav/site/mySite/shared/Documents/Consultation/Opinions/2015/15-09-11_Data_Ethics_EN.pdf

European Union (2016, 24 April) [accessed 1 August 2017] Regulation 2016/679/EU [Online] http://ec.europa.eu/justice/data-protection/reform/files/regulation_oj_en.pdf

Heidegger, M (1977) The question concerning technology, in *The Question Concerning Technology and Other Essays*, ed. W Lovitt, pp. 13–39, Harper & Row, New York

Hudson, SD and Husack, DN (1979) Benn on privacy and respect for persons, *Australasian Journal of Philosophy*, 57 (4), 324–29

Johnson, D (1999) *Ethical Issues in Engineering*, Pearson, New Jersey

Plato (2009) *Phaedrus*, Oxford University Press, Oxford

van der Sloot, B (2015) Privacy as personality right: why the ECTHR's focus on ulterior interests might prove indispensable in the age of 'big data', *Utrecht Journal of International and European Law*, 31 (80), 22–50

Warren, SD and Brandeis, LD (1890) The right to privacy, *Harvard Law Review*, 4 (5), 193–220

Introduction to ethical concepts and frameworks

02

What will we cover in this chapter?

In this chapter we will:

- Introduce fundamental concepts of ethics.
- Outline how these fundamental concepts and frameworks shape our approaches to ethical decision making.
- Introduce the concepts of normative theories of business ethics, including stakeholder theory.
- Highlight the challenge that is emerging in terms of the understanding of ethics in the context of information management, and the importance of these foundational concepts.
- Outline why the conflict between technological innovation and ethics exists, and why it is an important balance to get right in an increasingly 'data-rich' society.
- Introduce the concepts of the ethic of society, the ethic of the organization, and the ethic of the individual as different perspectives on ethics.

Introduction

The number of blogs, articles, comments and other publications dealing with the question of ethics in information management is increasing. Much of this has been in response to the encroachment onto data privacy rights by some high-profile technology companies, as well as wider issues of ethical information handling and business practices in a variety of businesses. Looking at search trends for the term 'data ethics' going back to 2010 and setting it as a reference point, we see a strong and steady trend of increasing frequency of searches (Figure 2.1).

However, when we drill into the data, we see some worrying trends. First, while there has been a 1,350 per cent increase in searches for the term 'big data ethics' since 2010, the increase in frequency of searches for the information on the fundamental concepts of ethics ranges between 250 per cent and 700 per cent during that period, which would suggest we have a handle on these fundamental issues. However, when we look at the top-ranked searches associated with the 'data ethics' search term, we find that the relative ranking of searches for questions such as 'what is ethics?' and 'what are ethics?' are solid performers. So, despite an increase in recent content on the topic, and an evident increase of interest in the topic, people still struggle with the fundamental question of 'what is ethics?'

This is a question that philosophers have wrestled with for millennia. Information management professionals recognize the importance of having an agreed definition of a concept. But a full analytical retrospective of the history of the philosophical discourse of ethics is outside the scope of this book. But, in the same way as we would not write a book about data modelling without explaining some of the underpinning mathematical and logical concepts behind that discipline, this chapter aims to provide you with an *operative definition* for ethics that will form the basis of further discussion in this book and when thinking about ethical issues in information management. In developing this operative definition, we are conscious of cultural bias in our definition (an emerging ethical issue itself in the fields of AI and machine learning) and will endeavour to provide a holistic definition that considers perspectives from other cultures.

On the topic of bias, if you visit the Free Online Dictionary of Computing (Free Online Dictionary of Computing, 2016) and search for the term 'ethics', it returns an extensive discussion of the topic of 'computer ethics'. Our experience in working with and teaching ethical information management concepts is that a better approach is to ask: 'what is ethics?' and build from there. The data we referred to earlier bears out our experience. Jumping in to a discussion of applied ethics without a grounding in some of the basic concepts, terms and modes of thinking would be like asking you to compete in a martial-arts tournament after watching a few Jackie Chan movies.

Figure 2.1 'Data ethics' search terms

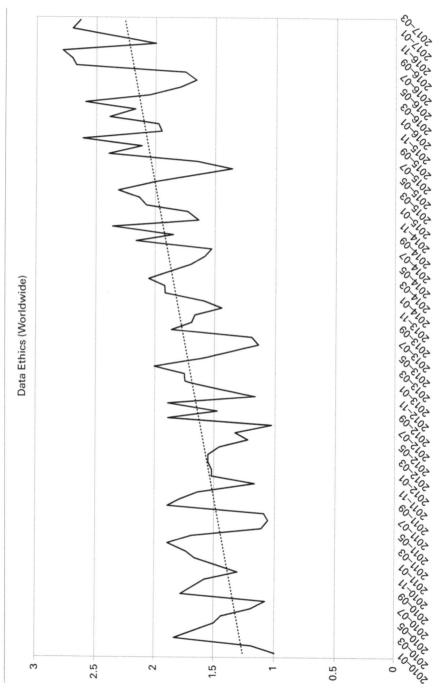

Data Ethics (Worldwide)

Many of the definitions for 'ethics' we encounter in the context of information management discussions present it as a set of principles and practices to help people decide if their conduct is good and bad. This may belie a computer-science bias in the definition. Ethics is not simply about defining what behaviour is good or bad, a binary choice between two options. Ethics is concerned with describing or defining the 'good', and understanding how do we decide what is 'good'. What tools and models do you have to help you do this? There are several broad categories of approaching how to define what is 'good' or what is the 'right action'. In formal philosophy, you might tend to follow a single approach down the garden path, testing the limits of the approach with thought problems, and looking for a logical, defensible theory. In the actions of day-to-day life, however, you tend to balance a mix of approaches without necessarily realizing it, making connections with and drawing on rules and frames of thinking you will have been exposed to through your education and culture.

What you need to be able to do in an information management context is to understand the inputs into your personal ethical algorithm and be able to understand what formal ethical rules, principles and approaches you are applying in your day-to-day management of information and information systems, and how you are forming your 'ethical algorithm'. This awareness of first principles and how you are applying them can also help you to describe your ethical reasoning to others, either inside your organization or outside it. In many respects, this need to be aware of ethical principles and be able to explain how you are applying them is not too different from the need for algorithmic transparency in big data and artificial intelligence.

Ethical theories you should know about

In this section, we look at a few schools of thought in the world of ethics and try to formulate a core definition for information management professionals.

Virtue-based ethics

Virtue ethics are the oldest of the three major normative theories of ethics. In this ethical norm, a good decision or correct act is one that a virtuous person would make or do in that situation. In Western philosophy, the ancient Greek philosophers Plato and Aristotle are seen as the founders of virtue ethics. In ancient Chinese philosophy, the founding philosophers for virtue ethics are Confucius and Mencius.

The ancient Greek and Roman philosophers tended to emphasize this school of thought, which approaches ethics through the lens of self-improvement, virtues being desirable or 'good' character attributes. To oversimplify, the aim of virtue ethics is to embody or live in harmony with the moral virtues valued by a culture or society. An ethical person acts in a way that makes them a better person. According to Aristotle, acting in accordance with virtue results in a well-lived life, '*Eudaimonia*', or 'happiness'. We see echoes of this in the teachings of a variety of religions and a host of cultural norms around the world that promote the doing of 'good works' as a manifestation of ethical conduct, and all of whom echo the concept of a balance between extremes as being the hallmark of virtuous behaviour. Aristotle (Aristotle, 2000) identified a range of virtues, and aspects of virtuous behaviour, in his writings. For example, one of these was the virtue of courage: 'The man who flies from and fears everything and does not stand his ground against anything becomes a coward, and the man who fears nothing at all but goes to meet every danger becomes rash.'

If you think about this virtue in a modern information management context, this could be applied to the adoption of new technologies and methods for obtaining or analysing information. The person who says no to any change becomes a coward, but the person who rushes in and adopts new technologies with no concern for danger becomes rash. The 'golden mean' is a risk-based approach, where the value of the information management capability is recognized, but the risks are also acknowledged, and appropriate measures are taken to address valid fears rather than ignore them.

One criticism of virtue ethics is that our values and understandings of 'virtues' are culturally bound. Different cultures have different focuses on what they consider to be moral goods or virtuous conduct. Which 'virtues' are valued over others may be different in different times, cultures and subcultures, so a focus on virtue ethics in a global context may need to engage with the relativist aspect of what is considered 'virtuous'. These cultural differences obviously exist between different countries and ethnic cultures. However, they can equally arise in the context of the cultural frame of an industry or social subculture. For example, the virtue perspective of a technology-focused person might differ from that of a more human rights-focused individual. However, as Martha Nussbaum has pointed out, the 'first principles' approach of Aristotle when spelling out his virtues does provide a basis to align the perspectives on virtue from a range of cultures (Nussbaum, 1988).

CASE STUDY Running with scissors

Daragh has regular debates with Dr Cathal Gurrin, Associate Professor of Computer Science at Dublin City University.[1] Cathal's research is in the area of personal data analytics. For over a decade, Cathal has been wearing and working with a range of wearable sensors and devices to log and record a range of aspects of human existence and experience. Cathal's focus is on the use of technology to improve and better the lives of people through augmentation of their memories with technology. Daragh comes from a position that technology should not unduly impact on the rights and freedoms of people in society, and the mass deployment of what is essentially a surveillance technology needs to balance both the benefits to the individual and the potential impacts on the wider community.

As Cathal puts it: 'Daragh's the guy who is always telling me not to run with scissors', while Daragh bemoans Cathal's research as being 'obsessed with building bigger, sharper scissors'.

When Daragh analysed why there was an apparent conflict of virtue between his view and the views of Cathal, he realized that they were both talking about applying technology in a way that makes people's lives better, but that they just had different perspectives on what that meant and what that required.

Case study questions

While this case study describes a debate among old friends, it highlights some interesting questions that can arise in the development of new technologies and the line between research and commercialization:

1 Can you think of a technology or a use of technology that might have sounded good as a research concept but had unintended consequences?

2 What types of controls exist, or should exist, to ensure academic researchers think about the potential negative aspects of their research?

3 Can you think of examples of academic studies using information or information technologies that give rise to potentially negative outcomes for society in the absence of robust ethical controls?

Deontological ethics

Another understanding of how to decide right action is based on our under-standing of rules, whether moral duties commanded by a deity, or through a theory of 'universal' rules or laws. The word 'deontology' comes from the Greek words for the study of 'duty'. Deontological ethics are based on choosing your action according to your duty to act in accordance with these universal laws of what is right.

German philosopher Immanuel Kant was a famous deontologist who (among other things) developed a philosophical system that looked to deter-mine universal ethical laws in the way we might consider the law of gravity (Stanford Encyclopedia of Philosophy, 2016). He formulated what he called the categorical imperative – formulated as ultimate, unconditional rules for moral conduct determined by objective reason. As an ethical framework, Kant's formulations of the categorical imperative directly apply to contem-porary ethical questions about privacy and human rights. In this book, we will focus on his first and second formulations of the categorical imperative.

Kant's first formulation of the categorical imperative: 'Act only accord-ing to that maxim whereby you can at the same time will that it should become a universal law.' In real-world practice, this can be interpreted as, 'Sauce for the goose is sauce for the gander.' If I create a set of rules or code of behaviour that applies to other people but not to myself, it is not a valid rule according to this formulation. Regarding questions of informa-tion privacy, we can see this formulation as a response to the argument that 'if you have nothing to fear you have nothing to hide'. Are people who are saying this willing to apply their argument universally? Are the state or corporate actors – who argue that people should have no reason not to open all our data to view and give up our rights to privacy – equally willing to be completely transparent with their own information and actions?

The ultimate transparency of a surveillance state, whether imposed by a government or arising from commercial enterprises, also removes autonomy and dignity. Without the ability to preserve the privacy of one's thoughts and actions one is in a continual state of exposure, comparable to having no choice but to walk down the street naked. The fact that in some situations one prefers to remove all one's clothes (eg a nudist beach or in the shower) does not defend against the removal of that choice.

The question of autonomy and informed consent, the ability to choose whether to share information or not, brings us to Kant's second formulation of the categorical imperative. Kant's second formulation of the categorical imperative is a foundational argument for human rights. As such, it is a useful check for the foundations of decisions made in information management and design of data processes: 'So act as to treat humanity, both in your own person, and in the person of every other, always at the same time as an end, never simply as a means.'

A right action does not simply treat people as commodities, but always ensures their autonomy and dignity as human beings are preserved. This ethical law (or imperative) provides a rule of thumb for right action, in which understanding whether an action is ethical or not is founded in respect for the human as an autonomous person with the right to choose and act in their own capacity. This foundational principle centres upon respect for human dignity. The second formulation of the categorical imperative provides a clear and simple framework, a checkpoint that aligns with the concerns that modern technological advances may violate human rights and dignity.

Consider the implications of this principle for 'freemium' business models of many online services where users effectively pay with their personal information. This is often summed up in phrases like: 'If you are not paying for the product, you *are* the product.' Are these business models treating people simply as commodities, or are they somehow acting to treat people as an end in themselves, not simply as a means to an end? Consider the announcement by Google that they were to begin linking people's offline shopping transactions to online searching activity (Neidig, 2017) to track whether online adverts are leading to real-world purchases. Is this treating people as an ends or a means?

Deontological ethical frameworks primarily focus on ethics in the intent behind action or the 'rightness of an act' rather than the outcomes of an act. In the case of framing an applied ethics for the design of data processing and information management, these ethical principles can be a clear foundational starting point. The result of your actions are less important in a deontological framework than the fact that you took the right action, following a defined set of rules or an ethical code in making that decision.

But right intent is only part of the equation. It is also extremely important to consider the consequences of an action or designed process, whether the consequences (or outcomes) in question are intended or unintended. An ethical framework for modern information practices will need to ensure that the individual's rights or human dignity are upheld in the outcomes of the actions and processes designed. As modern information management processes increase in complexity and capacity, the risk of unintended outcomes that violate the rights of the person increases. These risks must be considered in planning and design, so that possible controls and design changes might be introduced to mitigate the risk of treating individuals as a means rather than an end.

Consequentialist ethics and utilitarianism

Deontological ethics are often contrasted with consequentialist ethics. Consequentialist ethical frameworks look at the outcomes of actions rather than the intent behind the actions. As an ethical framework, consequentialism is goal-focused rather than rule-focused. In consequentialist ethical theories, the consequences of your actions are what determine whether it is a good action or not. While the intent and following the rules is more important than the result of the action from a deontological view, in consequentialism the ends justify whether the means were right. Utilitarianism is one of the best-known forms of consequentialist ethics. It is most closely associated with the works of the philosopher John Stuart Mill (Stanford Encyclopedia of Philosophy, 2016). Under a utilitarian view of ethics, we must act to maximize human welfare and minimize harm. One of the best-known popular-culture expressions of utilitarianism is Spock in *Star Trek*: 'The needs of the many outweigh the needs of the few or the one' (Meyer, 1982).

However, if the outcomes of an action are what counts, a consequentialist framework would allow clearly unethical or immoral acts up to and including murder, if the benefit was great enough. If you follow this garden path to its logical conclusion, if the organs of a healthy person would save the lives of five people in need of organ transplants, it would maximize the benefit and thus be ethical to murder the healthy person in order to save the lives of five.

You can see the results of this kind of thinking in the decision by the United States military to drop atomic bombs on Hiroshima and Nagasaki. As a consequentialist decision, the argument would be that the extreme destruction of the act minimized harm by ending the war quicker, thus resulting in fewer casualties. However, the complexity of follow-on consequences quickly compounds, and it is easy to risk becoming paralyzed by consideration of possible downstream effects.

We also see this in our consulting work where people in organizations rationalize the excessive processing of personal data or acquisition of data on questionable legal grounds on the basis that their data analytics process will have a benefit to society. Another example where this arises is in the context of CCTV or other forms of surveillance technology, where the argument is often put forward that the maximum benefit to society arises from a sacrifice of rights to data privacy.

Another problem with utilitarianism as an ethical framework is that the argument of 'maximizing benefit and minimizing harm' doesn't necessarily mean that benefit and harm are evenly spread. What if the 'maximized benefit' benefits only a few?

The common good and justice-based ethics

Justice ethics look to increase justice. In this framework, an ethical act looks to treat all human beings equally, increasing justice. Justice would be one of the virtues common to many approaches to virtue ethics, but as it is looking for an outcome of increasing justice, contemporary justice is a consequentialist framework (Stanford Encyclopedia of Philosophy, 2017).

In a 'common good' ethical frame, also known as social justice, the actions of individuals and organizations should contribute to the greater good of society. The common good has its origins in the work of classical ethics, but has found more modern discussion in the works of philosophers such as Rawls in the form of ethical concepts based on social justice (Velasquez et al, 1992). At the most basic it can be defined as: 'The common good, then, consists primarily of having the social systems, institutions, and environments on which we all depend work in a manner that benefits all people' (Velasquez et al, 1992).

An example of 'common good' or social justice-based ethics in action at a macro level would be the provision of social services such as affordable (or free) public healthcare. It provides a public benefit but ensures equality of access, ensuring that the promotion of health is distributed equally, otherwise healthcare would only be available to the very rich. It is no coincidence that 'justice' is one of the core ethical principles in the Belmont report's guidelines (National Commission for the Protection of Human Subjects of Biomedical and Behavioral Research, 1979) for the protection of human subjects in medical research.

Stakeholder theory versus shareholder/stockholder theory

One area of business ethics concerns the question of to whom an organization has moral or ethical obligations. This is encapsulated in two competing schools of thought: stakeholder theory and shareholder/stockholder theory. These different perspectives directly affect the focus of the organization when assessing the appropriateness of any course of action.

Stockholder or shareholder view is the more traditional view of the corporation and its role. It narrowly focuses on a corporation's fiduciary obligation to increase value to its shareholders by maximizing profits while complying with law by avoiding fraud. This approach views shareholders as the economic engine of the organization and the only group to which the firm must be socially responsible. As such, the goal of the firm is to maximize profits and return a portion of those profits to share-holders as a reward for the risk they took in investing in the firm. It is often referred to as the Friedman Doctrine as it was framed by Milton Friedman (Friedman, 1962) as follows: 'There is one and only one social responsibility of business – to use its resources and engage in activities designed to increase its profits so long as it stays within the rules of the game, which is to say, engages in open and free competition, without deception or fraud.'

In effect, shareholder theory says that the primary objective of the organization is to make money for its shareholders, and as long as it stays within the rules (or does not get caught breaking them), anything goes. While a dominant theory in business management, the problem with share-holder theory is that it can drive short-term behaviour by managers whose performance bonuses and salaries are usually linked to the bottom-line performance of the organization (Spicer, 2014). These criticisms echo the thoughts of W Edwards Deming, one of the pioneers of the quality manage-ment movement, who famously described short-term focus on tangible numbers as being one of the 'seven deadly diseases' of modern management (Deming, 1986).

Stakeholder theory broadens focus to an organization's fiduciary duty to not just an organization's shareholders, but an organization's stakehold-ers. This includes a duty to balance the interests or legal and moral rights of all the organization's stakeholders, both internal and external (Freeman, 2010; Phillips, 2005). Stakeholders are those who have a vital interest in the corporation, both those who affect the organization and those who are affected by it. This may include owners, managers and employees of a company internally, and external stakeholders such as shareholders, customers, suppliers, creditors, the government or regulators, and society in general, and even the natural environment. Organizations need to identify their legitimate stakeholders and prioritize them, finding the best balance of potentially competing or conflicting interests in order to make the right decisions for the organization. These priorities should include ensuring that the rights of stakeholders are not violated.

In a paper by Smith and Hasnas on the application of normative theories of ethics to information management, they describe one of the key functions of stakeholder theory as being to develop the 'algorithm' to balance the competing interests of different stakeholders (Smith and Hasnas, 1999). We will return to Smith and Hasnas later in this book to explore some of the other ideas in their paper, as they apply to actually putting ethical informa-tion management into practice.

You might consider shareholder and stakeholder theory as being expressions of a commercial ethical virtue in the ethic of the organization.

Common elements of ethical frameworks

As we mentioned in describing virtue ethics, different cultures around the world prioritize different 'virtues'. While philosophers may look for universal ethical values, it is important to remember that in practice there is no one universal ethical framework or understanding of ethical priorities. We navigate overlapping relative ethical frameworks daily, negotiating how our own understanding of what is right and good is like or different to the understandings or ethical frameworks of other people and groups of people.

The ethic of society

Various human groups develop their own norms, including ethical norms. These norms may deprioritize or remain blind to certain things that other cultures consider vital to ethical behaviour.

Societal groups and cultures develop common ethical frameworks shared within that society or culture. 'Cultures' or societal groups may be very large constructs, such as our understandings of national cultures or even larger geographical constructs such as our distinction between 'Eastern' and 'Western' cultures. Cultures or societies may be much smaller subunits, down to families.

One example of an ethical value for which organizations will encounter different interpretations globally is the differing cultural understandings of the relationship of the individual and society, and the resulting effects on the concept of 'privacy' as a value. In cultures that were greatly influenced by the values and philosophies developed in Europe during the 'Enlightenment', privacy as a concept is seen as fundamentally enabling the ability of the individual to develop himself or herself as a fully rounded personality – both with regard to how you present yourself to society but also how you develop your 'inner self' and formulate your independent moral and social philosophy. Privacy allows for that space in which you can formulate the thoughts and opinions you might later choose to express, or not to express, to others.

While we may often find common ground across cultural and societal groups, within a group people tend to develop a certain shared understanding of priorities and of what is 'right'. At a global level, we can see this in differences between cultural understandings of the individual's relationship to the larger social group. Ultimately, the 'ethic of society' affects the expectations that people in that society have of, for example, the way things should work, or the way that information systems should support humanity.

The ethic of the organization

Organizations develop their own culture and values or ethical norms. As a body of people within a cultural construct, every organization develops its own organizational culture. The cultural tone for an organization is often set from the top, as leaders set the organization's values and priorities. To a greater or lesser extent, these values may be very like the values of the larger society the organization developed in, but the organization may also develop different priorities and values (Figure 2.2).

Some organizations value ethical standards – such as altruism or the focus on benefit to society – more than others, but in all cases there is a drive to find a balance of priorities and values that result in a functional organization. If the cultural values or ethical framework of the larger society and the cultural values of the organization do not match, this can cause friction between the outcomes, driven by the decisions made in the organization and the expectations of society.

One broad example that often causes problems is an organizational ethical framework that primarily focuses its attention on the bottom line

Figure 2.2   The relationship between societal ethics and organizational ethics

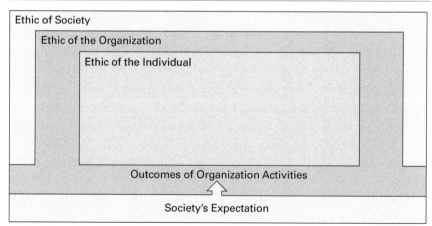

of the business at the expense of broader social impacts. Examples of this behaviour might include illegal dumping of waste, inappropriate acquiring of customer data, or sourcing products or raw materials from illegal or inappropriate sources.

If the organization supports and enables ethical decision making, this can support the success of the organization. Ethical information management and ethical decision making are increasingly being recognized as a competitive advantage in a competitive global market. Virtues and values such as trustworthiness, beneficence, fairness or justice, respect for privacy, and accountability promote good relationships between the organization and its stakeholders and sustainable business models. Public exposure of ethical breaches in information management and business practice have adversely affected not just the reputation but the bottom line of several large global organizations, driving demand for clear codes of ethics across multiple sectors, from automobile manufacturing to machine learning and AI.

The ethic of the individual

When considering ethics for information management, we as individuals are negotiating our particular place in our organizations as well as within society. Our personal ethical development is strongly influenced by the cultural frameworks we developed within, and our relations to the ideas, people, organizations and cultures we interact with daily. You may be influenced by these ethical frameworks, but you may also be influencers. Individual people may have higher ethical standards or a clearer ethical vision than the standards and expectations of the surrounding societal ethical framework. These people may be visionaries and leaders, driving cultural change or refining the cultural understanding of what actions are ethical.

One of the challenges we face in organizations is to align the balance between the organizational ethic with the societal ethic in a way that supports the ethics of the organization's stakeholders both within the organization and in society. How your personal ethical views are formed is an important factor in this context. How you express your personal ethic, and how you align it with the ethic of the organization, is a critical aspect of responsible information management.

Chapter summary

In this chapter:

- We introduced some of the foundational theories of ethics that need to be considered in the discussion of ethics in the context of information management.
- We introduced the ideas underpinning stakeholder theory and other normative models of business ethics, which are important to understand in the context of understanding why organizations, and people in organizations, make the ethical choices that they do.
- We introduced the concepts of the ethic of society, the ethic of the organization and the ethic of the individual, and highlighted some of the issues that can arise when there is a disconnect or misalignment between these factors.

Questions

1 What ethical approach set out here best describes your personal code of ethics?

2 How are ethical values communicated and instilled in the organization you work in, or in the school you attended (or are attending)? What are those ethics?

3 How might a stockholder/shareholder-theory approach to business ethics create challenges for you working in an information management function? What sort of ethical conflicts might arise?

4 If you were asked to implement an information management system or practice that would be beneficial to the bottom line of the organization, and would result in a bonus payment for you, but you knew the practice would impact on the rights or welfare of others, what would you do?

Note

1 See https://www.linkedin.com/in/cgurrin – Cathal and Daragh have been friends for over 30 years. The debate described has raged for half of that time. Daragh is winning.

Further reading

There are a lot of excellent books on ethics and ethical concepts available. After all, this is a field of study that is as old as humankind. Among the books we would recommend for further reading are:

Boone, B (2017) *Ethics 101: From altruism and utilitarianism to bioethics and political ethics, an exploration of the concepts of right and wrong*, Adams Media

Scalambrino, F (2016) *Introduction to Ethics: A primer for the Western tradition*, Kendall Hunt, Dubuque

Scrutton, R (2001) *Kant: A very short introduction*, Oxford University Press, Oxford

Phillips, R (2003) *Stakeholder Theory and Organizational Ethics*, Berrett-Koehler Publishers, Oakland

Yu, J (2009) *The Ethics of Confucius and Aristotle: Mirrors of virtue*, Routledge, New York and London

References

Aristotle (2000) *Nichomean Ethics*, 2nd edn, Hackett Publishing, Indianapolis

Deming, WE (1986) *Out of the Crisis*, MIT Press, Boston

Free Online Dictionary of Computing (2016) [accessed 5 February 2018] Computer Ethics [Online] http://foldoc.org/ethics

Freeman, RE (2010) *Strategic Management: A stakeholder approach*, Cambridge University Press, Cambridge

Friedman, M (1962) *Capitalism and Freedom*, University of Chicago Press, Chicago

Meyer, N (1982) *Star Trek II: The Wrath of Khan*, Paramount Studios

Neidig, H (2017) [accessed 1 August 2017] Privacy Watchdog Asks FTC To Investigate Google's Offline Shopping Tracker, *The Hill* [Online] http://thehill.com/policy/technology/344604-privacy-watchdog-asks-ftc-to-investigate-googles-offline-shopping-tracker

Nussbaum, MC (1988) [accessed 1 August 2017] Non-Relative Virtues – An Aristotlean Approach [Online] https://www.wider.unu.edu/sites/default/files/WP32.pdf

Phillips, R (2005) *Stakeholder Theory and Organizational Ethics*, Berrett-Koehler Publishers Inc, San Francisco

Smith, JH and Hasnas, J (1999) Ethics and information systems: the corporate domain, *MIS Quarterly*, **23** (1), pp 109–27

Spicer, A (2014) [accessed 1 August 2017] Why Shareholder Value Is 'The Dumbest Idea In The World' [Online] http://edition.cnn.com/2014/01/24/business/davos-shareholder-value-is-dumbest-idea/index.html

Stanford Encyclopedia of Philosophy (2016) [accessed 1 August 2017] John Stuart Mill [Online] https://plato.stanford.edu/entries/mill/

Stanford Encyclopedia of Philosophy (2016) [accessed 1 August 2017] Kant's Moral Philosophy [Online] https://plato.stanford.edu/entries/kant-moral/#CatHypImp

Stanford Encyclopedia of Philosophy (2017) [accessed 1 August 2017] Justice [Online] https://plato.stanford.edu/entries/justice/

Velasquez, M, Andre, C, Shanks, T and Meyer, MJ (1992) [accessed 1 August 2017] The Common Good [Online] https://www.scu.edu/ethics/ethics-resources/ethical-decision-making/the-common-good/

Ethics, privacy and analytics   03

What will we cover in this chapter?

In this chapter we will:

- Introduce concepts of ethics in data science and data analytics.
- Look at the ethical issues in analytics from multiple different perspectives. We will first look at the obvious challenges inherent in analytics and privacy and the potential for analytics processes, whether by intent or mishap, to infringe on the privacy of individuals. This is a fundamental area of concern as it spans a multitude of other analytics scenarios and it is one that organizations and individuals struggle with constantly.
- Explore how ethical issues in the application of big data in education have raised issues around the ethics of data acquisition about students, but also ethical questions around the potential for analytical bias, equity, and the impact on student expression and pedagogical decision making.
- Provide an overview of the ethical issues that can arise when applying data analytics to the electoral process. This will look at how the aggregation and analysis of voter data can have significant benefits for the electoral process, but also carries with it immense risks and concerns as well as an increasingly public dark side when combined with other aspects of data science and behavioural manipulation.
- Consider the ethics of big data in the context of the technologies and capabilities being evenly distributed and whether it is appropriate that societies or communities cannot benefit from these capabilities merely due to cost and access to technologies. If the processing of data is supposed to serve mankind, is some of mankind missing out?

At the end of the chapter we will discuss a case you are almost certainly familiar with – the use of analytics and reporting in the automobile industry to generate misleading and inaccurate reporting of vehicle emissions for the purposes of passing emissions tests. We will share with you what this example tells us about the importance of ethical alignment between society, organizations, and individuals within the organization, and how that can impact on the ethics and efficacy of analytics and data science endeavours. The case study is on ethics in analytics in the context of Volkswagen's emissions scandal, which affected the global automobile industry, resale values for certain types of cars (eg diesel engine vehicles), and assumptions in emissions models used by governments for motor taxation policies and compliance with emissions targets to combat global warming.

Analytics and data science: an ethical challenge

Data analytics has evolved rapidly in the last few years in parallel with the growth in the technical capabilities to capture, log, store and process ever larger volumes of data. We have seen the evolution of the humble statistician to the lofty role of 'Data Scientist', and we have seen organizations looking for ways to capitalize on the potential that exists to capture previously unheard-of volumes and types of data.

As discussed in Chapter 2, the growth in interest in data analytics and the associated technologies has been lagged somewhat by the interest in the ethics of data analytics and data science. The interest in the technology and its potential has raced ahead of the consideration of the ethical issues that might arise as a result of these technologies, resulting in risks to society that might not have been fully appreciated by the developers of these tools and technologies.

The potential impact on elections around the world of the application of analytics technologies to influence voters and election outcomes (Bright, 2017) is but one example of this emerging ethical dilemma for data analytics. The potential impact on personal data privacy because of the integration and consolidation of data sets also raises potential ethical issues as well as legal compliance challenges. The 'gaming' of vehicle engine-analytics processes resulting in the misreporting of actual emissions of greenhouse gasses is also an example of ethics in action in analytics and data science.

Of course, what is required is not a new form of ethics, but an evolution of existing ethical principles. We need to build from first principles in terms of the ethical frameworks we are applying to data, and ensure that the results that arise from our analytics capabilities are the results we would desire for individuals and society.

What is data analytics?

Before we dive too deep into a discussion of the ethical issues in data analytics, it is important that we have a core definition of what data analytics is in this context. This is important, as many of the fundamental ethical questions we are now encountering arise out of the nature of the analytics capabilities that the underlying technologies give rise to.

To help frame the discussion of information management disciplines, we will refer throughout this book to the Data Management Body of Knowledge (DMBOK) developed by DAMA International (DAMA International, 2017). The DMBOK defines 10 key knowledge domains for information and data management professionals. We will refer to the DMBOK in more detail in Chapter 5. For readers unfamiliar with the disciplines of data science and 'big data', we address these in more detail as part of that overview in Chapter 5.

However, for the purposes of this chapter we will combine these functions under the umbrella banner of 'data analytics'. Partly, this is to reflect the reality in modern organizations that the line between retrospective reporting (business intelligence) and forward-looking analytics (data science) is increasingly blurred, with technology implementations in organizations increasingly combining both the 'traditional' analytics functions of data warehousing with the emerging technologies of data science and big data. It is also a pragmatic choice given that, from the perspective of people who might be affected by the outcomes of the processing, the specifics of the technology are not the primary concern. For the same reason, in Chapter 4 we will discuss the implications of machine learning and artificial intelligence aspects of data science.

The ethical issues in data analytics

Data analytics raises a range of ethical issues and questions that need to be considered, particularly as organizations are beginning to apply or to mature their big data and data science capabilities. As Giovanni Buttarelli, European Data Protection Supervisor, put it:

> Human innovation has always been the product of activities by specific social groups and specific contexts, usually reflecting the societal norms of the time. However, technological design decisions should not dictate our societal interactions and the structure of our communities, but rather should support our values and fundamental rights. (European Data Protection Supervisor, 2015)

The challenge we face with analytics capabilities is ensuring that their implementation actually does support our values and fundamental rights. This is particularly the case given the granular detail of information that can be obtained in the current Information Age, let alone the potential of technologies such as the internet of things. Remember, at the time of writing it is only 10 years since Steve Jobs persuaded us to put a GPS-enabled audio-and-video-recording device in our pockets with the birth of the iPhone.

We will start our discussion of ethics in analytics by reviewing what the DAMA DMBOK says about the importance of 'tone at the top' in analytics and data science in the context of best practice in ethics.

'Tone at the top' and analytics

In this context, the 'tone at the top' refers to the strategy of the organization and the contribution that analytics, reporting and data science can make to that strategy. In the context of traditional data warehousing, the DMBOK (DAMA International, 2017) tells us that we should 'begin with business goals and strategy'. In the context of data science and big data, we are told that an 'organization's big data strategy needs to be aligned with and support its overall business strategy and business requirements'. This alignment to strategy also implies an alignment to the values and ethos of that strategy, and ethics (the 'tone from the top') has a role in relation to how that strategy is interpreted and what actions or tactics are deemed acceptable to achieving those strategic goals. This overarching ethical view of what is/is not acceptable, or what the emphasis is in the organization from an analytics perspective, is often referred to as the 'tone at the top'. As Deloitte Consulting (Deloitte, 2014) put it: 'In the context of an ethics and compliance programme, the tone at the top sets an organization's guiding values and ethical climate. Properly fed and nurtured, it is the foundation upon which the culture of an enterprise is built. Ultimately, it is the glue that holds an organization together.'

In many respects, this highlights one of the ways in which machine-learning strategies can appear to mimic human behaviour. If you focus solely on the stated goal in the strategy of the organization, you are applying a reinforcement learning strategy. As a result, you might achieve that result in a manner that is unexpected, unethical or illegal.

For example, if the strategic objective of the organization is to increase profitability by reducing the number of customers it costs more to serve than they generate in revenues, you might try to achieve that goal by sending promotional materials for your competitors to those portions of your customer base on whom you are making a net loss. To do this, you would need to have the data available to calculate the profitability of the customers, but also have data about your competitor's products and services so you can craft an attractive offer for your negative-value customers to migrate. Setting aside for one moment the question of whether such a practice would be legal, the question must be asked if it is *ethical* to adopt that type of approach to achieving the goal.

In this context, ethics can be thought of as analogous to a supervised learning model that helps you ensure alignment between the strategic goals of your organization and your data strategy to support those goals, and clarity of boundaries for what types of actions will be acceptable to achieve those goals. If directly off-loading your negative-value customers to your competitors is not ethically acceptable, how then would you achieve the overall objective of increasing average profitability of your customers? From an analytics perspective, you might try to identify opportunities to sell complimentary services or to sell them higher-margin services, or you might need to look at what is driving costs in the support and maintenance of those customers – for example, are they using the call centre (expensive contact channel) as opposed to engaging online or through self-service channels?

This highlights the dependency between analytics, ethics and data governance. When it comes to analytics and data science, our experience working with clients has been that a tone from the top that is emphasizing the technology over the information, or the value to the organization rather than balancing the value to the organization's customers or community, or that adopts a 'mission from god' approach to the acquisition and integration of data for analysis tends to be a strong indicator of ethics or compliance issues further down in the organization's analytics and information management functions.

Big data-driven education

Big data and data science promise incredible benefits in domains such as education. A brave new world of education is being heralded as schools, educators and government education departments look to capabilities of data analytics, sensor-based measurement and data gathered from learning

management systems or other classroom tools to develop improved historical reporting of achievement, but also to improve predictive analytics to
support learning interventions and, it is promised, improve learner outcomes
and achievement.

For example, Purdue University (Willis, 2014) has, for several years, used
a tool called Course Signals that uses predictive analytics to identify which
students are at risk of doing poorly. They use data such as:

- student demographics;
- academic history;
- engagement with online resources;
- current course performance.

This data is used to assign the learner to a risk group based on an algorithm.
Based on the analysis, learners are sent a notification of whether they are
in a red, yellow or green category. If you are red, that means the computer
says you need to pull up your socks and get some help. Yellow means you
have been categorized as falling behind, and green means you're doing okay.
Instructor feedback follows on performance and where to go next, if an
intervention is needed.

On the face of it, this is a successful use of analytics and predictive modelling to support learner attainment and learner retention. Purdue reported
overall gains in retention of students over four years. Students who did not
take part in a course linked to the Course Signals initiative had a retention
rate of 69.4 per cent. Students who had at least one course that was linked
to Course Signals had a retention rate of 87.42 per cent, and students who
had two or more Course Signals had retention rates in excess of 90 per cent.
This is despite the SAT scores for students coming into Purdue – and taking
more than two courses linked to the Signals programme – being lower than
for the group that had no Course Signals courses (Arnold and Pistilli, 2012).
In addition, student performance was higher on final course grades. Arnold
and Pistilli report that there was a 10.37 per cent increase in As and Bs
awarded on courses that were using Course Signals compared to the same
courses in previous years before the programme was introduced. They also
reported a decrease in lower grades and course withdrawals compared to
previous years. Despite the apparent success, Purdue has recently announced
(Purdue University, 2017) that the Course Signals technology will not be
available after December 2017 due to a vendor decision to decommission
the platform.

The initial reports looked laudable and impressive. The use of an analytics-based approach to learner support in a third-level institution seemed to work. Or did it? This apparently strong evidence has been criticized in the academic community as potentially confusing causation and correlation. A key question that has been raised by reviewers is whether students were retained because they took more courses linked to Course Signals, or whether they took more courses linked to Course Signals because they had been retained (Caufield, 2013; Essa, 2013).

The challenge of verifying the causal effect of learning analytics outcomes has been highlighted as a key challenge for the adoption and acceptance of the technology, with concerns raised about the lack of attention to ethics in the design and execution of studies in the effectiveness of learning analytics (Ferguson and Clow, 2017). In a blog post in 2013, one commentator queried whether the 'tone at the top' from Purdue, who had licensed Course Signals to a commercial partner to sell to other universities, might have posed an ethical issue in how they promoted the headline data that had since been called into question (Feldstein, 2013).

Indeed, the early adopter hype seems to have begun to fade for learning analytics. In addition to the concerns about whether learning outcomes are improved, or the impact on the privacy of students, or the impact on equality, there is a growing recognition that the use of big data and analytics in education can fundamentally affect the pedagogical approach of the university.

It is increasingly clear that learning analytics approaches and technologies have been adopted in the higher-education sector at a faster pace than the discussion of the ethical issues surrounding their use (Roberts et al, 2016). Again, it appears that 'tone at the top' may be a contributor to ethical issues in this context, with Roberts et al identifying that the 'increasingly competitive nature of higher education to quickly fulfil government demands in creating nationally and globally competitive graduates may serve as an explanation for the rapid expansion of learning analytics without student involvement'. Universities, competing for students and decreased government funding, may be using the lure of the latest technological supports and 'best teaching methods' to attract students and, hopefully, retain them.

Up until now, institutions have largely focused their efforts on institutional aims such as performance assessment, financial planning and admissions tracking. These are largely achievable with effective data warehousing and business intelligence capabilities. The application of data-science approaches promises the potential for student benefits such as insight into their own habits and learning strategies, along with personalized learning plans and the provision of timely interventions and supports. Such smart learning is heralded as a key to promoting efficacy and equality of learning.

One of the risks identified by researchers, however, is that use of algorithmically generated personal learning plans might have an impact on pedagogic approaches in education. The decisions of the machine can only be made based on the data the machine has access to. This may serve to limit rather than enhance the pedagogic experience and may make it harder for students, parents and society to exercise agency and choice and demand accountability (Zeide, 2017).

However, the accuracy of outcomes will depend on the representativeness, accuracy and relevance of data that is included in the models for analytics, and the algorithms that are applied. Data quality issues become potentially life altering if an incorrect value for you in the data set labels you as being in difficulty or, equally, labels you as being not in need of assistance when you are (Zeide, 2017). Likewise, the promise of more equitable education outcomes could be undermined by flaws and biases in the underlying algorithms and may incorporate historic patterns of inequity. These historic patterns can in turn create a self-fulfilling prophecy where, because a student fits a variety of criteria that the algorithm has determined are indicative of poor outcomes, the student may become demoralized by the labelling.

Zeide also points out that the 'current approach to big data analytics presumes more data is better, leading to the expansion of types of information collected about students and increasingly creating spaces of pervasive surveillance' (Zeide, 2017). This has a chilling effect on student expression and diversity, which in turn has a potential long-term impact on our society in terms of the independence of thinking and creativity of the members of that society. In many respects, this is the same type of consideration as exists when we consider the chilling effects of privacy-invasive analytics in the wider context, only in this case it has the potential to curtail future choices and opportunities. The research suggests that students feel more vulnerable in data-driven learning environments and this can impede academic performance, particularly among minorities.

If we consider this from the perspective of Kant's second formulation of the universal imperative, as discussed in Chapter 2, it seems that higher education may have an ethics problem when it comes to the adoption of learning analytics. The students risk getting lost in the mix, risking becoming a means to an end rather than an end in and of themselves. (To put this in context, your humble scribes of this book are both self-directed learners who make connections among topics by discussing with people from other disciplines. We shudder to think how we might have been labelled in a system such as Course Signals.)

Ethically, it is remiss not to include the considerations of students in the assessment of analytics in a learning environment. Despite the many academic papers in this area, there has been very little research on student attitudes. This is consistent with our experience in other areas of big data, including electoral analytics. Of the research that exists (see Roberts et al, 2016), several consistent themes emerge around awareness, privacy, accuracy of data, the potential impact on independence of learners and of learning, the potential for inequality because of only some students benefiting, and the importance of an effective governance structure for data that has a strong ethical base.

The overarching conclusion that emerges from the research is one of the importance of including students early in the decision-making process about big data and learning analytics in order to develop a 'student-centric' approach to meet student learning needs (Roberts et al, 2016).

We will leave the final word on this to Elana Zeide (Zeide, 2017): 'It is important that the changes wrought by big data in education are not made unknowingly and inadvertently by thoughtlessly implementing new technologies. They should instead be the result of considered choices sufficiently transparent to permit public scrutiny.'

Big data in the electoral process

Recent political developments have cast a light on the role of big data and analytics in the electoral process. The ability for political parties, or companies working on their behalf, to obtain, ingest, and analyse vast amounts of data about individuals, their interests, their hopes, their likely voting intentions, and more, has created a perfect ethical storm for information management professionals. This ethical storm embraces both the traditional data warehousing and business intelligence aspects of analytics, but it is increasingly clear that the data science and predictive analytics dimensions create a potential danger to democratic processes worldwide.

The traditional data warehousing and business intelligence aspect of this is relatively simple. A political party can acquire copies of voter rolls in most countries. In some they can obtain copies of the records of who actually voted. In the Irish political system, and many others, each candidate historically held data individually for their own electoral purposes rather than this being a centralized resource for the party machine. But increasingly political parties are centralizing the storage of that data in voter management systems that can include case management (for constituent queries), records of when you were canvassed in an electoral campaign and your stated voting intention or position on the issues. In the United States, this data is supplemented with data sets from third-party data brokers to develop an incredibly rich view of who you are, what you care about, and what is the best time to contact you.

Politicians and political parties have been doing this type of data gathering and statistical analysis of voters, drawing on the practices of market segmentation in commercial advertising, at least since the era of John F Kennedy. However, the recent increase in the types, granularity and the frequency of update of data about voters that are available now – as a result of social media and other technologies – means that savvy politicians, just like Kennedy, are seeking to apply the methods and practices of business to the political game.

Over the past five years, people interested in data-enabled political campaigning have become increasingly enthusiastic about the ability to create a 'single view of constituent' and use it to target political messaging and get out the vote, following the successes of the Obama presidential campaigns. Obama emulated his predecessor JFK in harnessing and using data and analytics tools more effectively than previous campaigns or his competitors (Lynch, 2012; Shen, 2013).

Over the same period, we have seen the number of users of social media platforms increase, new platforms emerge, and the continued evolution of data analytics capabilities and data-gathering capabilities – all of which now has the potential to be aggregated with the more traditional data that political parties would acquire to support micro-targeting of messages to voters. Platforms such as Google and Facebook provide services, driven by analytics and algorithms, that can target messages effectively even to people that the political parties do not have a detailed dossier on already (Armerding, 2016; Talbot, 2016).

Research published in 2013 by researchers at University of Cambridge (Kosinski, Stillwell and Graepel, 2013) showed that anonymous Facebook likes from US Facebook users could successfully predict, with substantially high degrees of probability, people's voting preference, sexual orientation and whether they were Caucasian or African American. This research highlighted just how much information people are willingly providing for algorithms to ingest and process to reveal intimate traits about political views, religion, intelligence levels and other factors.

Two significant electoral outcomes took place in 2016 and 2017 that have been attributed to the data analytics and targeted political advertising that capitalized on the 'filter bubble' effect that is generated by social media and algorithmically generated news feeds. Both the election of Donald Trump in the United States and the UK Brexit vote are credited to the use of data analysis and other techniques by data analytics companies working in both campaigns. The analysis allowed for online advertising to be directly targeted at voters, so a voter whose profile indicated they had a particular bias on a particular issue was shown the message that was most likely to generate a response in favour of the candidate.

There is an interesting parallel between the use of analytics and big data in elections and their use in education. The debate is about whether predictive analytics and other techniques that are alleged to have been applied in the Trump and Brexit campaigns worked versus other more traditional campaign methods (Mathieson, 2017; Doward and Gibbs, 2017). Both the Clinton defeat and the Brexit vote can equally be explained by poor campaigning on the part of the sides that lost each vote, and other factors unrelated to data and analytics. For example, a national public radio (NPR) analysis identified some key issues in Hillary Clinton's campaigning, including a failure to engage directly with voters (as she had done in her Senate campaign in 2000), a reactive campaign slogan that echoed Trump's, and a number of other factors (Montanaro, 2016). In the context of Brexit, there was a lack of awareness among voters that the Conservative Party position was actually to remain in the EU; there were mixed messages from other political parties, in particular Jeremy Corbyn; and there was a media frenzy around the Conservatives about their internal politicking and not their campaigning, and the impact of prolonged media misinformation about the EU, particularly in UK tabloids (Behr, 2016; The Economist, 2017).

However, the simple fact is we don't know for certain if these analytics techniques and the targeting of voters worked, or if they alone swung elections. Voters were targeted with messages that focused on specific issues and fears. The targeted voters tended to exist in a state of 'low-information', either through limited access to information, limited ability to compare and analyse information, or through the operation of 'filter bubbles' created by algorithmic filtering of content and search results. In that context it is all too easy for confirmation bias ('this must be true, all the sources I use are telling me the same thing') and other cognitive errors to affect decision making. The answer to the question of 'did misuse of data analytics affect elections' has to be 'it's complicated'. Research and investigation by activists such as Paul-Olivier de Haye (de Haye, 2016) highlight some worrying aspects of the Trump election and how these tools might have been used to influence people in these 'low information' states. But, as de Haye says, the evidence is compelling but not conclusive.

The other parallel concerns the views of the people who are ostensibly the focus of this analysis and targeting. As with the education sector there is very little research on voter attitudes to this kind of analysis. A few years ago, we did a Privacy Impact Assessment for an Irish political party voter-data-management system. We could only identify a few pieces of research that were addressing voter-data analytics from the voter perspective. However, they were all broadly consistent in their message. Voters didn't like it. One of the papers we identified (Turow et al, 2012) was very blunt: 64 per cent of Americans said their likelihood of voting for a candidate they support would decrease if they learn a candidate's organization buys information about their online activities and their neighbour's online activities and then sends different messages to each of them; 85 per cent said they would be angry if Facebook used profile information they had set as private in order to send targeted political adverts to them.

US voters didn't like micro-targeting back in 2012. The key issue that US voters reported having back in 2012 was a lack of information about what was being done with their data, and a lack of control over how that data is used. Of respondents surveyed by Turow et al (2012), 65 per cent wanted to know what a campaign knew about them when targeting an advert; 76 per cent said they wanted to know where the data came from. They also had extreme opinions on the selling and sharing of data without informed consent: 91 per cent said it was not okay for a candidate's website to sell their information; only 38 per cent objected when an opt-in option is given.

Turow summarizes the Annenberg research as follows: 'What we have is a major attitudinal tug of war: the public's emphatic and broad rejection of tailored political ads pulling against political campaigns' growing adoption of tailored political advertising without disclosing when they are using individuals' information and how.'

This highlights the information asymmetry problem that many commentators on electoral data analytics have raised in the context of the 2016 US election and the 2016 Brexit referendum. People are largely unaware of how their data is used in electoral analytics and electoral campaigning. Again, we have a classic Kantian ethics problem. As with the use of analytics in education and learning, it appears that the people are being treated as the means to an end, rather than an end in and of themselves. We also see a 'tone at the top' deficit from an ethics perspective. Politicians insist they want to hear the voice of the people and respect the will of the people. But, when it comes to data analytics, the voters' voices appear to be drowned out by the siren call of the algorithmic solution.

Looking at this from the perspective of the life cycle of analytics, we find the following ethical questions can arise:

1 **Acquisition** – is the level of transparency about what information is obtained, how, and where it is obtained from by political parties appropriate? Does the electorate have appropriate controls over how their data is used?

2 **Analysis** – when combining and linking data in the analysis process, are there appropriate safeguards in place to prevent ethical breaches and to ensure compliance with relevant legislation?

3 **Action** – what action will be taken based on the analysis? Is it ethical or appropriate to fuel social or political division at the extremes, curtailing debate, and reinforcing ideologies through an increasingly targeted algorithmic filter?

This is a critical ethical and social dilemma for the Information Age. Whether analytics or psychographic targeting based on your Facebook likes and the ratio of cat pictures to birthday greetings in your Twitter timeline worked in the last cycle of elections, the analytic capabilities and targeting capabilities are getting better. If politicians are going to carry out psychological profiling of you in an experiment to see if they can get your vote in the ballot box, then many commentators feel that, at a minimum, they should be obtaining informed consent, just like real psychologists and scientists.

Data privacy laws like the EU's data protection regime may provide some legal structures to mitigate this ethical dilemma (Zanfir, 2016). It would likely require explicit consent from each individual voter for the processing of a specific set of data. As the manipulation of people's voting preferences is an order of magnitude more impacting on the other fundamental rights of an individual than persuading them to buy a particular brand of breakfast cereal, it is likely that this type of processing would fall afoul of a number of provisions in the General Data Protection Regulation. The remedies to the concerns raised by US voters in 2012 can be found in EU legislation, it seems.

However, the evolution of analytics in the political sphere has tracked the commercial sphere since the invention of the printing press. The technologies used to nudge us to buy certain brands are evolving, as is their application in electoral campaigning. The stakes and implications are higher in this context, however, because breakfast cereal doesn't set the socioeconomic policies of our countries.

Analytics and privacy

The balancing of personal data privacy rights against the interests of an organization to execute its functions or sell its services is one of the highest-profile minefields for ethics and analytics. Indeed, when we discuss this topic with peers, clients or at conferences it can be difficult to steer away from privacy as a topic and to discuss some of the other ethical aspects of big data and data science. As you have seen in the discussion of analytics in education and in electoral processes, privacy concerns and people's awareness of what data about them is being processed are a common area of concern.

As of January 2017, there are 120 countries with data privacy laws and a further 30 with proposed legislation (Greenleaf, 2017). But as Mandy Chessell, writing for IBM, has pointed out (Chessell, 2014), increasingly the legislation can lag what is technically feasible. She is not alone in that view. This widening gap and disparity of power between individuals and organizations collecting and collating data about them is where the ethical challenges of data privacy come into play, particularly where there is a perceived gap in the legislation or, in the case of the EU's General Data Protection Regulation, the legislation is framed as a risk management approach to privacy and requires the organization to adopt its own assessment of whether its approach to protecting the privacy of the individual is sufficient.

It is beyond the scope of this book to give a full analysis of all the aspects and issues of data privacy in an analytics context. For now, we will consider the privacy implications of data analytics in the context of the analytics life cycle (Figure 3.1). While you might not be directly responsible for or in control of the acquisition or action stages in the life cycle, the choices made by others in those stages of the life cycle affect whether your analytics processing is ethical or legal.

Acquisition

It is a commonly agreed principle of data privacy that information about people should be obtained fairly and processed in a transparent manner.

Figure 3.1   The analytics life cycle

This is enshrined in the OECD's Fair Information Practices (OECD, 2013) and is a key principle in the EU's Charter of Fundamental Rights (European Union, 2000), the General Data Protection Regulation (GDPR) and the other data privacy laws around the world.

The ethical questions around transparency at the point of data acquisition include more than just how much you are going to tell people about processing, but also how you are going to tell them. The GDPR (European Union, 2016) explicitly requires that the information provided should be accessible, understandable and intelligible (Recital 39). This raises challenges when we consider the variety of methods by which data about people can be acquired, particularly when it is not being obtained directly from the affected individual. A key point that needs to be considered about the ethics of acquisition is accessibility. Issues such as the level of literacy of the people whose data you are going to be processing, or whether they are colour blind, all need to be considered.

The derivation of data about people using machine learning and other analytics techniques such as text analytics also raises potential ethical issues in relation to transparency. This is particularly the case when the machine-learning algorithms use unsupervised or reward-based learning strategies and may do things that are unforeseen by even the developers, or may codify inherent biases that could lead to incorrect or inaccurate data being recorded about people.

Analysis

When we enter the analysis phase of the analytics life cycle it is important to consider the ethics of compatibility of processing with the original purposes. Simply because you have data available to analyse, it does not necessarily mean you can or should be doing the analysis. This is highlighted in the principles of purpose limitation and purpose specification in global standards for data privacy principles (European Union, 2016; OECD, 2013).

This is an important ethical checkpoint as regulators are increasingly expecting organizations to have documented their decision-making processes for this type of compatibility test. This highlights the critical relationship between information ethics, analytics and data governance. Clear rules need to be defined about 'how to decide how to decide'. Another key ethical checkpoint is the requirement for processing of personal data to be both necessary and proportionate. This will affect your approach to data acquisition, but it will also affect how you will design your analytics process in a variety of ways, including, but not limited to, how you select data and what level of granularity of data you will use in your analysis.

The question of whether the data you are processing is personal data is also important. This relates to the ability of the organization to identify individuals directly or indirectly from the data, irrespective of the presence of tangible personal identifiers such as names or addresses. The combination of data sets, even anonymized data, can eventually result in individuals being identifiable in the data. For example, Facebook can identify people in images even where their faces are obscured, based on other physical characteristics (Glaser, 2017), and increasingly analytics processes on images and video are being used to infer people's emotions and mood in images and videos.

Think of it as being like the end of the movie *The Usual Suspects*, where the character Verbal Kint is being interrogated by police about a gangster, Keyser Söze, who masterminded a violent hijacking. Rather than the infamous Keyser Söze being a different person who Kint is afraid of, Kint is revealed at the end of the movie to be Keyser Söze, and his statement about the events in the movie is revealed to be based on items he has seen around the office of the police officer who was interrogating him such as the brand name on the coffee cup the police officer is drinking from. Based on the small items of data from different sources, a rich profile of an individual can be created. Given enough data points, analysis will prove that you are indeed Keyser Söze, and we also know if you are happy about that fact. The key ethical challenge in analytics though is what the impact on people this type analytics process will have. Will it affect their agency and choice? Will it restrict their access to services or information? Much of this comes down to how the output of the analysis will be put into action.

Action

'Action indeed is the sole medium of expression of ethics', according to Jane Addams (Addams, 1902), a pioneering US social reformer of the early 20th century. This is as true in analytics as it is in any other domain. As we have seen in our examination of education and electoral data management, it is often how the data will be used that drives many of the ethical issues and privacy issues that arise in analytics.

It is important to consider the legal or equivalent effects that your analytics processes will have on the affected individuals. This test of the balance between the data privacy rights of the individuals whose data you are processing and the organization conducting the processing is essential when there is a lack of clear legal basis for your processing such as contractual obligations, consent or a legal requirement. The Article 29 Working Party, the collegiate body of European Data Protection Supervisory Authorities, has issued extensive guidance on the considerations to include in such a balancing test (Article 29 Working Party, 2014). This guidance is a useful reference for ethical assessments of analytics processes.

There are countless examples of organizations that have failed to manage legal and ethical issues in the life cycle of a data analytics and big data context. In the introduction to this book we discussed the Samaritans Radar app and the fallout from the ethical questions of that application's use of text analytics to identify people who were potentially suicidal or in need of assistance (Orme, 2014). A more recent example is the introduction by Facebook of almost exactly the same type of technology combined with an AI component to proactively identify users who may be manifesting or expressing suicidal intent. Unlike Samaritans Radar, the Facebook system alerts appropriate first responders rather than other individuals who may be trolling the affected individual. Facebook have announced that the system will operate everywhere apart from in the EU, and they have also confirmed (at the time of our writing this chapter) that there is no way for people to opt out of this processing and monitoring. The exclusion of the EU is on the basis that automated processing of data relating to physical or mental health is more highly regulated in the EU, but Facebook's announcement appears to miss that all Facebook users outside the United States and Canada are customers of Facebook Ireland and, as such, are protected by EU data privacy laws. More troubling is the lack of any ability for a person to opt out of the monitoring (Constine, 2017). Equally concerning is the lack of transparency from Facebook about how their AI monitoring in this context actually works. In effect, by reason of geography, individuals now find themselves subject to monitoring of their mental health by a private corporation that has not disclosed how their monitoring works and will not provide an opt out (Ruiz, 2017). This raises an obvious risk of unintended consequences: without trust in the tool, at-risk people may simply decide against sharing emotionally revealing or suicidal posts, which serves to undermine the effectiveness of the existing human-driven reporting processes for content of this type.

Another example of the potential ethical issues that can arise is highlighted by the recent revelations that an Irish government agency had been trying for almost a decade to get access to data from mobile-phone operators in order to track the movements of tourists visiting the country. Despite repeated feedback from the Irish data privacy regulator that there was no legal basis for the processing, the agency has persisted to seek access to the data. This essentially amounts to a mass surveillance regime for the purposes of analysis of tourist movements. However, it would not only capture tourists but would also include any business travellers, or any person living along the border between Northern Ireland and the Republic of Ireland. Significant questions exist about the necessity and proportionality of this approach to generating tourism statistics (Edwards, 2017).

A key feature of an ethical approach to data privacy in an analytics context is the recognition of the need to ensure a balance between the data privacy rights of the individual and the objectives of the organization throughout the analytics life cycle. From a legal compliance perspective, this type of analysis only comes into consideration when there is no other grounds for carrying out the processing such as consent or a legal obligation and the data controller is relying on what is referred to as their 'legitimate interest'.[1] However, from an ethics perspective, in all cases it is a useful checkpoint to ensure that the processing is being done in a way that most appropriately balances rights, duties and obligations. It is an unfortunate truth that sometimes things can be done in a way that is perfectly legal but may not be entirely ethical.

The Article 29 Working Party has issued guidance (Article 29 Working Party, 2014)[2] on the balancing tests to be applied when an organization is seeking to rely on the legitimate interest ground to justify processing of data. The working party suggests that organizations consider both their interests and the interests of the affected data subjects as being on a spectrum ranging from insignificant to compelling. Compelling legitimate interests may, subject to appropriate safeguards and controls, justify an intrusion into the privacy of the individual. The role of safeguards is significant in assessing the balance of interests. The more 'investment' the data controller has made into safeguards – such as awareness and education about the processing (transparency), technical and organizational controls, data minimization etc – the higher the potential that there will be a balancing of interests. Of course, this depends on the context of the processing and the context of the types of information that are proposed to be processed. The balancing test for postal marketing to a customer is likely met by: 1) letting them know that if the order is from you then you will send them marketing materials; and 2) providing them with a simple means to opt out or decline the communications. The balancing test for a pizza chain selling the order history of customers to an insurance company for the purposes of calculating premiums is likely to be much harder given the impact on the rights and freedoms of the data subject (for example: how would the insurance company know if you had eaten those three deep-pan pepperonis on your own or not?).

The guidance on the balancing test is relatively straightforward and is detailed in the Article 29 Working Party's opinion. The process of conducting the assessment ultimately forces organizations to consider if they are viewing the individual as a means in and of themselves or purely as a means to an end. It requires you to consider less privacy-invasive methods and invest in appropriate privacy-enhancing controls such as anonymization, user access controls, or differential privacy in your analytics processes to strike the right balance. When working with clients we often whiteboard the perspective of the organization and the perspective of the customer using a version of the four-box model illustrated in Figure 3.2.

The future is here, it's just not evenly distributed

Another aspect of ethics in analytics is the issue of access to the analytics tools and technologies. Data science and analytics has a disproportionately large benefit for developing countries. Unfortunately, the digital dividends that come with technologies such as data analytics tools have lagged the developments in other areas. This is compounded when free software requires expensive hardware to run or presume an always-on, high-speed internet connection.

As we develop our analytics technologies and capabilities, we need to keep in mind the digital divide in the world. It is an ethical choice that needs to be made in terms of capability and equality of access to the same potential benefits of analytics. Bruno Sanchez-Andrade Nuño is a data scientist who

Figure 3.2   Balancing test matrix

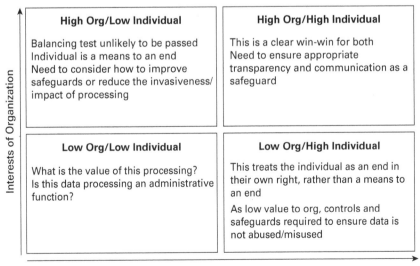

has worked with the World Bank on development projects. In a blog post in July 2017 (Nuño, 2017) he describes the idea of 'Cheap Data Science': 'Cheap Data Science is then the design principle of gracefully degrading to a modest computer and poor connectivity. It's okay if it takes more time, or you need to bundle your internet needs. The important thing is that you don't leave out those without that MacBook Pro or internet connection.'

Bruno's blog post describes how he has struggled to do cheap data science in developing countries, including the difficulties posed by online courses that use video and other technologies for interactive e-learning that simply will not work in a bandwidth-starved country. As Bruno puts it: 'Still, it feels to me that much of the latest data-science progress use frameworks that are just unable to run on slow computers.'

The ethical issue that Bruno is describing is not a million miles distant from the same issues that give rise to algorithmic bias. When the teams designing and evolving the next generations of data science tools have a frame of reference for the world that cannot comprehend not being able to simply log in to an Amazon AWS or Microsoft Azure, for instance, and spin up a virtual machine, while at the same time downloading data sets and the analytics tools you want to use, and simultaneously watching the training video for the latest release of the software you will be using, then we have one key ingredient for a digital divide. When you are in a position where, if your laptop is running slowly you can simply go online and order a new one, or go to the store and buy a higher-specification machine that day, we have another key ingredient for a digital divide.

In Bruno's blog post he writes that he is worried that the advance of data science is creating unnecessary barriers to entry in terms of hardware requirements and infrastructure requirements, which risk depriving a segment of the world's potential data scientists of access to the tools and technologies they need to bring about life-changing improvements for them and their communities.

Is it ethically responsible and sustainable to only design and build software that only works in the First World? While not an ethical issue that arises from the use of data in an analytics environment, this is a fundamentally ethical and moral issue where conscious or unconscious decisions taken about the design of technologies can affect the fundamental rights of others. Addressing this might simply mean that politicians in developing nations can also choose to ignore how their citizens want to have their data processed during elections, or it might allow a school or college to implement a student tracking system that may or may not work. Or it could help with processing of data to track infectious diseases before they take hold, or process data from a smartphone-based chloro-phyll tester to help predict crop yields and make farming more efficient.

Ethics and regulatory reporting

One of the applications of analytics technologies and methods is in regula-tory or consumer reporting. There are many scenarios in business where the output of processes must meet certain standards or a product or service cannot be brought to market. Often in these contexts, governments, industry bodies or regulators define standards that need to be complied with. Where there is a significant financial opportunity at stake organizations might be tempted to tell a white lie or bend the truth or cook the books a little. This highlights the importance of 'tone at the top', as discussed by Deloitte (Deloitte, 2014), and it is a key issue in the context of car manufacturers who designed software and analytics processes in the engine management system of vehicles so that they would perform differently under laboratory test conditions compared to their performance in the real world.

The Volkswagen case study below is a good example of the clever application of analytics technologies to detect how the different drive char-acteristics of a test lab versus a real road can be in the pursuit of an unethical objective. It also highlights the impact of the 'tone at the top', and also the impact of organization culture in ensuring that data analytics processes do not result in unethical or illegal outcomes.

CASE STUDY Volkswagen

To summarize the known facts of the Volkswagen case: Volkswagen installed software in their engine management systems that could detect when it was being tested and then switch into test mode and give significantly lower emissions results than any driver could hope to achieve in the real world. In this way, Volkswagen would be able to pass emissions standards tests without the cost or performance impacts that would arise if the engines functioned at that level all the time. In 2007 the manufacture of the engine management component had raised concerns about the legality of using the software. Volkswagen managers at various levels in the organization were aware of the cheat devices, including their CEO. The EPA in the United States investigated Volkswagen and discovered the cheat devices. In addition, Volkswagen has been under investigation in other jurisdictions and has had to do a mass recall of vehicles in the United States. The company faces criminal charges, and one former manager has pleaded guilty to conspiring to mislead regulators (Carey, 2017; Morgan and Hall, 2015; Atiyeh, 2017).

Referring back to Figure 3.1, we can apply an analytics life-cycle perspective to the Volkswagen case. It is easy to see where the information management ethics issues arise.

Acquisition

Volkswagen procured software and installed it that changed the characteristics of the engine during testing. That was a calculated attempt to generate data that did not match real engine performance for the purposes of the emissions testing processes. Management were aware of this and it had approval, it seems, from the CEO down.

Analysis

Volkswagen did not interfere with the analysis process being undertaken by regulators. It was outside of their control. All they could do was create data for input (through the 'cheat device') that they knew would fall within the acceptable parameters in the analytics process.

Action

The purpose of the emissions testing was to ensure the vehicle met the required standards under relevant environmental regulations. If the vehicle did not pass the tests, it could not be sold. However, the analysis led to other actions. Environmentally concerned car purchasers relied on the emissions data when making purchasing decisions. Governments signing climate-change agreements and making pledges to tackle climate change used the emissions data to forecast their emissions footprint into the future as part of their climate-change plan.

In short – there were a lot more people relying on the accuracy and quality of the emissions data than just the EPA and its sister organizations in the EU.

From one perspective, the analytics teams and information professionals who figured out how to develop the cheat device were acting entirely in alignment with company culture and ethos – Volkswagen has been revealed as 'confident, cutthroat and insular' (Ewing and Bowley, 2015). The cars had to pass emissions tests – this was the requirement defined, and it was met. The ability of the customer to rely on the emissions data appears not to have featured in the thinking. 'Volkswagen had become a place where subordinates were fearful of contradicting their superiors and were afraid to admit failure', according to Ewing and Bowley.

In an echo of the previous example scenarios, we see a clear 'tone at the top' ethic about the value of accurate and reliable data, and another example where people, the people buying the cars or breathing the exhaust fumes as they walk past the cars, were not considered as stakeholders in the analytics process. They were a means to an end – the profitability of Volkswagen through the sale of cars, not an end in and of themselves, a happy customer whose ecological concerns and choices should have been recognized by Volkswagen and supported through the provision of reliable emissions data.

Case study questions

1 What was the societal impact of Volkswagen's emissions-cheat processing?

2 Why do you think individual engineers might have allowed this to happen or gone along with the development of the emissions-cheating software?

3 What was the ethical balancing test that Volkswagen might have applied to their decision making?

Chapter summary

In this chapter we have looked at the ethics of analytics from a number of perspectives:

- We looked at the inherent challenges of ethics in the design of analytics processes.

- We introduced a simple three-step life cycle for analytics (acquisition, analysis, action) and discussed the ethical issues that can arise at each stage.

- We discussed how the development of big data analytics in education raises a number of ethical issues relating to privacy, autonomy, and also the potential for causation or correlation errors when attributing the success or otherwise of analytics processes.

- We examined the ethical issues that can arise when applying data analytics to the electoral process, in particular in light of the increasingly public dark side when combined with other aspects of data science and behavioural manipulation.

- We discussed the importance of ensuring that analytics technologies and practices that can add value to society are capable of being evenly distributed in society, particularly in areas where access to fundamental technologies such as modern computers, electricity or internet access might be limited.
- Finally, we looked at the ethical issues that arise when an organization decides to ensure its analytics processes always give the desired answer – we did this in a review of the Volkswagen emissions scandal.

Questions

1 Is it true to say that, in any type of data analytics, there is an impact on people, either through the acquisition of data, the type of analysis performed or the actions taken as a result of output of that analysis?

2 How does 'tone at the top' influence the governance of data analytics in your organization? If you are not working with an organization, how does 'tone at the top' affect analytics processes in a school or university?

3 Should data analytics professionals adopt an ethical principle such as: 'First, do no harm'?

4 What role does data privacy law have to play in helping to promote an ethical way of thinking about data and analytics?

Notes

1 The entity that is defining the means, purpose and objectives for processing is referred to as a data controller in EU data privacy law. Similar language exists in other jurisdictions.

2 The Article 29 Working Party is the collective body of EU data protection regulators and is convened under Article 29 of Directive 95/46/EC, the Data Protection Directive. This directive has been superseded by the Regulation 2016/679/EU (GDPR) under which the Article 29 Working Party will evolve into a more formally constituted group, the European Data Protection Supervisory Board, under Article 68 of the GDPR from May 2018 onwards.

Further reading

Bernal, P (2014) *Internet Privacy Rights: Rights to protect autonomy*, Cambridge University Press, Cambridge

Daniel, B (2015) Big data and analytics in higher education: opportunities and challenges, *BJET*, **46**, pp 904–20

Davis, K (2012) *The Ethics of Big Data: Balancing risk and innovation*, O'Reilly Media

Hasselbach, G and Tranberg, P (2016) *Data Ethics: The new competitive advantage*, PubliShare, Copenhagen

O'Neil, C (2017) *Weapons of Math Destruction: How big data increases inequality and threatens democracy*, Penguin Books, London

References

Addams, J (1902) *Democracy and Social Ethics*, Macmillan, New York

Armerding, T (2016) [accessed 1 August 2017] Big Data and Elections: The Candidates Know You – Better Than You Know Them [Online] http://www.csoonline.com/article/3095709/data-protection/big-data-and-elections-the-candidates-know-you-better-than-you-know-them.html

Arnold, KE and Pistilli, MD (2012) *LAK 12 Proceedings of the 2nd International Conference on Learning Analytics and Knowledge*, ACM, New York

Article 29 Working Party (2014) [accessed 1 August 2017] Opinion 06/2014 On the Notion of Legitimate Interests of the Data Controller [Online] http://ec.europa.eu/justice/data-protection/article-29/documentation/opinion-recommendation/files/2014/wp217_en.pdf

Atiyeh, C (2017) [accessed 3 August 2017] Everything You Need to Know About the VW Diesel-Emissions Scandal [Online] http://blog.caranddriver.com/everything-you-need-to-know-about-the-vw-diesel-emissions-scandal/

Behr, R (2016) [accessed 1 August 2017] How Remain Failed: The Inside Story of a Doomed Campaign [Online] https://www.theguardian.com/politics/2016/jul/05/how-remain-failed-inside-story-doomed-campaign

Bright, S (2017) [accessed 3 August 2017] After Trump, 'Big Data' Firm Cambridge Analytica Is Now Working In Kenya [Online] http://www.bbc.com/news/blogs-trending-40792078

Carey, N (2017) [accessed 4 August 2017] Volkswagen Executive Pleads Guilty in US Emissions Cheating Case [Online] http://www.reuters.com/article/us-volkwwagen-emissions-idUSKBN1AK1OY

Caufield, M (2013) [accessed 1 August 2017] A Simple, Less Mathematical Way To Understand The Course Signals Issue [Online] https://hapgood.us/2013/09/26/a-simple-less-mathematical-way-to-understand-the-course-signals-issue/

Chessell, M (2014) [accessed 1 August 2017] Ethics for Big Data and Analytics [Online] http://www.ibmbigdatahub.com/sites/default/files/whitepapers_reports_file/TCG%20Study%20Report%20-%20Ethics%20for%20BD%26A.pdf

Constine, J (2017) [accessed 1 December 2017] Facebook Rolls Out AI To Detect Suicidal Posts Before They're Reported [Online] https://techcrunch.com/2017/11/27/facebook-ai-suicide-prevention/

DAMA International (2017) *The Data Management Body of Knowledge*, 2nd edn, Technics Publications, New Jersey

De Haye, P-O (2016) [accessed 1 August 2017] Microtargeting of Low-Information Voters [Online] https://medium.com/personaldata-io/microtargeting-of-low-information-voters-6eb2520cd473

Deloitte (2014) *Tone at the Top: The first ingredient in a world-class ethics and compliance program*, Deloitte

Doward, J and Gibbs, A (2017) [accessed 1 August 2017] Did Cambridge Analytica Influence the Brexit Vote and the US Election? [Online] https://www.theguardian.com/politics/2017/mar/04/nigel-oakes-cambridge-analytica-what-role-brexit-trump

Edwards, E (2017) [accessed 1 August 2017] Regulator and CSO in Stand-Off Over Mobile Data [Online] http://www.irishtimes.com/news/ireland/irish-news/regulator-and-cso-in-stand-off-over-mobile-data-1.3156892

Essa, A (2013) [accessed 1 August 2017] Can We Improve Retention Rates By Giving Students Chocolates [Online] http://alfredessa.com/2013/10/can-we-improve-retention-rates-by-giving-students-chocolates/

European Data Protection Supervisor (2015) *Towards a New Digital Ethics*, EDPS, Brussels

European Union (2016) Regulation (EU) 2016/679 of the European Parliament and of the Council of 27 April 2016 on the Protection of Natural Persons with Regard to the Processing of Personal Data and on the Free Movement of Such Data, and Repealing Directive 95/46/EC (General Data Protection Regulation) [Online] http://ec.europa.eu/justice/data-protection/reform/files/regulation_oj_en.pdf

Ewing, J and Bowley, G (2015) [accessed 1 August 2017] The Engineering of Volkswagen's Aggressive Ambition [Online] https://www.nytimes.com/2015/12/14/business/the-engineering-of-volkswagens-aggressive-ambition.html

Feldstein, M (2013) [accessed 1 August 2017] *Purdue University Has an Ethics Problem* [Online] http://mfeldstein.com/purdue-university-ethics-problem/

Ferguson, R and Clow, D (2017) Where is the evidence? A call to action for learning analytics, in *LAK '17 Proceedings of the Seventh International Learning Analytics & Knowledge Conference*, ACM, New York

Glaser, A (2017) [accessed 5 August 2017] Facebook is Using an 'NRA Approach' to Defend Its Creepy Facial Recognition Programs [Online] http://www.slate.com/blogs/future_tense/2017/08/04/facebook_is_fighting_biometric_facial_recognition_privacy_laws.html

Greenleaf, G (2017) Global Data Privacy Laws 2017: 120 National Data Privacy Laws, including Indonesia and Turkey, *Privacy Laws & Business International Report*, **145**, pp 10–13

Kosinski, M, Stillwell, D and Graepel, T (2013) Private traits and attributes are predictable from digital records of human behaviour, *PNAS*, **110** (15), pp 5802–05

Lynch, M (2012) [accessed 2 August 2017] Barack Obama's Big Data Won the US Election [Online] http://www.computerworld.com/article/2492877/government-it/barack-obama-s-big-data-won-the-us-election.html

Mathieson, S (2017) [accessed 1 August 2017] Trump, Brexit and Cambridge Analytica – Not Quite The Dystopia You're Looking For [Online] https://www.theregister.co.uk/2017/03/07/cambridge_analytica_dystopianism/

Montanaro, D (2016) [accessed 1 August 2017] 7 Reasons Donald Trump Won The Presidential Election [Online] http://www.npr.org/2016/11/12/501848636/7-reasons-donald-trump-won-the-presidential-election

Morgan, T and Hall, M (2015) [accessed 4 August 2017] Volkswagen Crisis: Car Giant Warned Against Emissions Rigging Eight Years Ago [Online] http://www.telegraph.co.uk/motoring/car-manufacturers/volkswagen/11894672/Volkswagen-crisis-Car-giant-warned-against-emissions-rigging-eight-years-ago.html

Nuño, BS-A (2017) [accessed 1 August 2017] In Defense of Cheap Data Science [Online] https://medium.com/towards-data-science/in-defense-of-cheap-data-science-f630f248d400

OECD (2013) [accessed 1 August 2017] The OECD Privacy Framework [Online] http://www.oecd.org/sti/ieconomy/oecd_privacy_framework.pdf

Orme, J (2014) [accessed 1 August 2017] Samaritans Pulls 'Suicide Watch' Radar App Over Privacy Concerns [Online] https://www.theguardian.com/society/2014/nov/07/samaritans-radar-app-suicide-watch-privacy-twitter-users

Purdue Univeristy (2017) [accessed 1 August 2017] Course Signals [Online] https://www.itap.purdue.edu/learning/tools/course-signals.html

Roberts, LD, Howell, JA, Seaman, K and Gibson, DC (2016) [accessed 1 August 2017] Student Attitudes Toward Learning Analytics in Higher Education: 'The Fitbit Version of the Learning World' [Online] http://journal.frontiersin.org/article/10.3389/fpsyg.2016.01959/full

Ruiz, R (2017) [accessed 1 December 2017] Facebook Created an AI Tool That Can Prevent Suicide, But Won't Talk About How It Works [Online] http://mashable.com/2017/11/28/facebook-ai-suicide-prevention-tools/#pPNhE9_NBOqC

Shen, G (2013) [accessed 1 August 2017] Big Data, Analytics and Elections [Online] http://analytics-magazine.org/big-data-analytics-and-elections/

Talbot, D (2016) [accessed 2 August 2017] How Political Candidates Know If You're Neurotic [Online] https://www.technologyreview.com/s/601214/how-political-candidates-know-if-youre-neurotic/

The Economist (2017) [accessed 1 August 2017] How and Why Brexit Triumphed [Online] https://www.economist.com/news/books-and-arts/21713821-first-books-try-explain-shock-referendum-last-june-how-and-why-brexit

Turow, J, Delli Carpini, MX, Draper, N and Howard-Williams, R (2012) [accessed 1 August 2017] Americans Roundly Reject Tailored Political Advertising At Time When Political Campaigns Are Embracing It [Online] http://graphics8.nytimes.com/packages/pdf/business/24adco.pdf

Willis, JE (2014) [accessed 1 August 2017] Ethics, Big Data, and Analytics: A Model for Application [Online] http://docs.lib.purdue.edu/idcpubs/1/

Zanfir, G (2016) [accessed 1 August 2017] A Look At Political Psychological Targeting, EU Data Protection Law and the US Elections [Online] https://pdpecho.com/2016/11/14/does-eu-data-protection-law-apply-to-the-political-profilers-targeting-us-voters/

Zeide, E (2017) The structural consequences of big data driven education, *Big Data*, 5 (2), pp 164–72

Information ethics and artificial intelligence 04

Concepts and thought experiments

What will we cover in this chapter?

In this chapter we look at the broader questions of information ethics outside the specific aspects that directly impact on and affect humans. This chapter looks at the topics of artificial intelligence (AI) from two distinct tracks. The first track will look at the ethical design and operation of machine learning and intelligent systems, particularly in contexts that have significant impacts on people. The second track will consider the ethical implications that arise when we create a new 'intelligence' that is capable of autonomous learning. These issues are increasingly relevant for the practising data scientist and information manager and it is important that we develop some conceptual principles for addressing these issues.

At the end of this chapter you will:

- Be able to explain, in simple terms, how machine learning and AI work in modern computer systems.
- Be able to discuss ethical questions and issues that are raised by the nature of AI.
- Be able to discuss the importance of ethical thinking in the design, governance and evolution of AI.
- Be able to discuss the importance of algorithmic transparency.
- Demonstrate an appreciation for what science fiction can teach us about the ethical conundrums we will face as our use of AI expands.

Introduction

To constrain the discussion of ethics in information management to just those aspects that impact on and affect human beings directly is to take too narrow a focus. Ethical conduct and ethical ways of thinking affect fundamentally the evolution of the social and technical environment in which we live, work and socialize. Over the course of the last few years we have seen the world of 'decision support systems' evolve into the world of AI and machine learning. Increasingly, whole facets of our lives are being guided, influenced or outright directed by algorithmic processes, often without our knowledge or understanding of how these magic boxes actually work. Whether we understand how AI works or not though, we know it is important. Microsoft's 2017 Annual Report focused the company's vision and strategy on a 'new paradigm', the company focusing on 'best-in-class platforms and productivity services for an intelligent cloud and an intelligent edge infused with artificial intelligence'. This is just the tip of the iceberg. AI, algorithm-based decision making and machine-learning software are in many facets of our life, in our phones and digital assistants, in customer support functions, job applications, credit ratings, online restaurant reviews, search results and product recommendations. We are in the middle of a profound shift in how our societies operate, but our questions about the ethical aspects of these changes and 'what could go wrong' have not kept pace with our technological development.

Science fiction and popular culture are full of fictionalized images of artificial intelligence that colour the way we think about AI. Our fictional AIs, starting from Frankenstein's monster (artificial life) through HAL 9000 (the malevolent computer in Arthur C Clarke's *2001: A Space Odyssey*), Skynet (the all-seeing AI wiping out mankind in the *Terminator* movies), and Ultron (the AI created by Tony Stark in the movie *Avengers: Age of Ultron*, which sets about trying to destroy humanity in order to complete its programming to prevent wars), tell us stories about our fears that when we create intelligent beings in our own image we will create monsters and sow the seeds of our own destruction.

RUR (Rossum's Universal Robots), Asimov's robots, *Star Trek* and other narratives conceive of AI as created to be subservient to humans and grapple with how these 'human-like but not human' intelligences may need to be considered deserving of 'human' dignity and autonomy, grappling with questions of slavery, among other things. These fictional AIs frame some ethical questions that people involved in real-world AI are faced with on an increasingly regular basis. When the main antagonist of a story is an artificial being that is simply fulfilling its programming, the true 'villainy' is in the human programmers' failure to adequately assess risks and program the AI so that, given the inputs and programmed processing and decision making, the outcomes match expectations. Essentially, the villain of our fictional rogue AI narratives is bad information management, or information management that fails to take into account possible ethical implications.

Discussing AI: two parallel tracks

As mentioned at the beginning of this chapter, the discussion of information ethics in the context of AI must take two parallel tracks. The first track relates to the ethical design and operation of machine learning and intelligent systems that operate in the real world in contexts that have material physical, financial or legal consequences on people. The second track requires us to address the ethical issues that arise when we create a new intelligence that is capable of autonomous learning. Both tracks require us to first explain, in simple terms, how machine learning and AI work in modern computer systems. This may sound like an oxymoronic challenge, but it is necessary for us to have a common understanding of some core principles for the remainder of this chapter.

Defining AI

John McCarthy defined 'artificial intelligence' in 1956 as the science and engineering of making intelligent machines. One question we have to stop and ask ourselves when it comes to real-life ethical situations regarding AI is what we mean when we say 'intelligence'. Our main analogy we have for 'thinking' and for the idea of 'intelligence' boils down to how 'like us' things appear to be. When we try to judge the intelligence of animals, some of the things we look for include logic, pattern-recognition capabilities, object permanence, creative problem solving, language, and some form of recognition itself. At this point, we have developed computers to display or mimic some of these functions or capabilities in at least limited situations. But, we still would not say that these computers or programs have 'true' intelligence. So what do we actually mean when we talk about 'artificial intelligence'? Alan Turing found the question 'can machines think?' to be too ambiguous in definition, and proposed a test to see whether a human could tell a machine from a human in answers to questions (Turing, 1950).

The term 'artificial intelligence' is applied when a machine mimics the cognitive functions that humans normally associate with human minds. Examples of functions that AI has historically performed include optical character recognition, speech recognition and pattern analysis in large and complex data sets. For example, internet search engines are an example of an AI system that analyses and indexes online content as well as search queries input by people to helpfully predict what you might be searching for and to return content indexed and sorted by its likely relevance to the search terms you have typed in.

As computing power has increased in recent years, AI applications have found their way into our smartphones, our game consoles and our smart TVs. In recent years we have witnessed significant evolution of AI in technologies such as self-driving cars and self-navigating drones, and increasingly AI systems are being developed and deployed in areas where, historically, humans would have been deployed to conduct research and analysis such as stock-market trading (intelligent trading algorithms) and in law firms (electronic discovery, analysis of legal precedents, intelligent case management systems etc).

At its simplest, however, AI is best described as an area of computer science that deals with giving machines the ability to seem like they have human intelligence. For the purposes of practical discussion, we are conflating the terms 'artificial intelligence' and 'computational intelligence' (which some computer scientists will probably dispute), as it is impossible in a short chapter to do justice to a large and growing field with many branches, let alone leave space to discuss the ethical issues. Rather, we will discuss a few ethical questions related to impacts of AI-related functions such as heuristic classification, pattern recognition and machine learning, computational decision making, autonomous vehicles, and autonomous weapons systems.

Ethical issues in AI

With a general definition to give us a common understanding, what are the ethical questions related to AI? What issues arise for systems that are used to support decision making and other functions in the real world? Increasingly we are seeing the impacts of what is known as algorithmic bias. Just as with people, AI systems are often a product of the mental models that their parents give them. The cultural biases of those who define the seed rules and coding for a self-learning system can lead to that system repeating those biases in its processing of information and making of decisions.

We have adopted computational decision making based on machine learning without fully examining the ethical impacts of what data we use to train the algorithms. This has led to situations where, for instance, sentencing support systems give harsher sentences to ethnic minorities; insurance-risk scoring scores people of particular ethnicity as higher risk than their Caucasian neighbours; internet searches displayed to ethnic minorities disproportionately turn up results for predatory loan companies, profit colleges and low-paying job options; and there are many other situations that invisibly reinforce biased systems. These situations require proactive decisions to address systemic ethical impacts. You need to check your assumptions and blind spots.

Algorithmic law enforcement – an ethical dilemma

In 2016 journalists at ProPublica investigated the use of computational reasoning in predictive assessment determining risk of recidivism used to support decision making at multiple stages in the US criminal justice system, from determining bond amounts to sentencing. They found that risk scores assigned to people by COMPAS, a privately owned system, was 'remarkably unreliable' in its predictions, with clear racial disparities. COMPAS was nearly twice as likely to falsely flag black defendants as predicted to reoffend as it was white defendants (Angwin et al, 2016). Algorithmically derived risk assessments are intended to reduce human bias and increase equality in the criminal justice system, but Pro Publica's investigation suggests that a great deal of work is still required to ensure justice. These systems require governance, transparency and accountability in how results are derived, what metrics are used and how, and what results and impacts are prioritized.

The ethical question of training data sets

One ethical problem raised by the use of machine learning and big data for decision making is that bias introduced into the algorithm or through the data is invisible to us. While you may know that Carl's opinion on which restaurant in the area is best is coloured by the fact that he doesn't like Mexican food, you don't expect an algorithmic sentiment analysis to automatically rate Mexican restaurants lower than other reviewed restaurants because it takes in a corpus of online comments in which the word 'Mexican' is frequently collocated with the word 'illegal' in derogatory comments about immigrants. Unfortunately, this is an actual observed effect (Speer, 2017).

Numbers do not have the fuzzy values and built-in bias of language. But, when the numbers are based on pattern recognition of models built by language, and the data set used for training machines to recognize patterns is modelled on a system that has unequal outcomes, the result will be computational decision making that is inherently biased. This invisibility is compounded by trade secrecy. Companies consider their algorithms to be trade secrets, so what goes into the decision-making process and how results are derived remains secret even to those with the expertise to examine the source code.

These biases might be intentional, but far more often they are unintended and accidental. Models cannot replicate every single variable in the world, so the decisions you make on what is important or relevant for a decision will impact the output. Often a researcher or developer has simply made assumptions in their initial model based on their personal experiences and social points of reference. This is what JK Galbraith, the famous economist, referred to in his 1958 book *The Affluent Society* as 'the conventional wisdom'. What many fail to appreciate is that Galbraith was not being complimentary with that comment. The ethical issues that arise raise the need for effective controls. Identifying and removing potentially harmful ethical biases requires a rigorous quality control system. This involves not only checking the output to see whether it matches expectation, but critical self-reflection and 'red teaming' or having someone search for your assumptions or blind spots.

The question of how you train machine-learning algorithms is ethical. Algorithmic biases can arise from the set of data used to train machine-learning algorithms. For instance, facial recognition software has been shown to have more trouble with accurate identification of faces of people when they are of a different ethnicity or age group than the set of data its algorithms were trained on (Klare et al, 2012). While facial recognition technology has increased accuracy incredibly between 2012 and 2017, researchers and activists still note racial disparities, especially regarding higher inaccuracy in identifying black people. Code libraries used by many programmers to do common tasks often reflect the lack of diversity in the population of people contributing to the libraries, and this affects the diversity of the training sets used. Joy Buolamwini, a graduate researcher at MIT Media Lab, found that she was better recognized when wearing a white mask than her actual face. Peeling this back another level, cameras and the light balance in photography have historically been optimized for accurate and aesthetic recording of people with lighter skin. The machine you use and the lighting exposure you are yourself trained to consider optimal have their own preconditions that can affect people. As Buolamwini notes, 'default is not neutral' (Buolamwini, 2016, 2017).

Another inescapable issue where the default for input is not neutral and communicates systemic bias lies in the fact that much input for algorithmic decision making comes from human languages. Language is in itself a model of the world shaped by and shaping cultural models of reality. It is not a pure description of reality. The corpus of human expression in language reinforces that, by reflecting the biases and blind spots of the people using language to express their opinions and ideas. As we build models based on models, we risk reinforcing and amplifying the inherent inaccuracies.

Algorithmic bias and feedback loops

One particular problem is a feedback loop, which can happen when an algorithmic model that starts with an input based on inequality reinforces the model developed by its results. This creates a self-reinforcing pattern, which can result in increasing inequality while giving the incorrect impression that it is fair and unbiased because the decisions made are done purely through mathematic analysis of data and without the meddling of prejudiced humans. William Cheshire highlights another potential type of implicit bias caused by 'excessive conformity' in AI software analogous to human groupthink, which he labels 'loopthink' (Cheshire, 2017). Unfortunately, one law of computing hasn't changed: Garbage In, Garbage Out. When garbage slips into our models and our training data, automation will not clean it and may instead amplify it.

Machine learning has the capability of recognizing patterns and trends far more quickly, efficiently and far beyond the capacity of human processing. But, it does not have the ethical framework or critical self-reflection capability to recognize that the results of its calculations reflect human prejudice or the blind spots of the model, and may have a disproportionate impact on certain classes of people. When Microsoft created a Twitter chatbot and it learnt from the dregs of the internet to spout neo-Nazi slurs within the space of a day, it had little impact on people's lives (aside from a good laugh) and it was quickly and easily discontinued. But, that pattern is instructive on the risks of unintended results and impacts in creating a learning machine. When women are shown lower-paying job advertisements on Google than men (Datta, Tschantz and Datta, 2015), and hiring algorithms also evidence bias in the decision making regarding which résumés are even seen by hiring managers (Mann and O'Neil, 2016), then social impact is much higher.

Defining success: highlighting the need for algorithmic accountability

So, how do you determine whether your model is successful? What are your optimal outcomes? What do you prioritize? Cathy O'Neil suggests that for many businesses, revenue has been one of the most common indicators of success. But this metric is an absolutely horrible way to determine whether your model creates accurate, fair or just results, or whether the AI-driven processes affecting and even controlling people's lives are making their lives better and enhancing their dignity or reinforcing a spiral of oppression (O'Neil, 2016).

The question of how you determine the successfulness or accuracy of your model pairs with the question of accountability. Transparency is traditionally a way that has held decision makers accountable. However, as Maayan Perel and Niva Elkin-Koren have noted, even when private companies are willing to expose their trade secrets to examination, the complexity, learning capacities and sheer volume of the code can result in obscurity and incomprehensibility through excessive disclosure. They suggest that 'black box tinkering' – a technique that effectively tries to reverse-engineer an algorithm – is one tool for governance and accountability (Perel and Elkin-Koren, 2017). Anupam Datta, Shayak Sen and Yair Zick at Carnegie Mellon similarly examine causal quantitative input influence (QII) as a measure to assess the relative influence of the factors evaluated in an individual automated decision. They suggest combining QII with differential privacy in reporting as a way to aid transparency and algorithmic accountability (Datta, 2017; Datta, Sen and Zick, 2016).

Some requirements to ensure algorithmic accountability will include oversight and governance. You will need to consider checks and balances to ensure justice and that people's rights are preserved. Another question is whether your models, cognitive decision making or decision trees preserve people's dignity and autonomy as decision makers. Does your system result in funnelling people's choices in ways that reduce their ability to choose? Is there invisible censorship of results that limits access to knowledge or freedom of speech?

Principles for accountable algorithms

Members of FAT/ML, an organization dedicated to fairness, accountability and transparency in machine learning, suggest five guiding principles for ensuring accountability and mitigating harms and other undesirable impacts, providing guiding questions to ask and steps to take for each principle. FAT/ML suggests that you develop a 'social impact statement' and assess impact at the very least at the design, launch and post-launch stages of a process:

- Responsibility: there should be a clear path of accountability, with clear ways to redress adverse effects at an individual or societal level. Have a designated role who is responsible for this.

- Explainability: you should be able to explain how decisions were made and, in non-technical terms, the data that went into making those decisions.

- Accuracy: any sources of error or uncertainty in the algorithm or data sources should be 'identified, logged and articulated' to aid understanding of risk and mitigation procedures.

- Auditability: you should open your algorithm to third parties to audit code, documentation, application programming interfaces (APIs) etc.

- Fairness: you should ensure that the results of the decisions do not have disproportionate, discriminatory or unjust impacts when comparing across demographics.

Conceptually, this is very similar to the Privacy Impact Assessment and Ethical Impact Assessment process we will discuss in Chapter 10. The ethical principles articulated by FAT/ML are clearly reflected in the European General Data Protection Regulation, which in addition to core principles of accuracy and accountability, and supporting governance structures, requires that any automated decision that has a significant impact on individuals must have human oversight and be explainable.

Specific examples of developments in AI with ethical impacts

Driverless cars

The entry of autonomous vehicles or 'self-driving' cars on the market has resulted in practical collision of coding and ethics, as the philosophical thought experiment called the 'Trolley Problem' moved from a theoretical game proposing an abstract problem to the real-world design of vehicles that require coding for algorithmic decision making regarding what – or whose lives – to prioritize in event of a potential collision. Scholars, researchers and practitioners have been vigorously debating what it means and how to program a car to make ethical decisions. These problems have already hit the road, as a Tesla self-driving car was involved in a fatal crash in 2016 (Vlasic and Boudette, 2016). When it comes down to it, the development of autonomous cars is likely to increase safety on the roads and reduce fatal collisions. Humans are wonderful at multitasking, but not very good at driving safely. But the fact remains that in developing autonomous vehicles, you must confront the questions in planning, identifying and assessing risk, and coding for these edge cases in the design and creation of cars. This raises the question of accountability – who is responsible when an autonomous vehicle makes an 'error' resulting in harm?

Amitai Etzioni argues that we should not focus disproportionately on the 'outlier' trolley-problem scenarios, and that many of the ethical issues may be resolved by the development of an AI that reads the preferences of the human and imitates them within lawful societal constraints (Etzioni, 2017). Mercedes-Benz made a simpler but more controversial decision in October 2016, when they announced that they would prioritize the safety of their cars' occupants over that of pedestrians (Mandal, 2016). The questions we are now facing with autonomous vehicles will be raised in many other applications of AI as they develop.

Lethal autonomous weapons systems

Researchers such as Stuart Russell have noted that developments in the fields of AI and robotics have reached the point that lethal autonomous weapons systems (LAWS) are within reach – technically possible, if legally questionable. The components to make AI-driven autonomous weapons systems are in existence, or well on their way to development. One could conceivably combine several AI and robotics applications that are either already existing or are in close reach to design, for instance an autonomous aerial drone that could identify, assess, target and attack individuals. In an article in *Nature* in 2015, Russell made a clear call for the AI and robotics communities to take a clear ethical position on the possible developments of autonomous weapons. He notes that while the United Nations has held meetings on LAWS, leading to the possibility of a treaty in the future, in absence of a treaty he believes there is a risk of an arms race, resulting in developments of weapons that will compromise peoples' fundamental human dignity, and possibly leaving humans defenceless against weapons. Some experts believe that LAWS would lower the threshold for war. There is also the risk that, as with other weapons developments, LAWS may spread into civilian policing (Russell et al, 2015).

Who benefits? Justice and human dignity in AI development

William Gibson famously said that 'the future is already here, it is just unevenly distributed'. The implementation of AI without consideration of justice and equitable benefits may risk amplification of inequality regarding who benefits from applications.

Russ Altman, Professor of Bioengineering, Genetics, Medicine and Computer Science at Stanford, has discussed the potentially immense benefits of using AI-supported systems in medical research, analysis and diagnosis. In the same *Nature* article that Stuart Russell shared his concerns about LAW systems, Altman expressed concerns about the possible downsides of AI use in medical research. His comments reflect the Belmont Principles for medical research in raising concerns about the possible unequal realization of benefit. Without proactive action by those developing the technology and governing the systems in which it is used to ensure equality in implementation, there is a risk that the use of AI in these cases will not only amplify existing inequalities, but create new inequalities (Russell et al, 2015). This is a clear concern in the medical research community, as it echoes the reasons that ethical standards for medical research were developed.

One large structural ethical issue immediately facing us is the question of how we can ethically and sustainably implement AI-driven technology that fulfils functions that have until now required hiring humans. We are in another industrial revolution, with all the upheaval and human cost – as well as opportunity – that this entails. As discussed earlier in this chapter, the development of driverless vehicles has the potential for enormous benefits in safety and preventing loss of life. However, the widespread availability of self-driving vehicles will massively affect whole sectors of employment, including taxi and cab driving, as well as haulage. This does not mean we should try to stop technological progress, but we should consider the lives and livelihood of the people in these sectors and how to minimize harm while implementing progress in a sustainable manner. Far from simply replacing humans or human jobs, AI can be also be used to assist and augment human activities and experiences.

Dignity-enhancing applications

AI applications are being used to augment human experience, and some developments may be of great benefit to individuals and society. For instance, an engineer with Microsoft is developing a 'Seeing AI' application to use with 'smart' sunglasses, to augment the experience of people with visual impairments (Weinberger, 2016). A similar assistive technology named 'Drishti' was announced in July 2017 by researchers at Accenture, supported by India's National Association for the Blind. Drishti is described as smartphone-based assistive technology that can identify and narrate information to the user, including identifying obstructions, facial recognition and facial expression recognition, identification of currency, narration of text (Accenture, 2017).

These kinds of developments have great potential to enhance the dignity and autonomy and augment the experience of individuals living with various impairments or disabilities. However, these immensely beneficial technologies also bring with them other risks and potential ethical impacts that will require assessment, and risk or harm mitigation. For instance, 'Seeing AI' technology using facial recognition technology may have disproportionate invasiveness in processing biometric data of anyone within the range of the technology. These risks must be identified, balanced and mitigated during design and development.

What does AI tell us about us?

For the foreseeable future, at least, ethical questions about strong AI remain theoretical or fictional. Experts in the field generally agree that developments in AI are nowhere near the possibility of our fictional super-intelligent computers, 'true' or 'strong' AI. People such as Stephen Hawking and Elon Musk have raised warnings about the risks of super-intelligent AI; Hawking warned that such developments 'could spell the end of the human race', while Musk called it our 'greatest existential threat', referring back to the folkloric Faustian metaphor of 'summoning the demon' and losing control over the force you intended to have power over. As of yet, though, nothing has come near to passing the Turing test, and Luciano Floridi calls true AI 'not logically impossible, but utterly improbable' (Floridi, 2017).

Of course, this does bring us back again to the question of how we determine 'intelligence' or judge whether or not an entity has consciousness or sapience. Do we assume the necessity of being a carbon-based life form for consciousness? Considering that historically humans don't have a strong record of recognizing the dignity and autonomy of our fellow humans, and our assessment of animal intelligence tends to focus on comparison to cognitive functions based on the standard of humans, at what point should we be considering the possibility that we may in the future develop true AI without recognizing it? What outputs do we really expect? What models are we using?

Chapter summary

In this chapter we have examined some of the ethical issues that arise in the wider fields of information management, in particular the emerging fields of driverless cars and autonomous law enforcement systems. We discussed:

- The nature of AI.
- The sources of ethical risk in AI systems, including algorithmic bias and quality of training data.
- The risks of algorithmic bias and the impact on people.
- The importance of ensuring equality of access to advanced technologies that are beneficial to humankind.
- The potential risks to humankind from AI, and the importance of science fiction in helping us explore the ethical implications of AI.

Questions

1 What are our responsibilities in regard to AI?

2 How should we develop AI in relation to human roles and employment: replacement, automation or augmentation?

3 How do we determine 'true intelligence' as opposed to 'imitation'?

4 AI is an incredibly fast-moving field at the moment. How can we anticipate ethical dilemmas in the field?

5 How can we be transparent about black-box algorithmic decision making?

Further reading

Article 19 (2016) [accessed 1 August 2017] Algorithms and Automated Decision Making in the Context of Crime Prevention: a Briefing Paper, Article 19 – Free Word Centre, London [Online] https://www.article19.org/data/files/medialibrary/38579/Algorithms-and-Automated-Decision-Making-in-the-Context-of-Crime-Prevention-Final.pdf

Asimov, I (1976) *The Bicentennial Man and Other Stories*, Doubleday, London

Cave, S (2017) [accessed 4 August 2017] Intelligence: A History, *Aeon Essays* [Online] https://aeon.co/amp/essays/on-the-dark-history-of-intelligence-as-domination

Cheshire, WP (2017) Loopthink: A limitation of medical artificial intelligence, *Ethics and Medicine*, **33** (1), pp 7–12

Data Geek (2017) [accessed 8 May 2017] A Tour of Machine Learning Algorithms, *Data Science Central* [Online] http://www.datasciencecentral.com/profiles/blog/show?id=6448529%3ABlogPost%3A341501

Davies, J (2016) Program good ethics into artificial intelligence, *Nature*, **538** (7625), p 291

Deng, B (2015) Machine ethics: the robot's dilemma, *Nature*, **523** (7558), pp 24–26

Diakopoulos, N et al (2017) [accessed 4 August 2017] Principles for Accountable Algorithms and a Social Impact Statement for Algorithms, *Fairness, Accountability, and Transparency in Machine Learning* [Online] http://www.fatml.org/resources/principles-for-accountable-algorithms

Doctorow, C (2017) Algorithmic Decision-Making: An Arms-Race Between Entropy, Programmers and Referees, *Boing Boing* [Online] http://boingboing.net/2017/06/01/adversarial-computing.html

Etzioni, A and Etzioni, O (2017) Incorporating ethics into artificial intelligence, *Journal of Ethics*, **21** (4), pp 403–18

Gourarie, C (2017) [accessed 8 May 2017] Investigating the Algorithms That Govern Our Lives, *Columbia Journalism Review* [Online] https://www.cjr.org/innovations/investigating_algorithms.php

Hudson, L (2017) [accessed 4 August 2017] Technology Is Biased Too. How Do We Fix It?, *FiveThirtyEight* [Online] https://fivethirtyeight.com/features/technology-is-biased-too-how-do-we-fix-it/

Mateos-Garcia, J (2017) [accessed 4 August 2017] To Err is Algorithm: Algorithmic Fallibility and Economic Organisation, *Nesta* [Online] https://www.nesta.org.uk/blog/err-algorithm-algorithmic-fallibility-and-economic-organisation

Microsoft Corp (2017) [accessed 4 August 2017] Annual Report Pursuant To Section 13 Or 15(D) Of The Securities Exchange Act Of 1934 [Online] https://www.sec.gov/Archives/edgar/data/789019/000156459017014900/msft-10k_20170630.htm#ITEM_1_BUSINESS

Pasquale, F (2017) [accessed 5 February 2018] Toward a fourth law of robotics: preserving attribution, responsibility, and explainability in an algorithmic society, *Ohio State Law Journal*, **78** [Online] SSRN: https://ssrn.com/abstract=3002546

The Principled Algorithm (2017) [accessed 4 August 2017] Article Summary – Discussion Around Decision-Making Algorithms (Pt. 1) [Online] https://theprincipledalgorithm.com/index.php/2017/06/article-summary-discussion-around-decision-making-algorithms/

References

Accenture (2017) [accessed 4 August 2017] Accenture Develops Artificial Intelligence-Powered Solution to Help Improve How Visually Impaired People Live and Work [Online] https://newsroom.accenture.com/news/accenture-develops-artificial-intelligence-powered-solution-to-help-improve-how-visually-impaired-people-live-and-work.htm

Angwin, J et al (2016) [accessed 4 August 2017] Machine Bias: There's Software Used Across the Country to Predict Future Criminals. And It's Biased Against Blacks, *ProPublica* [Online] https://www.propublica.org/article/machine-bias-risk-assessments-in-criminal-sentencing

Buolamwini, J (2016) [accessed 4 August 2017] InCoding – In The Beginning, *MIT MEDIA LAB* [Online] https://medium.com/mit-media-lab/incoding-in-the-beginning-4e2a5c51a45d

Buolamwini, J (2017) [accessed 4 August 2017] Algorithms Aren't Racist. Your Skin Is Just Too Dark [Online] https://hackernoon.com/algorithms-arent-racist-your-skin-is-just-too-dark-4ed31a7304b8

Cheshire, WP (2017) Loopthink: a limitation of medical artificial intelligence, *Ethics and Medicine*, **33** (1), pp 7–12

Datta, A (2017) [accessed 5 August 2017] Did Artificial Intelligence Deny you Credit?, *The Conversation* [Online] https://theconversation.com/did-artificial-intelligence-deny-you-credit-73259

Datta, A, Sen, S and Zick, Y (2016) [accessed 4 August 2017] Algorithmic Transparency via Quantitative Input Influence: Theory and Experiments with Learning Systems [Online] https://www.andrew.cmu.edu/user/danupam/datta-sen-zick-oakland16.pdf

Datta, A, Tschantz, M and Datta, A (2015) [accessed 5 August 2017] Automated Experiments on Ad Privacy Settings, *Proceedings on Privacy Enhancing Technologies*, 2015 (1), pp 92–112, doi:10.1515/popets-2015-0007

Etzioni, A and Etzioni, O (2017) [accessed 4 August 2017] Incorporating Ethics into Artificial Intelligence, *The Journal of Ethics* [Online] doi:10.1007/s10892-017-9252-2

Floridi, L (2017) [accessed 4 August 2017] True AI Is Both Logically Possible and Utterly Implausible, *Aeon Essays* [Online] https://aeon.co/essays/true-ai-is-both-logically-possible-and-utterly-implausible

Klare, B et al (2012) Face recognition performance: role of demographic information, *IEEE Transactions on Information Forensics and Security*, 7 (6), pp 1789–1801

Mandal, S (2016) [accessed 4 August 2017] Mercedes-Benz Self-Driving Cars Will Prioritize Occupant Safety Over Pedestrians, *Auto World News* [Online] http://www.autoworldnews.com/articles/21462/20161011/mercedes-benz-self-driving-cars-will-prioritize-occupant-safety-over.htm

Mann, G and O'Neil, C (2016) [accessed 5 February 2018] Hiring algorithms are not neutral, *Harvard Business Review* [Online] https://hbr.org/2016/12/hiring-algorithms-are-not-neutral

O'Neil, C (2017) *Weapons of Math Destruction: How big data increases inequality and threatens democracy*, Penguin Books, London

Perel, M and Elkin-Koren, M (2017) Black box tinkering: beyond disclosure in algorithmic enforcement, *Florida Law Review*, **69,** pp 181–221

Russell, S, Hauert, S, Altman, R and Veloso, M (2015) Robotics: ethics of artificial intelligence, *Nature*, **521** (7553), 415–18

Speer, R (2017) [accessed 4 August 2017] ConceptNet Numberbatch 17.04: Better, Less-Stereotyped Word Vectors, *ConceptNet Blog* [Online] https://blog.conceptnet.io/2017/04/24/conceptnet-numberbatch-17-04-better-less-stereotyped-word-vectors/

Turing, AM (1950) Computing machinery and intelligence, *Mind*, **59,** 433–60

Vlasic, B and Boudette, N (2016) [accessed 4 August 2017] Self-Driving Tesla was Involved in Fatal Crash, U.S. Says, *New York Times*, 30 June [Online] https://www.nytimes.com/2016/07/01/business/self-driving-tesla-fatal-crash-investigation.html

Weinberger, M (2016) [accessed 1 August 2017] This Blind Programmer Wrote An App For His Sunglasses That Let Him 'See', *Business Insider UK* [Online] http://uk.businessinsider.com/microsoft-sunglasses-let-blind-man-see-2016-3?r=US&IR=T

Ethics in the Data Management Body of Knowledge

05

What will we cover in this chapter?

In this chapter we will:

- Introduce a baseline set of concepts for the profession of information management and its constituent disciplines, particularly for readers who are coming to this topic from a non-IT background.
- Provide a high-level overview of some of the information management disciplines as outlined by DAMA International.
- Introduce basic concepts of how these disciplines can support the management of information in an ethical manner, but also introduce how ethical issues can and will affect how these disciplines can and should be applied.
- Identify where ethical issues and questions can arise in the DAMA DMBOK.

We will not cover all of the DAMA Data Management Body of Knowledge (DMBOK) disciplines in this book. The purpose of this chapter is to provide a basic introduction to some of the key disciplines so that we can elaborate on their role in ethics elsewhere in this book (eg Chapters 4, 9 and 10). We suggest that readers looking for a more in-depth treatment of these topics and the broader DMBOK should seek out and acquire a copy of the DAMA DMBOK (see References for more details).

Introducing the DAMA DMBOK

The professional discipline of data management addresses the challenges of managing data and information as an enterprise asset, to better deliver value to an organization and its stakeholders. As with other asset management disciplines, this requires considering managing the data asset throughout the life cycle and considering its proper handling, from planning for acquiring or creation of the data through its maintenance and use and into its disposition once its purpose is concluded.

It is important to understand that the disciplines of data management are simply tools, in the same way as the software and technologies for information management. They can be applied efficiently and effectively for both ethical and unethical purposes. Ethical information management requires us to make conscious choices to apply these disciplines in an ethical way. While the disciplines of data management are ethically neutral tools, ethical decisions or norms often underpin its principles and disciplines as to what is considered valuable and what should be prioritized, and goals related to ethical principles such as trustworthiness of data, ensuring privacy and confidentiality of stakeholder data, ensuring integrity and quality of data, and accurately representing facts. As people in data-centred disciplines realize the increasing power of the data as an asset, we have realized both the increasing need to manage data properly and effectively as an asset to increase value for the organization, and the need to ensure that data is managed and handled ethically with regards to the effects on stakeholders and society in general, with a focus on minimizing any data-related risks.

The various data management disciplines are interrelated, touching upon each other in different ways. The Data Management Association visualizes this as a wheel of interconnected knowledge areas with different scopes and activities (Figure 5.1), while acknowledging that a two-dimensional representation of how the disciplines relate will not adequately model how the disciplines connect with each other.

Data governance

Data governance as a function is one of the areas that will most explicitly express an organization's ethical norms regarding data and data use, whether the organization's normative ethical framework is formally recognized and accounted for or not.

Figure 5.1   The DAMA DMBOK wheel

The DAMA DMBOK defines data governance as 'the exercise of and authority and control (planning, monitoring and enforcement) over the management of data assets' (DAMA International, 2017). We can understand this as parallel to civil government. At a civil or national level, government and laws facilitate societal enforcement of the agreed ethical norms of a nation or civil body. Laws and the legal system do not determine ethics; they codify decisions made as to what behaviour should be enforced, and provide a path for mediation and escalation in disputes. Ethical norms guide the formal decision and codification of what is considered a right action, and who has overriding rights in certain situations. We take decisions based on our ethical views, the codified laws, and any alleged infringement is decided on by an independent judiciary.

Data governance is an analogous system that enables an organization to determine what is considered proper action regarding data and data processes. It enables clear definitions, decision-making rights and responsibilities, and provides an escalation path or process of mediation or remediation when people have questions or disputes as to what should be done with what data, by whom and under which circumstances.

As a tool, data governance is ethically neutral and acts as a guiding function that facilitates appropriate decision making and enforcement capabilities. Historically, data governance initiatives have been used by organizations in response to legal and regulatory changes relating to information management. For example, a key driver for data governance in the financial services sector has been the data management requirements of regulations around capital adequacy for banks and insurers. In a broader context, the Sarbanes-Oxley Act in the United States and the General Data Protection Regulation in Europe each contain specific requirements for data governance. While the implementation of data governance in any organization must be based on defined principles for data management, which may in turn be grounded on ethical principles, the actual structural practices of data governance as a tool for management and oversight are the same whether or not the organization is pursuing outcomes that society would consider ethical.

In many respects, this echoes Heidegger's discussion of the ethics of technology, which require consideration of the thinking and principles that underpin the use of technology. We will explore the relationship between ethics and data governance in more detail in Chapter 9. For now, we will give a summary introduction to some of the core concepts of data governance so that you have a common frame of reference for those later discussions.

Key areas of focus for data governance

Data governance is a key enabling capability in organizations of any size. While the DAMA DMBOK (DAMA International, 2017) refers to concepts such as the Chief Data Officer or Chief Information Officer, the core concepts of good data governance are applicable to organizations of any size.

One of the core concepts that needs to be understood and embraced is that managing information is different from managing technology. To use a metaphor that Daragh has used in training courses over the years:

- Your organization is a kitchen in a fancy restaurant.
- Your customers expect a nice meal that tastes nice, looks nice and is at the right price.
- You don't deliver that by only looking at the sharpness of your knives and the number of rings on your cooker hobs.
- If your ingredients are not right, if the menu is not what you are actually serving, and if your brigade of chefs and kitchen porters don't know what they are supposed to do and when, your diners won't care how sharp your knives were.

TV reality shows featuring cranky celebrity chefs going into struggling restaurants to turn them around can help bring this message home. While they are edited and packaged for human drama, the one thing that is constant is that the basic technologies being used are, by and large, unchanging from episode to episode. How the use of those technologies is managed and governed, and how the other inputs into the process of producing a meal are managed and governed, and how the overall operation of the kitchen and the production line in the kitchen are governed – that is the difference between a kitchen nightmare and a tasty meal.

Figure 5.2 shows how the DMBOK sets out the conceptual view of data governance structures in the organization. A key part of this framework is an explicit separation of duties between the execution of functions ('Do things right') and the oversight of those functions ('Do the right things'). John Ladley, a leading consultant and author in the areas of data governance and information management highlights the importance of this separation of duties in his work (Ladley, 2012).

The framework in Figure 5.2 highlights the importance of organizations turning data strategy into action, but in doing so the opportunity arises for ethical dilemmas to present themselves. Traditionally, a key part of the governance of the transition from strategy to action is ensuring clarity of

Figure 5.2   Data governance in the organization

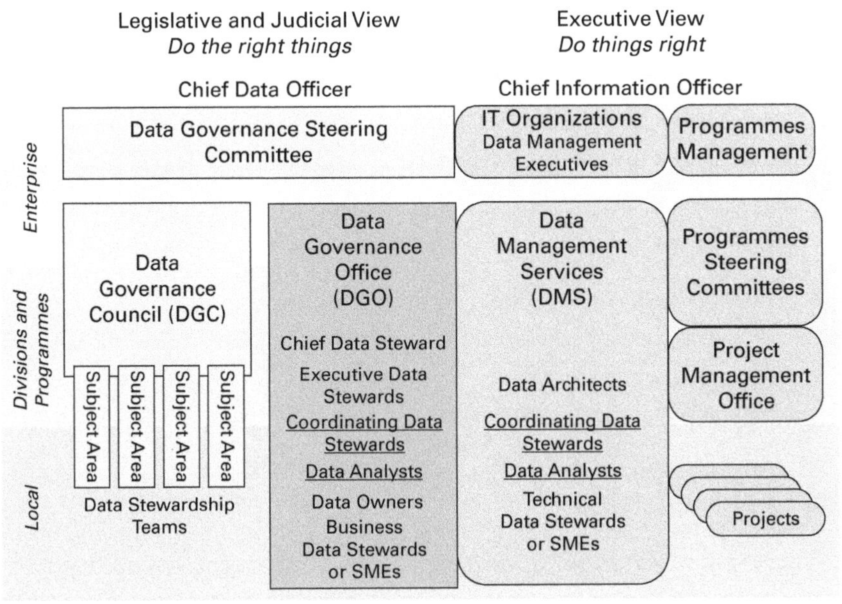

SOURCE DAMA International

data definition, clarity of roles, responsibilities, accountabilities for data, and implementation of appropriate technologies and tools to support the delivery of data-driven projects. The model outlined in Figure 5.2 is a conceptual ideal, but in most organizations most of these roles exist or are being brought into being. While the specific format and organizational design for these roles and functions may differ from organization to organization, the conceptual functions must still be there for data governance to be effective.

The DMBOK identifies a number of key tasks to be performed in this data governance framework, including, but not limited to:

- culture change and change management;
- shifting from an IT focus to an information focus (echoing the change recognized in the Amsterdam Information Model we will discuss in Chapter 7);
- introducing data stewardship ethos and practices;
- defining and improving the data governance operating framework for the organization;
- defining goals, principles and policies for data and data management in the organization;
- the goals for data management need to be aligned with business strategy;
- the principles being applied need to align with the organization's values and ethos;
- issue management and escalation;
- providing the arbitration (an 'honest broker') when there is an internal dispute about the meaning and purpose of data;
- supporting the organization in engagements with external stakeholders such as regulators.

Many of these tasks involve the definition of or reaction to ethical principles that are either developed internally in the organization or are imposed by external forces such as regulatory bodies or legislation. We examine this aspect in Chapter 9.

Data stewardship

A steward is a person who has a responsibility to manage the property of another person and may be held to account if that property is lost, stolen, damaged or misused. If you have ever rented an apartment or a house, you will have found language in your lease agreement that made you a steward of the property. You may have been required to maintain the property, or to refrain from doing things that would damage the property. You may have had to give an undertaking that you would not sublet the property without permission from the landlord.

Data stewardship is the term used to describe accountability and responsibility for the use of data assets in an organization. Data stewards 'manage data assets on behalf of others and in the best interests of the organization' (McGilvray, 2008). It can be a formal assignment or it can evolve through people organically trying to help an organization better manage its information. At the heart of the data stewardship concept is an ethical value that data is only held on trust and the processing being performed is for the benefit of someone else. This is consistent with the 'customer-centric' ethos of quality management systems.

The DAMA DMBOK identifies a number of different types of data steward depending on the complexity or size of the organization. Stewardship roles identified by DAMA include:

- **Chief Data Stewards** – who chair data governance bodies and can act as executive sponsors for data governance in the organization.

- **Executive Data Stewards** – these are senior managers who sit on a data governance council or steering committee.

- **Enterprise Data Stewards** – these are managers who have oversight of a data domain such as 'customer data' across the organization's business functions.

- **Business Data Stewards** – staff on the 'business' side of the organization who are subject-matter experts for a subset of the organization's data.

- **Technical Data Stewards** – staff on the IT side of the organization who are subject-matter experts on the technologies and technical disciplines that are applied in the organization to manage data.

- **Co-ordinating Data Stewards** – who lead and represent cross-functional teams of business and technical data stewards. These are particularly important in larger organizations.

Of course, theory and experience often differ slightly. Our experience is that data stewardship and the role to be performed is often better defined by the relationship that the individual has with the information assets of the organization rather than where in the functional hierarchy of the organization they sit. Based on Daragh's experiences in strategic information transformation roles and in regulatory governance roles earlier in his career, he developed

Figure 5.3   The 3DC framework

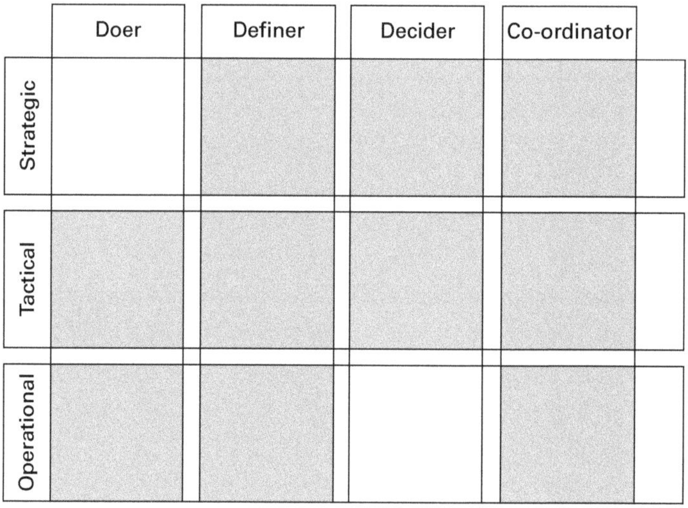

	Doer	Definer	Decider	Co-ordinator
Strategic				
Tactical				
Operational				

the 3DC framework for the consulting business we work in (see Figure 5.3). This framework defines four categories of data steward:

- **Doers** – who work with data on a day-to-day basis to deliver services or perform customer-facing tasks. They can be found at the front line (operational) and line management (tactical) level in the organization.

- **Definers** – who define the meaning and purpose of information. They exist at all levels in the organization. It is important that the strategic-level view of what data means or is to be used for aligns with how staff at the coal face of the organization understand this – or compliance or quality issues can arise.

- **Deciders** – who exist at the tactical and strategic management levels of the organization, from line management up to board level. Deciders are the people who make decisions about the meaning and purpose of information and are the escalation path for decisions on policies, rules, procedures and strategy.

- **Co-ordinators** – who operate at all levels in the organization, acting as facilitators for data-related discussion and debate and ensuring policies, standards and methods are communicated and understood consistently around the organization. They also act as 'honest brokers' resolving data-related issues or disputes internally. Often the co-ordinating function is one that is mandated by legislation. In other cases, the co-ordinator may be someone who steps into the role voluntarily or by default.

A formalized data governance framework in the organization serves to clarify the roles, responsibilities and accountabilities of staff in the context of these governance roles. A key aspect of the 3DC framework is that it doesn't matter where in the organization a staff member sits, it is their role and the actions they take, or should take, in relation to data that determine what their stewardship role is.

It is outside the scope of this book to cover more detail on data governance. The DAMA DMBOK contains a more detailed examination of the concept, and we provide some additional recommended reading at the end of this chapter.

Data architecture

Data architecture is a key enabler for data management, and the disciplines involved can also be key enablers for ensuring a good system, designing blueprints and specifications to define and express strategic data requirements, guide integration, and ensure alignment of system requirements with business needs. The artefacts produced through effective data architecture practices include specifications for the technology environment, data requirements, standards and protocols for data storage, integration, and for the movement and transformation of data in the organization. At a minimum, the data architecture should describe all the repositories and data flows that data takes through the organization's systems.

In defining and documenting a data architecture, the organization:

- Creates a readiness for including data in the development of new products or services because it knows what data it has and where it can be accessed.

- Translates business needs into data and technology specifications, so that the processes of the organization get the right data at the right time and in the right format.

- Supports effective alignment between the business functions of the organization and the IT function by developing a common reference language and shared blueprints for how and where data is used.

In effect, data architects are librarians who create and maintain the organization's knowledge about the data structures, processes and systems in the organization. A significant portion of what a data architect does in an organization is support and enable collaboration through the development of a common business vocabulary for the things the organization needs to know about and manage, and by engaging with other stakeholders to learn from, influence and educate them on the information systems landscape in the organization.

The development of different levels of architectural model for use with different stakeholders is a key part of this process. There are, in effect, four architectural perspectives (aka data architecture domains) that an organization needs to consider:

- **The enterprise business architecture** – how is value being created (or destroyed) for customers and other stakeholders? What are the business processes? What are the core organization capabilities? What is the business data vocabulary?

- **The enterprise data architecture** – how is data in the organization organized and managed? How do different concepts relate to each other? What is the definition of key data elements such as 'customer' or 'product' and where are they related to each other? What is the map of the flow of information in the data landscape in the organization?

- **The enterprise applications architecture** – what is the structure and purpose of the different software applications that exist in the organization? What data are they consuming? What outputs do they generate, and for whom?

- **Enterprise technology architecture** – what is the physical technology environment needed to enable the operation of the applications, the processing of the data and the delivery of business value?

While there are a range of standards for enterprise architecture such as TOGAF9.1 and ISO42010:2011, we have found in our consulting and teaching work that the Zachman framework is a model that is both complete and relatively straightforward for people to understand. The DAMA DMBOK (DAMA International, 2017) covers the detail of the Zachman framework in detail. For this chapter we will provide a quick summary and then discuss in more detail in Chapter 6 how it supports ethical information management.

The Zachman framework

The Zachman framework is an ontological model built around a six-by-six matrix of models that describe an enterprise (see Figure 5.4). The framework also captures the relationship between these different models at different levels of abstraction. The Zachman framework does not tell us how to document things or how to create the models that form the artefacts in the different cells, it just shows us what models should exist and how they are related to each other.

Figure 5.4 The Zachman framework version 3.0 (used with permission)

	What (Data)	How (Action)	Where (Location)	Who (Actor)	When (Event)	Why (Motivation)	
Executive	Inventory Identification	Process Identification	Distribution Identification	Responsibility Identification	Timing Identification	Motivation Identification	Scope Context
Business Manager	Inventory Definition	Process Definition	Distribution Definition	Responsibility Definition	Timing Definition	Motivation Definition	Business Concepts
Architect	Inventory Representation	Process Representation	Distribution Representation	Responsibility Representation	Timing Representation	Motivation Representation	System Logic
Engineer	Inventory Specification	Process Specification	Distribution Specification	Responsibility Specification	Timing Specification	Motivation Specification	Technology Physics
Technician	Inventory Configuration	Process Configuration	Distribution Configuration	Responsibility Configuration	Timing Configuration	Motivation Configuration	Tool Components
Enterprise	Inventory Instantiation	Process Instantiation	Distribution Instantiation	Responsibility Instantiation	Timing Instantiation	Motivation Instantiation	Enterprise
	Inventory Sets	Process Flows	Distribution Networks	Responsibility Assignments	Timing Cycles	Motivation Intentions	

We have had the delight of talking with John Zachman over the years about his framework and figuring out the complexities hidden behind the six-by-six matrix. The best way of explaining what it does and the objective of the framework is with a metaphor. The metaphor is that of a house under construction:

- The people who are having the house built have their perspective and view of the different aspects of the house. They will have a vision for what the house will be used for and the 'finished product'. They may have a sketched idea, or photographs of other houses they are taking inspiration from.

- The architect working with the family will have a more detailed representation of the house, showing all the aspects and elements in proportion. This formal design will highlight or require trade-offs from the family in terms of their perspective. Physics, space or building regulations may constrain the architect's implementation.

- Each of the trades working on the construction will have a different set of plans or a different perspective or view of what the defined blueprints mean. A plumber will see the house as a network of taps and pipes that need to be connected in the right way. An electrician will see plug sockets and light fittings that need to be installed.

- The quantity surveyor will see the volume of materials that need to be procured and the cost. That cost may result in changes to the design, which in turn can give rise to changes in the vision.

- The project manager will see dependencies between different stages of the build, where some tasks cannot be completed before others.

As any of us know who have watched home improvement programmes on television, if the various perspectives are not aligned there can be potential for drama, conflict, and what we call in consultant speak, 'suboptimal outcomes'.

The Zachman framework essentially links six communication interrogatives (the what, how, where, who, when and why of your organization) to the steps needed to turn an abstract concept into a real instance of that thing. These steps are presented in the context of different perspectives, similar to the different perspectives of the different parties to the house-building project described above. At each intersection of the interrogative and the perspective, a particular set of artefacts would be expected to exist.

Each cell of the Zachman framework represents a unique type of design and planning artefact. Each artefact represents specific answers to fundamental questions across the top, in the context of the different perspectives that exist in the organization.

For more information on the types of models and artefacts in the Zachman framework, we recommend the DAMA DMBOK as a starting point for further reading (please see the Further Reading at the end of this chapter for more details). In Chapter 6 we will develop the discussion of the Zachman framework further in the context of its role in supporting the 'designing in' of ethics into the information architecture of the organization.

Data modelling

Data modelling is defined in the DAMA DMBOK (DAMA International, 2017) as 'the process of discovering, analysing and scoping data requirements, and then representing and communicating these data requirements in a precise form called a data model'. In essence, it is the process of identifying the key things that the organization needs to manage information about, understanding how they are related to each other, and identifying any other business rules that need to be applied.

The process requires organizations to discover and document how their data fits together. This drives the development of a common data vocabulary, documents explicit knowledge about your data and your systems, and provides a reference point for communications during projects. The data model formalizes, in a concise manner, the definition of key data structures and relationships between things. It also helps define the boundaries and scope for data in a given context. The models that are produced form part of the corporate memory of how things work in the organization, so that as things evolve and are changed at a data level, there can be better governance and management of those changes.

A good data model is a powerful communications tool. When Daragh was working in the telephone company, his team were able to draw the logical data models of a number of the systems they were responsible for from memory in workshops. This helped focus discussion of requirements and simplified assessment of requests for changes.

Data models are made up of entities (things) and relationships (the high-level interactions between conceptual entities, detailed interactions at a logical level, and constraints at a physical level). Taken together, these can form a graphical representation of the things that are being managed by the organization and the relationship between them. For example, in a school setting, a TEACHER is an entity, as is a STUDENT and a COURSE. The relationship between a TEACHER and a STUDENT could be resolved through the COURSE:

Figure 5.5 An example of a logical data model

Data models are one type of artefact that is created in the Zachman framework, and there are different types of data model depending on what level of perspective you are applying within that framework. There are three basic categories of data model, each reflecting different layers of the Zachman framework:

- **The Conceptual Data Model** – this model describes the high-level business concepts. It addresses the executive and business manager layers of the Zachman framework.

- **The Logical Data Model** – this model describes the high-level business concepts, their attributes, and how they are linked together logically. This maps to the architect and engineer layers of the Zachman framework.

- **The Physical Data Model** – the physical instantiation of a database in the database system. This maps to the engineer, technician and enterprise layers of the framework as it reflects how the database is designed and implemented as a tangible thing.

For most business purposes, a conceptual or logical model is sufficient as it supports effective communication about data concepts. It is outside the scope of this book to provide a detailed overview of the more technical aspects of data modelling, in particular physical data modelling. We recommend the DAMA DMBOK (see the Further Reading at the end of this chapter) as a good reference to start from to learn more.

Data modelling and ethics

The ethical issues in data modelling are often related to the way in which we view the world and the bias that modellers can bring to the table, similar to the challenges of algorithmic bias in AI and analytics. These issues can arise in the most trivial of contexts such as the humble task of recording someone's gender in a database. They can also arise in the context of whether or not the model should be built at all.

Gender, and modelling for gender in databases, is one of the challenges that we set students when we are guest lecturing at universities. How many gender classifications are there? Is gender the same as anatomical sex?

Is gender identity the same as gender? The traditional approaches of a simple 'male/female' flag in your database simply do not work any more, particularly when many countries have enacted legislation requiring public-sector databases to be able to support the gender identity needs of citizens. It is only in recent years that standards have been defined for how this type of data might be captured (UK Information Standards Board for Education, Skills and Children's Services, 2016).

The UK Information Standards Board sets out a choice of three questions that schools might ask in relation to transgender students:

- Legal sex type – male/female/not applicable.
- Self-declared gender type – man/woman/other.
- Transgender type – yes/no/prefer not to say.

Rather than being three attributes of a person, they are defined as attributes of the person in the context of their relationship to an organization. This reflects the ethical challenge posed where a transgender person is in transition and may be presenting as a male in one organization's context and as a female in another organization's context. In this way, the ethical values of inclusivity and confidentiality are baked into the data model because they have been considered during the design and data definition.

The other context is whether data should be gathered or processed in the first place. For example, if your organization was developing a smartphone application that tracked the driving habits of people who downloaded it and provided rewards for good driver behaviour (eg not interacting with the phone while driving, average speed between two points within the speed limit, etc) you might be faced with a requirement to record the origin and destination GPS co-ordinates for each journey taken by the users of the application, and GPS co-ordinates for way points on the journey every 10 minutes, to calculate the average speed correctly. Safe drivers get points, so you need to have the data calculated to calculate the points the driver gets.

However, you are obtaining a significant amount of data from the smartphone app. By storing it all in the database you are creating a toolset for analysis of driving patterns that could single out individual drivers. Ethically, a data modeller should ask if this is the most efficient way to process this data and preserve the data privacy of the drivers. If the points scheme is based on average speed between two points and evidence of the device being handled or touched during that time, it may be more appropriate to model for distance travelled and average speed to be recorded, and to ask your smartphone developers to perform the calculations on the data on the device before transferring it to the database.

A third example comes from work we did for a client a number of years ago looking at voter canvassing systems, and it highlights the value of data modelling as a tool to support ethical decision making. As part of the Privacy Impact Assessment for the design and implementation of a voter canvassing database for a European political party, we developed a logical data model of the different entities, based on the identified data sources (see Figure 5.6). Based on the modelling exercise, we were able to show how data that, historically, was held in discrete files within the party organization would be combined in a way that would allow analysis to be run to identify how a person in a home had voted in the last round of elections. We flagged to the client that this risked breaching the fundamental principle of the secrecy of the ballot. Our client took a principled ethical decision to step back from the originally proposed level of data integration and analytics until a method could be found to avoid this potential breach of constitutional law.

These are just three examples. Ultimately, the data modelling function needs to align with the data governance function to ensure the right ethics principles are applied to the data models in the right way.

Data quality management

Data quality management is defined by the DAMA DMBOK as 'the planning, implementation, and control activities that apply quality management techniques to data, to assure it is fit for consumption and business purposes'. In effect, data quality management is the application of proven quality management principles to the management of information.

A data quality dimension is a measurable feature or characteristic of data. These dimensions can be objective (eg completeness) or they can be subjective (usability, transactability, reputation) or they can be highly contextual (accuracy, accuracy against surrogate source). Organizations have to identify what dimensions are important to business processes and can also be measured. The key aspect of what is being measured is that it should be linked back to a business risk or issue.

For example, if the blood group is not recorded correctly for patients in a hospital, this could result in potential treatment complications. Therefore, a hospital might require 100 per cent population of blood group and an accuracy level of 99.999 per cent for that data.

Data quality dimensions are used as inputs into data quality business rules. These rules describe how the data should be for it to be useful. They codify the expectation of quality of data and act either to prevent, detect

Figure 5.6 Example data model: political canvassing

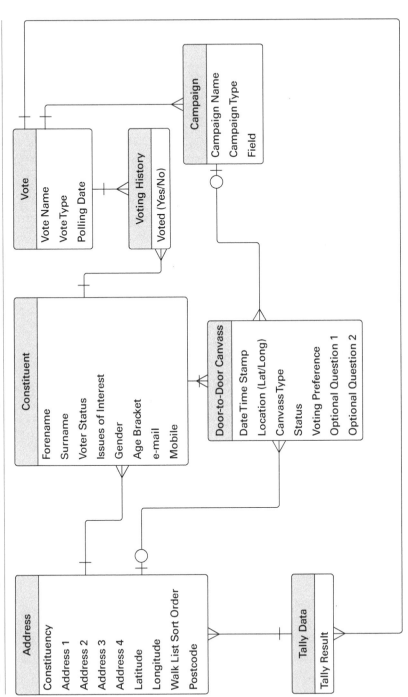

or remedy issues when they are identified. The DAMA DMBOK and other publications provide a range of examples of data quality business rules. For the purposes of this book, we will focus on what happens after a measurement has been taken of quality.

Data profiling is the process by which data is measured against defined business rules to identify issues in the data. A profiling tool will produce a statistical analysis of the data, which can be used to inform analysts about patterns of defect in the content and structure of the data. Depending on the business rule a value may be significant or not. For example, if a data-profiling exercise is expected to reveal that 100 per cent of all the rows in field X are null, but there are 20 per cent of the records that have values, this might indicate a problem in the data that needs to be investigated.

Ultimately, all data is the product of a process that captured or created it. Data quality management applies manufacturing process paradigms to understand the causes of poor-quality data and improve the quality of output data through improvements in the processes that capture and create that data, in order to remove the causes of error. However, studies and industry practitioner experience have identified a range of common causes for data quality problems. These include:

- a lack of leadership and appropriate governance;
- difficulty in justifying the required improvements;
- inappropriate or ineffective tools to measure the value of information;
- data-entry process issues, including inconsistent processes and lack of training;
- data-processing issues, including assumptions about data sources;
- data systems design issues, including data modelling issues;
- issues caused by hasty fixes.

Addressing these root causes requires the right approach to be taken both technically and ethically. During Daragh's time in the telephone company he often had to challenge managers who were blaming front-line staff for the creation of billing errors or other defects. Ultimately, the root cause of the defect did not always lie with the staff. There were often issues with bugs in software implementation, poorly defined business rules or poor-quality staff training. These were not in the control of the front-line staff members and instead were usually the responsibility of the managers who were trying to cascade blame down the hierarchy.

Ethics in information quality

The challenge here is more in relation to the ethic of quality in the organization. W Edwards Deming called on leaders in organizations to 'adopt the new philosophy' (Deming, 1986) of quality. That is an ethical principle. Organizations that are thinking in terms of quality systems and quality approaches tend to:

1 **Focus on the needs of their customers** – they make sure they identify and understand them, both customers and their needs, correctly.

2 **Drive out fear and encourage pride in a job well done** – blaming people for errors and failures of the overall system is counterproductive. While it might be tempting to blame the person nearest the symptom, often the root cause lies elsewhere in the organization.

3 **Focus on continuous improvement** – by incrementally improving quality and not resting on laurels, the organization can develop a sustainable level of quality.

In our work with clients we have seen the failure of the 'hero ethic' where staff are thrown at problems to fix them manually. A much better approach is to apply a quality ethic in the organization and focus on preventing the defects rather than just hurrying to scrap and rework data. This requires an ethical focus on the needs, wants and concerns of the stakeholders in that data, which could include internal and external customers, so that quality is designed in.

Another aspect of ethics in information quality management is the approach the organization takes to measurement and how that affects how quality is perceived. There is a line in an old song that says we need to 'accentuate the positive, eliminate the negative'.[1] In quality management terms that may mean measuring the successful outcomes and not tracking people on the defects that have been created but on the number of records that meet the required standard. This changes the ethic of quality improvement away from punishment for deviation from standard towards one of reward and recognition for good-quality outputs.

This ties into the wider ethical concepts of preserving and promoting human dignity. If you constantly highlight the failings of the organization, teams within the organization, or single out individuals as being below par, you can impact on morale and feelings of dignity at the micro and macro level.

Data warehousing and business intelligence

According to the DAMA DMBOK, data warehousing and business intelligence have been a key focus of most enterprise information management since the 1980s,[2] as technology became available to integrate data across the organization into a single repository. This triggered a revolution in reporting across organizations as data could be linked, cross-referenced, and applied to more complex automated reporting and decision support functions.

One of the drivers for the development of data warehousing was as a panacea for the proliferation of departmental decision support systems and reporting environments that were emerging as computing moved onto the desktop in organizations. These local 'data islands' were often collating the same data, albeit for different purposes, and it made logical sense to reduce the redundancy and duplication of data, improve consistency of information, and enable the organization to become more 'data driven'.

The data warehouse and business intelligence are the antecedent of the data lakes and 'big data' solutions that are emerging in the 'newer' fields of data science and big data. A data warehouse consists of two core elements: 1) a decision support database that integrates data from multiple sources both within the organization and from outside the organization; 2) a set of software programs that collect, extract, transform and load data from these data sources into the data warehouse.

A data warehouse may also incorporate smaller databases that contain defined subsets of the larger data warehouse for analytical or archival purposes. These 'data marts' form part of the overall data warehouse in the context of business intelligence and reporting processes.

Business intelligence refers to both the process of data analysis to understand organizational activities and opportunities as well as the technology and software that support this kind of analysis. The premise of business intelligence, according to the DMBOK (DAMA International, 2017), is 'that if an organization asks the right questions of its own data, it can gain insights about its products, services and customers that enable it to make better decisions about how to fulfil its strategic objectives'. The technologies used for business intelligence range from basic spreadsheet reports to business intelligence tools that enable querying, statistical analysis, scenario modelling and data visualization.

Other key tools for data warehousing and business intelligence include:

- **Metadata repositories** – used to manage the technical and business metadata from various systems.

- **Data glossary** – a description of data in business terms accompanied by technical metadata, and business metadata relating to such things as access rights and allowed uses.
- **Data and data model lineage** – it is important to know where the data has come from and what transformations or changes to the data may have occurred when moving from source to destination. Likewise, if data models are being changed or updated, it is important to understand the history of such changes.
- **Data integration tools** – software that supports the execution of data quality functions, defect resolution, and escalation of issues within the extract, transform and load processes of the data warehouse.

Applications of business intelligence tools include:

- **Operational reporting** – the use of business intelligence tools to track business trends over time and to identify trends and patterns that may be of use to the operational planning of the business.
- **Business performance management** – the formal assessment of key performance indicators (KPIs) and other metrics against business goals. End-of-quarter sales or revenue targets would be an example of business performance management reporting.
- **Self-service analytics** – providing access to business intelligence tools to the business stakeholders or function heads and their direct reports. The objective is to provide more timely insights into data by letting those closest to the front lines query data themselves to identify operational or strategic trends or opportunities.

While it may have evolved out of departmental reporting functions, business intelligence and data warehousing are fundamental data management disciplines found in most organizations. The key difference between what is traditionally thought of as business intelligence and the emerging fields of data science and 'big data' is that business intelligence has traditionally been retrospective – focusing on telling the organization what *has* happened, rather than predictive.

Increasingly, the move towards self-service business intelligence, and the 'consumerization' of business intelligence tools, has placed significant power on the desktop or tablet devices of business and IT professionals in organizations, combined with powerful statistical tools and data visualization capabilities. As such, the oversight and governance of business intelligence and data warehousing is evolving away from the traditional IT department.

When working with clients we break the business intelligence and data warehouse life cycle into three distinct phases, as illustrated in Figure 3.1 in this book. Each phase can give rise to different issues and challenges from a compliance, governance or ethics perspective. These phases are not part of the DAMA DMBOK but are part of our consulting methodologies:

- **Acquisition** – this describes the processes by which data is obtained or created by the organization and populated into the data warehouse environment. The methods and approaches used to obtain data or process data during this phase can impact on the quality of the data, the compliance of processing with relevant laws (eg data privacy laws) and could raise ethical questions.

- **Analysis** – this describes the processes by which the data is being analysed and interrogated. There is an old joke among statisticians that if you torture data long enough it will give you the answers you want. This highlights one of the potential ethical hazards in analysis. Other issues that might arise in the analysis phase can include the knowledge and ability of staff to use the data they have access to, in a manner that is compatible with relevant laws or standards. This is particularly true in the context of self-service business intelligence.

- **Action** – this describes the action that is to be taken based on the analysis outputs. Depending on the action to be taken, and the methods applied to taking that action, ethical or other issues may arise. For example, if you were to automatically fire the lowest-performing members of staff in your organization, based on a performance report, with no human review or intervention, this could raise ethical issues or issues of legal liability in some jurisdictions.

Ethical issues in data warehousing and business intelligence

We have looked at these issues in Chapter 3, but here we will examine them from the perspective of the practicalities of the DMBOK disciplines, where issues can often fall into the 'just because we can, does it mean we should?' category of ethical dilemmas and can relate to questions such as the sourcing of data from third parties, the inference of data from other data as part of the standardization of data or analysis of data, or questions over the management of access to data in the data warehouse, particularly where the organization has deployed self-service analytics capabilities.

In general, one of the key ethical challenges in data warehousing and business intelligence is the definition of and embedding of a culture of ethical analytics, particularly in the context of data privacy issues and risks, but also in the context of data being used for new and unforeseen analytics purposes.

Data science and 'big data'

Data science and 'big data' are the descendants of the traditional data warehouse and business intelligence capabilities in organizations. They are terms that are often misused and abused as technology jargon, and much of what is described as 'data science' is little more than modern business intelligence.

Data science has evolved from the historic disciplines of applied statistics. It deals with the capability to analyse and explore data patterns quickly and effectively. As already mentioned, where traditional business intelligence is retrospective in its focus, data science tries to infer future behaviours and outcomes based on historical patterns. Historically, this required application of statistical methods such as sampling of data to get a representative sample of a population to analyse.

Modern data technologies allow for the collection and analysis of much larger datasets, allowing data science to evolve from its statistical roots and integrate disciplines from pattern recognition, artificial intelligence, machine learning, data visualization, and more, to find new ways to analyse and extract value from data that is both retrospective (what has happened) and predictive (based on what happened, what will happen next).

'Big data' is a label applied to data sets that are large (volume), or have a wide range of variety (for example, structured and unstructured data, audio, video, documents etc), or have velocity (are produced at speed). This large, varied and rapidly changing data environment requires the tools and techniques of data science to enable the data to be analysed and meaning inferred. It is not surprising that many of the initial tools for big data emerged from the large internet companies such as Google, where they were used to help process the vast amounts of data generated from searches and from text analysis from people using services like Gmail.

Of course, the promises of deep science and big data depend greatly on the ability of the organization to manage that data. This has created a renewed focus on the effective governance and control of data. The management of the metadata associated with the various data sources, transformations, linkages and business rules applied to the data is an essential element of this.

According to DAMA, data scientists should follow the scientific method of knowledge refinement through observation, hypothesis formulation and testing, and the development of general theories that explain the results observed from the testing of their hypotheses. This is not often the case in organizations, however, where data science is conflated or confused with traditional business intelligence.

Some of the technologies and tools of data science and big data are:

- **Machine learning** – this is at the core of the advances in AI and is concerned with the construction and study of learning algorithms. These fall into three main categories:

  - unsupervised methods that rely on pattern recognition and identification;

  - supervised (general rules-based) learning methods based on generalized rules and statistical and mathematical modelling techniques;

  - reinforcement learning strategies, which are goal-based learning strategies driven by the algorithm achieving a defined goal, such as winning a game or some other defined task.

- **Sentiment analysis** – this uses technologies such as natural language processing or semantic analysis methods to understand what people are saying or writing, and to infer sentiment from that content (eg whether you like or dislike a particular brand of washing powder based on your Twitter activity). Sentiment analysis can also be linked to machine learning to identify changes in sentiment and infer the next action that might be taken or trigger an appropriate automated response.

- **Data and text mining** – this aspect of data science looks for patterns in data, and is effectively a form of unsupervised machine learning. These techniques are used to find hidden or unknown relationships between data by identifying patterns.

- **Predictive analytics** – this is an application of supervised machine learning in which the data elements are modelled and future outcomes are predicted based on the probability of that thing occurring, based on all the data in the model data. Predictive analytics methods are often used in areas such as share trading, where a predictive model triggers a share trade based on a reaction to an input variable when compared to the historic model. For example, if there are hailstorms in an area that grows sunflowers, the model may trigger the sale of sunflower-oil company shares as there will be a drop in profits due to the increased cost of the input materials (sunflowers), as the harvest of sunflowers has reduced after hailstorms in the past.

- **Prescriptive analytics** – this is another application of supervised learning that goes beyond simply predicting outcomes but to infer what actions might trigger what outcome. It is used in advanced decision support and risk management scenarios as it can identify what will happen and infers or implies why it will happen, highlighting the impacts of various options that might exist to avoid risk or seize opportunity.

- **Unstructured Data Analytics** – Unstructured Analytics uses a range of unsupervised learning approaches to analyse and codify information held in 'unstructured' forms such as electronic documents, images, video, etc. It commonly focuses on the inference of metadata tagging to link the unstructured data to structured data sets in the Data Warehouse.

The corollary for business intelligence in the data science and big data world are the disciplines of operational analytics and data visualization. Operational analytics applies predictive, prescriptive, and other machine-learning approaches to the live operational data streams of the organization. Examples of operational analytics include things like surge pricing in ridesharing services, real-time up-selling and cross-selling of products on Amazon, or in financial trading. Data visualization is the process by which we interpret concepts and data by using pictures or graphical representations. It can be as simple as a chart or a graph, or as complicated as a colour-coded visualization of data.

As with business intelligence and data warehousing, when working with clients we break down the data science and big data functions into three distinct phases. As before, we can encounter a range of issues from a compliance, ethics, technology or quality perspective. Of course, the details of what is in the scope of each phase differs between traditional business intelligence and more advanced data science. As the principles and practices for governance of data science are still evolving, these issues can often be more challenging to address:

- **Acquisition** – in addition to the actual obtaining of data, as we discussed in the context of data warehousing, a data science context needs to add the development of training data sets and the development of the business rule cascades that are applied in machine-learning/deep-learning contexts to this acquisition phase. In short, in addition to understanding how the data that is to be analysed has been obtained, it is necessary to understand how the rules and inferences that are being applied to the data through the various algorithms you might apply have been created as well. How this is approached can have significant implications for the results of analysis based on those algorithms. Only by understanding this can you ensure you are identifying and controlling for algorithmic biases that might lead to unexpected or unethical outcomes.

- **Analysis** – this describes the application of the analytics processes and algorithms to the testing of hypotheses in the data. This is the essence of the scientific method that data scientists should be applying. In our experience, a key element of the analysis phase in a data science/big data context needs to be the constant tuning and enhancing of the algorithms and associated processes based on the outcomes of the various hypothesis tests that are performed. For example, an algorithm to detect faces in a video may need to have its learning cascade and algorithms enhanced to take account of a child's face or bright lights or fast movement that might not have been in earlier data sets analysed.

- **Action** – as before, this describes the action that is to be taken based on the analysis outputs. The action taken may simply be to blur a face in a video, or it may be to provide fashion suggestions in a beauty app on a smartphone. Depending on the action, there may be ethical issues that arise, or there may be legal liability issues, or commercial impacts on your organization. For example, an error in an automated trading process could be costly. A bug in the automated trading systems of Knight Capital Group in 2012 cost the company $400 million dollars in a matter of minutes (Farrell, 2012). If the action taken as a result of your analysis is a data visualization, perhaps considering how that is presented and considering the accessibility issues that arise when relying on visual representations of data would be important from a quality and ethics perspective.

Ethical issues in data science and big data

The pace with which the fields of data science and big data have evolved, combined with the potential to analyse full population data sets rather than just samples, and the potential to infer and predict behaviour, all raise potential for ethical concerns, some of which we will explore in more detail in later chapters.

However, particularly in the context of the use of data science and big data technologies and methods in relation to data about or describing people, a significant area of general ethical concern is the gap between the data scientist ideal, as set out by DAMA in the DMBOK, and the practice on the ground. Scientists, particularly scientists who are engaged in experiments on people, need to comply with strict ethical codes. These codes do not yet exist for data scientists, who often forget that the data they are working with is data about people and the actions taken as a result of the analysis could have significant impacts on people. This highlights the need for a holistic framework to support the integration of ethical concepts into day-to-day data management activities. Without this, we risk remaining at a point where ethics is the thing that is done by someone else in the organization, just as information quality was a decade ago.

There is a range of other issues we will cover in Chapters 6 to 11, but for this chapter we leave you with the question of whether it is ethical to produce data visualizations that cannot be read or interpreted by colour-blind people. Or, for that matter, to rely only on a data visualization that cannot be read by a visually impaired person.

Chapter summary

As information professionals we should seek to ensure that, in the words of the European Union's General Data Protection Regulation, 'the processing of personal data should be designed to serve mankind' (European Union, 2016). In this chapter we:

- Discussed the ethical neutrality of information management disciplines, in that they can be equally applied to processing activities that are ethical as to processing activities that are unethical.

- Introduced the DMBOK wheel and the various data management disciplines identified by DAMA.

- Examined, at a high level, some of the more relevant DMBOK disciplines in which ethical issues can arise.

- Outlined how ethical issues can arise, and can be addressed, at different phases of the data warehousing and data analytics life cycles.

- Identified how the application of information management disciplines such as data modelling can help bring to light potential ethical issues during the design phase of a project or proposed processing activity.

- Discussed how ethical questions outside the core scope of an information management discipline can impact the overall ethical nature of the processing activity.

The other disciplines in the DAMA DMBOK can give rise to ethical issues relating to the method and manner of execution of the discipline or arising from the impact and implications of decisions that are being taken relating to the definition of and management of data.

Questions

Several questions arise that warrant further consideration by the budding information ethicist. These are a starting point for further discussion:

1 What is the role of personal ethics in defining and shaping organizational ethics and linking that to the information strategy of the organization? Is it appropriate to have an ethical value of pride in a job well done when that job involves the processing of data to ship contraband and illegal weaponry around the world more efficiently?

2 Information security is a key function in the organization. While we have not discussed it in this chapter, is it ethical to instal keyloggers on company computers to have access to information about what staff are doing in the organization at all times? Why do you take that view?

3 How might the policies of an organization in relation to document and content management raise ethical questions? For example, if a government organization has been given the only copies of medical records for people who had undergone questionable medical procedures for the purposes of a redress scheme, would it be ethical for the organization to destroy those records rather than returning them to the survivors?

Notes

1 Information about the song can be found here: http://bit.ly/2v6uoOz.

2 Daragh likes to remind people that the first published paper on the architecture of an information warehouse was published in 1988 in the *IBM Systems Journal*, 27 (1), by Barry Devlin, a fellow Irishman.

Further reading

We recommend the following books for further reading on information and data management topics addressed in this chapter:

English, L (2009) *Information Quality Applied: Best practices for improving business information, processes, and systems*, Wiley, Chichester

Ladley, J (2012) *Data Governance: How to design, deploy, and sustain an effective data governance program*, Elsevier, San Francisco

McGilvray, D (2008) *Executing Data Quality Projects: 10 steps to quality data and trusted information*, Morgan Kaufmann, Boston

Redman, T (2016) *Getting In Front On Data*, Technics Publications, New Jersey

Seiner, R (2014) *Non-Invasive Data Governance: The path of least resistance and greatest success*, Technics Publications, New Jersey

Simsion, G (2004) *Data Modelling Essentials*, 3rd edn, Morgan Kaufmann, Boston

References

DAMA International (2017) DAMA DMBOK, *DAMA DMBOK – Data Management Body of Knowledge*, Technics Publications, New Jersey, pp 381–85

Deming, WE (1986) *Out of the Crisis*, MIT Press, Boston

European Union (2016) [accessed 1 August 2017] *Regulation 2016/679/EU* [Online] http://ec.europa.eu/justice/data-protection/reform/files/regulation_oj_en.pdf

Farrell, M (2012) [accessed 1 August 2017] Knight's Bizarre Trades Rattle Markets [Online] http://buzz.money.cnn.com/2012/08/01/trading-glitch/?iid=H_MKT_News

Ladley, J (2012) *Data Governance: How to design, deploy, and sustain an effective data governance program*, Elsevier, New York

McGilvray, D (2008) *Executing Data Quality Projects: 10 steps to quality data and trusted information*, Morgan Kaufmann, Boston

UK Information Standards Board for Education, Skills, and Childrens Services (2016) [accessed 1 August 2017] ISB Standards Guidance: Sex, Gender and Trangender – Data Capture [Online] https://data.gov.uk/education-standards/sites/default/files/ISB-Standards-Guidance-Sex-Gender-and-Transgender-Data-Capture-v2-0.pdf

Developing an ethical architecture for information management

06

What will we cover in this chapter?

In Chapter 5, we introduced the Zachman framework as part of our discussion of information architecture as a fundamental data management discipline in the DMBOK. In this chapter, we look at how this ontology of artefacts and different levels of perspective on information management can help address some of the key challenges we face when trying to put ethical concepts into operation in an information management context.

By the end of this chapter you will understand:

- Fundamental concepts underpinning the Zachman framework.
- The importance of the ontology to defining, assessing and understanding the impact of ethical principles for information management.
- The importance of an ontological approach to information management and information ethics.
- The importance of an architectural approach to information ethics to ensure ethical issues and risks posed by processing activities are identified and mitigated in the design of processing activities and technology implementations.

Information ethics and architecture – what is the connection?

One of the common complaints we see surrounding ethics in information management is that the challenges that are raised are often complex and require, or are initiated by, changes in organizations, technical capability or in society's expectations. People and organizations struggle at times to deal with complexity and change. Understanding and assessing the impact of a change on an already complex network of information management systems and capabilities can be difficult for us. As John Zachman puts it: 'A quick review of the history of all the known disciplines that deal with complex objects (things) reveals that change starts with the engineering descriptions of the things' (Zachman, 1996).

What organizations often lack as part of their information strategy or information architecture is a formal description of what the ethics of the organization are and how they cascade through the different representations and perspectives on the information systems and processes that the people in the organization work with. An architectural approach is one proven approach to doing this in a structured way.

The Zachman framework is described by John Zachman as an ontology. From a philosophical perspective, ontology is the branch of philosophy that deals with the nature of existence and being, and the ultimate substance of things (Collins English Dictionary, n.d.). Who we are, how we relate to each other and our surrounding environment is at the heart of the philosophical study of ontology. In an information architecture context, an ontological approach deals with the nature of the enterprise as expressed in its information strategy and systems. Part of the discussion of how you, and your organization, relate to others and to your environment is the ethical model that you are applying to that conduct. Therefore, an ontological approach to managing information in the enterprise must include explicit consideration of the moral and ethical models that are to be applied as part of the management of information in that organization.

Logicians understand the term 'ontology' slightly differently. They define an ontology as the set of entities that are presupposed by a particular theory about being or reality. What are the things that need to be considered? How are they related to each other in the context of this theoretical model that has been constructed to describe the reality that is being addressed? This provides a mental map that allows for rational discussion of concepts using agreed-upon terms. As with the philosophical perspective, though, an information architecture needs to define a set of 'things' that are being described in the context of a framework for that architecture. Part of that set of things that need to be described and related to other parts of your information architecture are the ethical concepts and precepts that need to be described, understood and applied at each level of perspective you are dealing with.

Zachman uses the term 'ontology' correctly in its philosophical and primary logical sense when he describes his framework for information architecture as an ontology. Of course, this can lead to confusion in an information management context and AI context as the term 'ontology' has become used in an information science context to mean the structuring of knowledge about things by subcategorizing based on identified attributes or essential qualities. From a philosophical and wider library science perspective, that more closely aligns with the definition of a taxonomy than an ontology.

This confusion has led to some criticism of the Zachman framework for not being complete enough in its description of the framework to constitute an ontology. One of the main reasons cited is that there is no description of how the basic concepts outlined in the Zachman framework can be broken down into their composite objects. However, it is worth noting that one of the pioneers of the use of the term 'ontology' in knowledge sharing and AI clearly states that his use of the term 'is certainly a different sense of the word than its use in philosophy' (Gruber, 1992).

According to Gruber, 'ontology is a technical term denoting an artefact that is designed for a purpose, which is to enable the modelling of knowledge about some domain, real or imagined' (Gruber, 2007). The Zachman framework is designed to model knowledge about the universe of enterprise architecture components and provide a framework within which more detailed models can be developed at each level of perspective within each communicative interrogative domain. Rather than being prescriptive of how to break out the composite objects within each level of the framework, the Zachman framework identifies a set of things that will need to be defined and described in more detail. It then provides a conceptual relationship across the categories of things (the different levels of perspective) that indicate that they need to be considered together at that level. A further conceptual dimension is found looking vertically within the different domains of things down the different levels of perspective. In this way, the actual instantiation of things that describe the concepts at that level in the architecture is linked thematically to one of the key interrogative questions that underpin the ontology.

While many other approaches to defining information architecture exist, and while there are many ontological frameworks for breaking out in more detail many of the primitive artefacts identified by the Zachman framework, it is the philosophical perspective on ontologies in the Zachman framework, rather than the more recent information science perspective, that makes it particularly useful as a framework for figuring out how to define and instantiate an architectural model for ethics in information management. The problems we face are complex and arise in an era of unprecedented change in information management capability and the potential impact of information and how it is used, or abused, on individuals, communities and society as a whole.

Zachman and the allegory of the cave

One of the challenges we all face in changing how we think about information management and information ethics is that very often you will perceive your portion of the information architecture from the perspective of your professional discipline or background. This can lead to confusion and miscommunication about what is really being discussed. Ironically, the discussion of whether the Zachman framework is an ontology or not is actually a good example of this.

This brings to mind the Allegory of the Cave (Plato, 2017) in which Plato describes Socrates discussing the effect of education on the nature and behaviour of people. In this story, Socrates described a group of people who have lived chained to the wall of a cave, facing the wall. They see shadows on the wall from objects that are passed in front of a fire that is behind them and they give names to these shadows based on their field of perception. Socrates argued that a philosopher was one of these prisoners, who had simply broken free of his chains and understands the shadows on the wall as being just one representation of reality rather than reality itself.

In an information management context, our chains are often the professional disciplines or functions we are performing and the bodies of knowledge or methodologies associated with those functions, and the biases that we bring to the discussion from those perspectives. In the absence of a means of expanding our perspective, a data modeller will consider things through the perspective of data modelling, a process architect will perceive things from the perspective of process modelling and execution, and a data scientist will perceive things through the lens of data science methodologies and practices. The Zachman framework provides an ontological representation of the world outside our respective 'caves', all of which may have their own ontological and taxonomical models for the disciplines and activities that are undertaken at different levels of detail in that domain. It provides an ontological construct to recognize the horizontal dependencies of the different disciplines that need to be aligned in an effective enterprise information architecture.

In Plato's recounting of Socrates's fable, the prisoner who escapes their chains has to learn to adapt their perception of things, at first turning away from the bright lights outside the cave, but ultimately being able to look at the sun itself. It is only when they can look at the sun that they can begin to think about what it is and how it relates to the experience of the prisoner. In the context of ethical information management, the 'sun' is our motivation for gathering and processing data in the first place. John Zachman provides an ontological model within which the motivation and reasons for processing can be linked, through the communicative interrogatives and the different perspectives of information management in the organization, to specific categories of 'thing' that need to be created and managed in the organization to ensure that ethical considerations are applied appropriately.[1]

We introduced the Zachman framework in Chapter 5 (see Figure 5.4). Here (see Figure 6.1), for completeness, we reproduce John Zachman's original framework graphic, with his permission. The version we referenced in Figure 5.4 is a simplified representation that we will use for the purposes of the rest of this chapter.

Ethics in the Zachman framework

John Zachman defines 'architecture' as 'the set of design artefacts, or descriptive representations, that are relevant for describing an object such that it can be produced to requirements (quality) as well as maintained over the period of its useful life (change)' (Zachman, 1996).

As we have already discussed in Chapter 5, the Zachman framework is a six-by-six matrix that maps the interrogatives (what, how, where, who, when and why) to different levels of perspective in the organization. The intersection of these interrogatives (row) and the perspectives (column) represents a unique category of design artefact. Each artefact represents how the specific perspective answers the fundamental question in that context (DAMA International, 2017). For certain types of design artefact, there may be a hierarchical relationship of components of that object, which may have architectural models which define how those elements are assembled. These still need to fit within the overall enterprise architecture. The job of the architect, according to Zachman, is to 'be meticulous to ensure that every sub-part is architected to fit within the super-part', so that they can be sure

Figure 6.1 The Zachman framework, adapted

	Data	Action	Location	Actor	Event	Motivation	
Executive	Inventory Identification	Process Identification	Distribution Identification	Responsibility Identification	Timing Identification	Motivation Identification	Scope and Context
Business Manager	Inventory Definition	Process Definition	Distribution Definition	Responsibility Definition	Timing Definition	Motivation Definition	Business Concepts
Architect	Inventory Representation	Process Representation	Distribution Representation	Responsibility Representation	Timing Representation	Motivation Representation	System Logic
Engineer	Inventory Specification	Process Specification	Distribution Specification	Responsibility Specification	Timing Specification	Motivation Specification	Technology Physics
Technician	Inventory Configuration	Process Configuration	Distribution Configuration	Responsibility Configuration	Timing Configuration	Motivation Configuration	Tool Components
Enterprise	Inventory Instantiation	Process Instantiation	Distribution Instantiation	Responsibility Instantiation	Timing Instantiation	Motivation Instantiation	Enterprise

SOURCE adapted from John Zachman, with permission; www.zachman.com

to avoid 'semantic discontinuities, network anomalies, or rule inconsistencies' across the enterprise as a whole (Zachman, 1996).

Ethical models for organizations are no different in this regard to any other form of model. They can have a hierarchical or ontological architecture of their own that translates general precepts and principles of ethics into more granular representations of those precepts or principles. At different levels of perspective the way in which that ethic is expressed may differ. But where in the framework would ethics sit? Do we need to define another column in the ontology to reflect ethics as a type of thing that needs to be understood and managed? Thankfully we do not. For a model that was defined long before the current discussion of ethics in information management, the Zachman framework has already defined a communicative interrogative that can capture the questions of ethics, and which Zachman recognizes as being impacted by issues of granularity in the modelling of responses – the 'Why' (Zachman, 1996).

Zachman originally defined the 'Why' column of the framework to address the goals, strategies and means of the organization (DAMA International, 2017). Writing in 1997, David Hay described this column as concerning 'the translation of business goals and strategies into specific ends and means' (Hay, 1997). Hay goes on to say that this 'can be expanded to include the entire set of constraints that apply to an enterprise's efforts'. Ethics are just another form of constraint that would apply to the efforts of the enterprise. As such, the concept of the ethical information architecture sits within the 'Why' column as both a positive interrogative ('Why are we doing these things?') and as a negative interrogative ('Why are we not doing these things?'). The answers to these questions need to be cascaded and reflected in the different perspective rows of the framework and will influence and impact on the design of artefacts elsewhere in that row.

Of course, the potential scope of ethical principles and precepts that might need to be considered in the 'Executive' perspective (Row 1) is immense. In this context, it is important to consider what we mean by the 'Enterprise' and what its boundaries are. Zachman identifies a key characteristic of the boundary of an enterprise as being the point at which the organization operates as a stand-alone, self-contained unit. The 'Enterprise' would be defined by the business functions and assets, integrated in support of a common mission or objectives. This raises an architectural issue, however, when we are considering ethical issues as there will be ethics that are the 'ethic of society' and ethics that are the 'ethic of the organization'. There will even be 'ethics of the individual'. We have referenced this before and will examine it in more detail in Chapter 9. For now, we will confine ourselves to accepting that there are ethics and ethical perspectives that are external to the organization (the 'ethics of society') and those that are internal to the organization (the 'ethics of the organization'). The ones you need to architect for are the ethics of the organization. However, as these principles may evolve as society's ethic evolves, you need to be able to support both the complexity of ethics and the potential for change in your approach.

When we start thinking about how ethics can be implemented in an architectural construct, we very quickly find ourselves having to think about how ethics translates into action in the context of the different perspective levels that exist in the enterprise ontology defined by Zachman. To put it bluntly, we need to very quickly get out of philosophy and into engineering and doing, via the medium of architecture. This echoes the sentiment of Jane Addams who we introduced in Chapter 3, who pointed out in her writings that our actions are the only way to evidence our ethics.

Motivation

The 'Motivation' column of the framework (Figure 6.2) is where the examination of how you translate philosophy into action through an architecture needs to start. Looking at the different levels of perspective on motivation, we can begin to identify the types of artefact that might be created at each level. It is significant to note that in the original version of the Zachman framework we reproduced in Figure 5.4, Zachman identifies artefacts in the 'Motivation' column as including:

- Motivation Types at Row 1.
- Business Ends and Business Means at Row 2.
- System Ends and Means at Row 3.
- Technology Ends and Means at Row 4.

In Row 1 of the Zachman framework, our discussion of ethics in the enterprise is focused on identifying what the ethics and values of the organization actually are. At this level, we might begin to think about normative theories of ethics such as stakeholder theory, or shareholder theory, or even social justice/common good. This is the executive-level scope and context for *every other ethical decision that is taken in the organization*. Ethical considerations are one of a number of motivation types that can exist for an organization and it is at this level that we see the manifestation of normative theories of ethics such as shareholder theory versus stakeholder theory.

Figure 6.2 Ethics in the Zachman framework

	Data	Action	Location	Actor	Event	Motivation	
Executive	Inventory Identification	Process Identification	Distribution Identification	Responsibility Identification	Timing Identification	Motivation Identification	Scope and Context
Business Manager	Inventory Definition	Process Definition	Distribution Definition	Responsibility Definition	Timing Definition	Motivation Definition	Business Concepts
Architect	Inventory Representation	Process Representation	Distribution Representation	Responsibility Representation	Timing Representation	Motivation Representation	System Logic
Engineer	Inventory Specification	Process Specification	Distribution Specification	Responsibility Specification	Timing Specification	Motivation Specification	Technology Physics
Technician	Inventory Configuration	Process Configuration	Distribution Configuration	Responsibility Configuration	Timing Configuration	Motivation Configuration	Tool Components
Enterprise	Inventory Instantiation	Process Instantiation	Distribution Instantiation	Responsibility Instantiation	Timing Instantiation	Motivation Instantiation	Enterprise

SOURCE adapted from Zachman Framework, version 3.0

As we look at the lower-level perspectives from Row 2 to Row 4, we see how we need to plan in an architectural way for consistency in how ethics and values are communicated in the enterprise, particularly in the information management function:

- Row 2 requires business managers to align the philosophy and ethos espoused at Row 1, Column 6, with day-to-day 'doing' of things in the organization. Inconsistency and incongruence arises here where the day-to-day processes and practices espoused by management do not match with the values that are promoted by the executive scope and context. For example, if an organization states at the executive level that it values and protects the personal data of its customers and employees, a mismatch can arise when business managers in the organization adopt the view that dealing with privacy issues is someone else's job, like the Privacy department or Legal. Zachman explicitly labels the artefacts to be defined here as 'Business Ends' and 'Business Means', echoing the language of classical ethicists such as Kant.

- Row 3 requires clear representation of the values in the design of the logic of the internal systems (information systems and people systems). The logic of that design and the internal alignment with the executive values and the business management definition is what helps reinforce and embed the values in the organization. For example, if an organization says that it values the opinions and feedback of its customers but penalizes staff for spending longer than 90 seconds on a customer-service call, there is a disconnect that weakens the ethic of the organization. At this level, Zachman discusses the idea of 'System Ends' and 'System Means', alluding to the need to begin modelling ethical rules into systems and data architecture constructs.

- Row 4 relates to how ethical values might find themselves embedded in the specification of how things get done in the organization. The 'technology physics' that Zachman refers to can equally be applied to the people in the organization and the constraints on how they might behave. At this level, Zachman still refers to 'Ends' and 'Means', but in the context of the actual design of the information management technology platform in the organization.

- Row 5 and Row 6 reflect the actual implementation and instantiation of ethics in the organization in actual process implementation and process execution. Ultimately, it is at this level that the true measure of the ethical motivation of the organization is manifest, as the sole medium of expression of ethics is the actions that are performed.

The way in which the organization architects the definition of and communication of ethics and ethical values in the organization establishes a set of constraints on the behaviour of the enterprise. If these are not defined and executed in a semantically congruent way, there is scope for misinterpretation or incorrect internalization of the ethics of the organization by staff. As such, the translation of ethical principles into ethical practices is often a challenge in most enterprises and should be undertaken in a structured manner and not left to chance. We will now look at each of the rows in the Zachman framework in turn to examine how ethical factors can be instantiated in the overall ontology that Zachman defined.

The 'Executive' perspective

The ethical motivation of the organization impacts on the approaches applied and actions taken in the context of the other intersections of interrogative and perspective. For example, at the 'Executive' (Row 1) perspective (see Figure 6.3), the ethical motivation of the organization can impact on the gathering of data and what data is obtained or processed as part of the 'data inventory'.

One of the key areas organizations often struggle with is identifying the ethical issues that might arise with the data that they are proposing to process. These ethical issues are often related to the question of whether the data identifies, relates to or impacts on people. A clearly defined ethical-principles artefact that identifies the ethical motives and motivations of the organization can help you frame these discussions in terms of identifying what data you have that contributes to the achievement of those ethical values or which require care in processing to avoid infringing on the ethical principles you have identified for the organization. This can help avoid the 'it's not data about people' argument that can often bog down ethical change in information management. It allows you, through your executive-level definition of ethical motivation, to identify that the data your organization is processing can be used to have either a positive or negative impact on people.

Apple is a good example of this impact as they have historically lagged in the analytics space compared to Google with their Android operating system, because they do not harvest personal data about their customers from their devices in the same way and have only begun to do so in earnest when they could engineer privacy-respectful and privacy-enhancing ways of doing so, such as differential privacy or the development of on-chip analytics and AI capabilities – so raw data never leaves the person's device (Glance, 2017).

Figure 6.3 Ethical motives on Row 1 of the Zachman framework

	Data	Action	Location	Actor	Event	Motivation	
Executive	Inventory Identification	Process Identification	Distribution Identification	Responsibility Identification	Timing Identification	Motivation Identification	Scope and Context
Business Manager	Inventory Definition	Process Definition	Distribution Definition	Responsibility Definition	Timing Definition	Motivation Definition	Business Concepts
Architect	Inventory Representation	Process Representation	Distribution Representation	Responsibility Representation	Timing Representation	Motivation Representation	System Logic
Engineer	Inventory Specification	Process Specification	Distribution Specification	Responsibility Specification	Timing Specification	Motivation Specification	Technology Physics
Technician	Inventory Configuration	Process Configuration	Distribution Configuration	Responsibility Configuration	Timing Configuration	Motivation Configuration	Tool Components
Enterprise	Inventory Instantiation	Process Instantiation	Distribution Instantiation	Responsibility Instantiation	Timing Instantiation	Motivation Instantiation	Enterprise

Contrast this with Facebook's struggles with the ethical management and use of data that has resulted in experiments on users to see if bad news affects their mood (shock: it does) (Phipps, 2014) or the introduction of services such as 'Life Stages' (which removed privacy controls on content and showed it to people who claimed, without any validation, to be in your school) (O'Keefe and O Brien, 2016; TeenSafe, 2016).

Ethical considerations at the 'Executive' level should also guide the identification of actions that will be taken using data. This can also be seen in the example of the Samaritans Radar application we discussed in the Introduction, and in the context of the deployment of AI by Facebook to achieve similar goals, which we looked at in Chapter 3. In the context of Samaritans Radar, while the intent was good (Marrins, 2014) it is open to question whether this mass surveillance approach to mental health support was an action that was compatible with the Samaritans' core values of privacy, confidentiality and respect for the individual.

By considering the ethical motivation at the 'Executive' perspective, we can identify that disconnect, which ultimately resulted in the Samaritans pulling the Samaritans Radar app entirely due to the privacy concerns that were raised and which were not addressed in the design of the app (Lee, 2014). Likewise, in the context of the Facebook AI processing, we can see that at the 'Executive' level, Facebook have recognized that the processing of data relating to physical or mental health by automated means is subject to more stringent controls in Europe, but they appear not to have considered if the use of an 'always on' monitoring of people's posts to make decisions about mental health will support or undermine the objective of helping people by discouraging them from sharing such information on social media.

Similarly, the ethical values and motivations of the organization can impact on the decisions that are taken at the executive level regarding the location where data is processed or stored, and the identification of the responsibilities that the organization may have regarding the data, or regarding when certain actions or processes might be invoked or triggered. For example, an organization may adopt an ethical policy of not using certain companies for their data processing or not processing data in certain jurisdictions. This may result in the organization losing money or market opportunities. On the other hand, an enterprise may choose to change its product or service offerings in certain markets in response to market opportunity (eg lower levels of regulation) or in response to legal requirements in a jurisdiction. An example of this is Apple's recent decision to pull Virtual Private Network (VPN) apps from their App Store in China (Molina, 2017).

This has raised questions about Apple's commitment to its ethical stance on data privacy (Holt, 2017).

As we explore in more detail in our discussion of ethics and data governance, a key element of the architecture and design of ethical frameworks in an information management context is the identification of responsibility and accountability for ethical issues involving data. This is a Row 1 Column 4 consideration in the Zachman framework. What is it that your organization is responsible for at the end of the day? At what point might your ethical vision and values be constrained by external factors such as legal or regulatory constraints? Or at what point should your organization seek to go beyond the 'letter of the law' and promote a higher ethical standard? Who in the organization is ultimately responsible, and what are they responsible for? It is at this point that the 'tone at the top' issues referred to in Chapter 3 begin to emerge, as the statement of identified ethical motivation defined in Row 1 Column 6 is either congruent with or incongruent with the identified responsibilities in Row 1 Column 4.

Apple's decision in July 2017 to pull VPN apps from its App Store is a good example of this type of incongruity. Apple have historically positioned themselves as strongly protective of the data privacy of their users. Speaking in 2010, Steve Jobs encapsulated the value as: 'Privacy means people know what they are signing up for – in plain English, and repeatedly' (Bergen, 2016).

In 2015, Tim Cook drew another line in the sand regarding data privacy and encryption in a speech to EPIC's Champions of Freedom event in Washington DC, a speech in which he explicitly addressed the issues of encryption, privacy and security, and the morality of undermining privacy rights (Panzarino, 2015). However, critics of Apple contrast their stance in the case relating to an iPhone used by mass murderers in San Bernardino California (Queally and Bennett, 2016) with their actions over VPNs in China (Tepper, 2017).

In the former case, Apple engaged in extensive legal action to prevent the FBI requiring it to engineer a 'master key' for all iPhones without a clear legal basis for the request. In the latter case, Apple has stated that the Chinese situation is different as there is legislation in China that requires VPN providers to register with the government and obtain a licence and Apple were required to remove apps that do not meet these Chinese regulations. In an explanation given on an earnings call, Tim Cook went on to express Apple's hope that, over time, the Chinese government would loosen restrictions and that Apple believed in engaging with governments, even when they disagree with them (Tepper, 2017). On that call, Cook also stated: 'We strongly believe participating in markets and bringing benefits to customers is in the best interests of the folks there and in other countries as well.'

This highlights a key area of responsibility identification at the executive level. Apple appear to have identified that their ethical motivation is constrained by a responsibility as a company to comply with the laws of the jurisdictions they operate in. Apple also sees withdrawing from markets as being something that curtails their influence and their ability to bring benefits to customers, in addition to costing them money and market share (the shareholder-value normative ethic at play). In that context, it seems that Apple have determined that the use of engagement and lobbying to push back against enacted laws and regulations that impinge on personal privacy or freedoms is as valid an executive responsibility as litigating when governments or government agencies seek to step beyond what their legal powers and rights to infringe on data privacy might be, and that being active in a market is a lever to help them influence improvements in the ethical drivers of society over time.

The 'Business Manager' perspective

Row 2 of the Zachman framework is concerned with translating the mission of the enterprise into more detailed representations and models. In the 'Motivation' column (Row 2, Column 6) you would expect to see some tangible definition of what ethical behaviour looks like in the organization (see Figure 6.4). It is the level at which organizations start defining a range of things, from what the data they are processing in the organization's business functions will be, to how the process steps necessary to achieving business functions will be executed, where that will be done and who will do it.

The ethical motivation of the organization needs to be defined and codified at this level into meaningful statements of principle and policy. As David Hay wrote in 1997, Row 2 is the level at which the motivations of the organization are 'translated into the specific rules and constraints that apply to an enterprise's operation' (Hay, 1997). In the context of the ethical motivation, this means defining at the business management level clear business rules and policies for ethical conduct in the information environment. These rules may be defined as part of a statement of business values, a core business ethics policy, or as part of information security or data privacy policies in the organization. However, as these documents are rarely prepared by the same functional areas of the

Figure 6.4 Ethics in Row 2 of the Zachman framework

	Data	Action	Location	Actor	Event	Motivation	
Executive	Inventory Identification	Process Identification	Distribution Identification	Responsibility Identification	Timing Identification	Motivation Identification	Scope and Context
Business Manager	Inventory Definition	Process Definition	Distribution Definition	Responsibility Definition	Timing Definition	Motivation Definition	Business Concepts
Architect	Inventory Representation	Process Representation	Distribution Representation	Responsibility Representation	Timing Representation	Motivation Representation	System Logic
Engineer	Inventory Specification	Process Specification	Distribution Specification	Responsibility Specification	Timing Specification	Motivation Specification	Technology Physics
Technician	Inventory Configuration	Process Configuration	Distribution Configuration	Responsibility Configuration	Timing Configuration	Motivation Configuration	Tool Components
Enterprise	Inventory Instantiation	Process Instantiation	Distribution Instantiation	Responsibility Instantiation	Timing Instantiation	Motivation Instantiation	Enterprise

organization, often the sum of the parts can be less than the whole, with inconsistencies, incongruities, or simply no explicit consideration given to information ethics.

Also, in the context of the ethical motivation of the organization, many of these documents are drafted at such a high level as to be more accurately classed as Row 1 Column 6 artefacts, as they describe the ethical values and priorities of the organization or profession rather than getting into anything resembling an 'engineering definition' of those ethical behaviours. This is particularly the case outside of professional fields where there is an absence of defined disciplinary sanctions for breaches of ethical standards. In these cases, professional bodies may define codes of ethics for their members (which is arguably an externality influencing the organization rather than being something the organization can architect for), or enterprises may define an internal ethics code. However, absent some form of meaningful sanction, these codes have been found to be 'aspirational, inspirational and a basis for ethical reflection' (Sturges, 2009). Sturges examined the formal documentation of codes for information ethics. He found that many of them defined the scope of the ethical discussion quite narrowly to issues of data privacy, copyright and confidentiality, or even simply not breaking the law. These are the *identification* of principles, so belong in the 'Executive' perspective.

Many organizations are beginning to examine the concept of an information ethics forum to translate identified ethical principles into defined ethical actions and practices in their organizations as part of their overall information governance model. While this is to be welcomed, it does not necessarily address the issue of translating identified principles (Row 1) into defined policies and actions (Row 2). What is required is for management to define a formal framework at this level that allows managers to confirm the following:

- I can clearly explain to others how my functional area supports the ethical mission and vision of the organization.

- When I'm faced with an ethical issue or conflict between values I know where to go for help in resolving the situation.

- Essential information about ethical issues and priorities flow from management to staff.

If a framework to answer these questions is defined at the 'Business Manager' level, with clearly defined triggers and pathways to escalate ethical questions to the 'Executive' level, then the enterprise will have had to address the question of responsibility definition for information ethics in the context of responsibility in the wider information architecture (Row 2 Column 4). The challenge for organizations is to define their ethical values and motivations clearly enough at this level for business managers to make informed decisions and choices. This requires the elaboration of high-level ethical values into meaningful principles that can be applied in day-to-day practices and processes. This will feed into the definition of the overall data governance framework for the organization, which we discuss in Chapter 9.

To enable the enterprise to discuss and manage ethical issues consistently, there will need to be a consistent definition of the data inventory in the organization from a *business* perspective (Row 2 Column 1). This definition of data inventory will need to address the definition of metadata for all the entities and 'things' that the organization needs to manage. This will need to include both defined terminology such as 'What is a customer?' as well as more abstract business rules for the identification of categories of data, such as personal data or data relating to ethnicity, gender or physical or mental health, which might raise ethical concerns. Of course, as data does not exist in a vacuum, this will require consideration of the definition of the actions and processes that are taken with that data (Row 2 Column 2) and how it might lead to unethical behaviour or support an outcome that is unethical in its impact on individuals. These assessments will often need to go beyond addressing the questions of whether data is 'personal data' or whether it describes, defines or represents a person or people, to whether the application of that data in a process context, and the outcomes or impacts of that processing, is in line with the ethical values of the organization.

One way in which this might be manifest is the definition of data that is 'off limits' for certain processing activities or purposes, even if it exists in the information architecture. This can arise because of legal restrictions placed on the processing of data, but can equally arise from an ethical decision. For example, as a result of a Privacy Impact Assessment we conducted with a government department, they identified that for a certain set of analytics purposes they did not require granular identifiable data, but for other purposes they did. By carefully defining the entities in the data inventory, and associating them to the context of the processes they are used in, the client identified how their ethical value of only infringing on the privacy of identifiable people where necessary and where proportionate could be best achieved.

Finally, the definition of the 'when' and 'where' of processing should be constrained by the definition of ethical principles. Examples of ethics dictating where organizations might conduct business are manifold, often backed up by legal obligations around trade sanctions or restrictions. Examples of ethical artefacts we would expect to see in this context would include business policy decisions about what technology platforms to use for processing of data (eg use of cloud versus on-premises, criteria for the selection of cloud providers) or the decisions not to allow data to be processed in certain jurisdictions or countries or third-party providers. In practice, organizations may find some of this is defined in general business ethics policies or enforceable legal obligations such as trade sanctions. However, in other cases it can be a simple moral policy decision (Row 2 Column 6) that constrains the decisions that business managers might take in other contexts.

For example, when our company, Castlebridge, was looking to redevelop our website and improve our e-commerce capability we looked at several potential third-party platforms. A key ethical principle in the business is we 'walk the talk' on data privacy issues, so we absolutely had to ensure that data transfers out of the EU were going to jurisdictions to which such transfers were allowed. One platform stood out as being potentially useful to us, but as we researched it further we identified that the company had taken an aggressively neutral stance on other users of the platform who used it to sell products that funded race-hate groups in the United States and elsewhere. This was all despite repeated calls from other companies using the platform, and despite the views of their own employees on the need for a policy on the promotion of hate speech through the platform, and despite their own terms of service (Reville, 2017). We felt we could not ethically be associated with that platform, given its ethical ambivalence on a key issue. That business policy decision had an effect on the overall technical architecture for the site, and affected the business model we would adopt for the distribution of white papers and other publications.

The 'Architect' perspective

As we move down the perspectives of the Zachman framework we begin to identify more granular and tangible things that demonstrate ethical information management at work. At the level of the 'Architect' perspective (see Figure 6.5), the 'Motivation' column is seen in the traditional information management context as being where 'business rules are expressed in terms of information that is and is not permitted to exist' (Hay, 1997) and which constrain the design of the database and the processes to create and update data in an information system. This is the level at which the business planning is cascaded into defined business-rule models and the design of data flow models, logical data models, and the specification of data access roles and responsibilities.

Figure 6.5 Ethics in Row 3 of the Zachman framework

	Data	Action	Location	Actor	Event	Motivation	
Executive	Inventory Identification	Process Identification	Distribution Identification	Responsibility Identification	Timing Identification	Motivation Identification	Scope and Context
Business Manager	Inventory Definition	Process Definition	Distribution Definition	Responsibility Definition	Timing Definition	Motivation Definition	Business Concepts
Architect	Inventory Representation	Process Representation	Distribution Representation	Responsibility Representation	Timing Representation	Motivation Representation	System Logic
Engineer	Inventory Specification	Process Specification	Distribution Specification	Responsibility Specification	Timing Specification	Motivation Specification	Technology Physics
Technician	Inventory Configuration	Process Configuration	Distribution Configuration	Responsibility Configuration	Timing Configuration	Motivation Configuration	Tool Components
Enterprise	Inventory Instantiation	Process Instantiation	Distribution Instantiation	Responsibility Instantiation	Timing Instantiation	Motivation Instantiation	Enterprise

So, if the 'Architect' perspective is concerned with developing operative models for the enterprise in the contexts of the data, the processes, the actors involved, and the other interrogatives that describe the ontology for the enterprise, how do we model the ethical motivation for the organization in Row 3 Column 6? The solution here is not radically different to the question of how we might define or describe a business rule for when data may or may not be accessed for a particular purpose, or how we might define a rule for determining if data is of an appropriate level of quality for the purpose for which it will be used.

The key point is that, just like a business rule for data, the business rules for ethics need to be consciously designed and documented and a definition of what is 'good' needs to be formulated and communicated. One approach is to identify desired behaviours, model them, and describe them in a way that is communicable within the organization (see Chapter 3 for more on this). Another approach is to formalize clear policies and procedures for ethical conduct that create 'stop and think' checkpoints in the execution of other architectural functions at this level of perspective. Finally, identifying stories and examples of the ethical behaviour you want the people in your organization to demonstrate, and examples of how common ethical issues can be addressed, are essential. But just like any other architected or designed thing, the quality of the outputs from the process depends on the inputs, which are driven by the higher-level perspectives in Column 6.

When discussing ethics, the proof of the pudding is in the actions taken and outcomes that are delivered. In this context, the way in which the ethical model influences the models that are produced for data, process and accountability in the organization are essential. The expression of ethics will be manifested in the design principles that are applied in the context of each of the other columns in the Zachman framework. This may include issues like:

- accessibility standards for the representation of data in data models or in reports ('Data');

- definition of standards for on-boarding of data from third-party sources ('Data'/'Actor');

- definition of roles, responsibilities and accountabilities for data and access to data in the context of processes ('Actor');

- standards for the use of data-storage technologies or cloud platforms ('Actor'/'Location');

- the models used to define algorithms and machine-learning processes ('Data' and/or 'Process').

Ultimately, the 'Architect' perspective of the Zachman framework is the level where the enterprise starts to define the day-to-day models for how things get done with data in the organization. It is essential that there is clear alignment with strong ethical models of behaviour in the definition of these other models. Absent a clearly articulated and defined ethical model for enterprise information, however, these other models retain the potential to deliver unethical, or at best ethically questionable, outcomes. Whether it is failing to test to see if the technology in a soap dispenser can detect non-Caucasian skin tones, or producing data visualizations that are unintelligible to the colour blind, to failing to introduce controls against gender bias in selection algorithms, these are all symptoms of an absence of an ethically aligned architectural perspective that defined appropriate standards.

The 'Engineer' perspective

The 'Engineer' perspective in the Zachman framework addresses how things are actually specified in the context of any project, process or system in the enterprise. This is the level of the technology model. It is the level at which the models that are defined in the organization are translated into functioning software, executable business processes, and actionable responsibilities and accountabilities. This occurs through a design process that is informed by the models and rules identified and applies them in the context of a particular system or process. In the context of the ethical motivation (Row 4 Column 6) this means translating abstract ethical concepts into tangible requirements for the operation and behaviour of a system or process. These requirements in turn affect the specification of the data inventory in question, the process steps that are to be taken, and the specification of responsibility and accountability in the execution of the processing activity. It will also require the specification of requirements around the location of processing (what servers or other technology will be holding the data) and the rules for triggering the execution of the process.

The problem from an ethical perspective is that this is often the level at which organizations start addressing the implementation of new systems or technologies without first ensuring an appropriate ethical model is defined that will feed the technology requirements. It is at this level that companies like Facebook find their data-science teams altering algorithms to see if exposure to bad news makes people sad, or where organizations like the Samaritans adopt text analytics and sentiment analysis technologies without determining how they might be best used to achieve the ethical objectives of the organization.

The 'Technician' perspective

Penultimately, we consider the perspective of the technician, the level at which the specific programs and execution processes are created and configured in the enterprise. The challenge here is to build and configure the enterprise's technology in such a way as it meets the specification, conforms to the architectural models, meets business requirements and enables execution of strategic vision. There is not a lot to say here, other than that the ability of the organization to process and manage information in an ethical manner depends on how well the technician implements and configures the programs and coding to give effect to the processes and processing.

Of course, this includes people generating business intelligence reporting, training AI applications, implementing chat bots, as well as implementing databases, data interchange processes, and other 'traditional' information systems implementation tasks. In the context of trends such as self-service business intelligence, how the analytics environment is configured to ensure that individuals only have access to data that is legally or ethically permitted is also a consideration. This can, and should, include assessing if the specification of data extracts or data transfer processes contain excessive or irrelevant data that might create a legal or ethical exposure for the enterprise.

Again, we often see data privacy or data ethics breaches arising in organizations because a 'Technician'-level focus was adopted absent any other models being defined or perspectives being considered. This results in technology that might work wonderfully but does not integrate with other parts of the organization's IT systems, or which operates at odds with the stated ethical and regulatory controls that the organization may aspire to have in place. W Edwards Deming described this symptom as being what arises when everyone attempts to apply their 'best efforts' to addressing a problem without a broader 'theory of knowledge' to apply to the analysis of need and specification and implementation of solution (Deming, 1986).

The 'Enterprise' perspective

In the context of the Zachman framework this perspective is what the customer sees of the organization, the instantiation at a point in time of the different interrogatives in the context of an interaction with the individual. The outcomes delivered and experience of the individual of their interactions are ultimately the hallmark of the enterprise's information management capabilities. Likewise, the perception of ethical conduct, and the alignment between stated objective and actual delivery and execution of values, is also determined through what the individual experiences when interacting with the organization, and the impact that the processing of information in that instance has on the rights and freedoms and choices of the individual or of society.

Granularity and the enterprise

Looking back at the questions raised by the different responses by Apple to requests from US law enforcement to develop a capability to unlock iPhones versus their withdrawal of VPN apps from their App Store in China, you are probably wondering how that fits into the Zachman framework from an ethical perspective. The question of how such questions might be considered in the ontology highlights a key point about the Zachman framework regardless of whether we are discussing ethics or some other aspect of the enterprise.

The focus of the Zachman framework is the definition of those things that are *within* the enterprise. There are concepts, influences and obligations outside the organization's perimeter that it may seek to influence but, ultimately, are beyond its control. This is not a flaw in the ontology, but rather it is a feature of the level of granularity where the ontology defined by John Zachman is focused. Zachman himself highlights this in his 1996 article describing the framework (Zachman, 1996). In that article, Zachman tells us that 'the level in the hierarchy in which an object functions as a standalone, self-contained unit is the level that constitutes a natural boundary for integration'. He goes on to highlight that this is a choice that 'is made on the basis of manageable scope versus jurisdictional authority'. In short: it is based on the boundary between the things the organization can control directly in a manageable way and those things that the organization can, at best, seek to influence and other externalities that influence the organization.

In his article, Zachman describes this as 'the issue of granularity', bemoaning the fact that the legacy of the information management and data-processing profession has been a focus on the lower levels of architectural granularity. He tells us that:

> Regardless of our intention and even if we have been employing the best architectural techniques by using model-driven approaches to systems development, if the implementation was architected at the program, system, application or departmental levels, we inadvertently or sometimes even deliberately introduced substantial discontinuity and redundancies into the enterprise data, the network and the business rules (columns 1, 3 and 6).

When considering information ethics, you are facing a similar granularity problem in the architecture, which you will increasingly see manifesting in AI, analytics and other information management disciplines or initiatives. If the implementation is architected at the program, system, application or departmental level you will inadvertently or sometimes even deliberately introduce discontinuity into the enterprise. This highlights the need for a coherent ethical 'tone at the top' from an ethics perspective (Row 1 Column 6), as is borne out by research by organizations such as Deloitte (Deloitte, 2014).

Implementing ethical architecture: common challenges

One of the challenges that is faced in implementing ethical approaches to information management in organizations is that the traditional 'information managers' are at the level of the 'Engineer', or at best at the 'Architect' level. Just as there are developers of systems and information management processes who do not consider ethical issues, there are others who recognize the need to engineer information systems ethically. What they often lack is clear guidance on what that should be and what 'ethical' means in the context of a given process, a given set of data, or a given context of location or timing. As we have seen in our discussion of the Zachman framework, the reason for this angst is more often than not that the business management or executive leadership layers of the organization have not engaged with the ethical aspects of their information management strategies. The value of an ontological information architecture approach such as Zachman's is that it is very easy to point to a Row/Column intersection and show that there is something missing at these levels to provide the guidance and parameters for decisions and actions at lower levels in the framework.

Another challenge that is faced, particularly in organizations that are operating in a multinational or multijurisdictional context, is that there can be cultural difference around ethical values or how those values should be expressed in systems and processes in different jurisdictions. This is a granularity issue that relates to the 'Motivation' column and the 'Location' column of the framework. In the context of the Zachman framework we would expect to see clear statements and guidelines from the 'Executive', identifying the locations, identifying responsibilities, and identifying the ethical principles and values of the organization and the local variations that are acceptable.

From an ethical perspective, the organization needs to align its ethical architecture internally in a way that both supports 'higher principle' ethical positions as well as meeting legal obligations in any jurisdiction the enterprise operates in. While the enterprise may have control over its expression of ethics internally, it may find that external legal obligations constrain or curtail the expression of those ethics in practice. Apple's response to VPNs in China appears inconsistent with their previously stated ethics and has required their CEO to explain the apparent dichotomy with their previously adopted positions. However, that is an example of an enterprise with a strong ethic of protecting personal data privacy having to respond to a legislative constraint on those protections. If you look at the response of tech giants such as Google or Facebook to the global trend of legislation protecting personal data privacy we can see the same effect from the opposite end of the spectrum. Both organizations have faced regulatory scrutiny in the EU over their approach to processing data about people. Practices and approaches that are legal in the United States and are executed in line with the internal ethics of the organization, all too often run into problems when tested against legislative frameworks that require higher standards of protection of personal data privacy.

So, while the impact on individuals is different in each case (Apple's decision risks reducing data privacy for their customers in China, at least for the foreseeable future; Google/Facebook find their business and information management practices under challenge), the end result is the same. Apple has indicated they will lobby to restore privacy protections in China. Google and Facebook lobby extensively against data privacy legislation and enforcement worldwide. They cannot control these things from an architectural perspective but they can seek to influence those things that are external to the enterprise architecture, to seek alignment between the internal ethical motivations of the organization and ensure congruence in the architecture for information management.

However, sometimes the enterprise must change, rather than the external world. With the trends in consumer concern and awareness about data privacy and data ethics, your organization and many others may need (or are already needing) to realign your internal information architecture to align with external forces. Those that do not, or cannot, risk being considered unethical actors in the Information Age.

Zachman, ethical architecture and the long-term vision

The Zachman framework is a powerful enterprise ontology that supports information architecture concepts but also gives a reasonably complete set of things that need to be considered when trying to give effect to ethics through action in the organization. While criticisms have been raised that the ontology is not an ontology in the computer-science understanding of the term, critics of Zachman also admit that they are using the term differently to how it would be used in philosophy.

John Zachman concludes his own 1996 paper on the Zachman framework by engaging in philosophical discussion of how life is a 'series of decisions'. His words are 20 years old at the time of this writing but are particularly prescient in the context of the threats to data privacy, fundamental rights, and equality of access and opportunity that are arising through the actively, or unthinkingly, unethical application of both legacy and emerging technologies:

> There are good decisions and bad decisions, urgent decisions and important decisions… but every decision has either short-term or long-term implications. There is nothing wrong about short-term or long-term decisions except, it is abundantly clear, **if you exclusively make short-term decisions and ignore the long-term implications there comes a time when you will live to regret it.** You are going to 'pay later'. (Zachman, 1996) (emphasis ours)

Chapter summary

In this chapter we examined the detail of the Zachman framework:

- You became more familiar with the basic construct of the Zachman framework ontology.

- You identified the importance of the 'Motivation' column and its referencing of motivation types and the means and ends for business, systems and technology.

- You became familiar with the concept that the execution of the motivation ends requires that conscious design decisions be made in other areas of the ontology across each level of perspective or abstraction. For example, avoiding exposing data to government surveillance as an ethical principle may restrict jurisdictions where data can be stored, affecting the 'Location' vertical.

- You developed an understanding of why ethical management of information has to be designed for and planned for rather than just hoped for.

Questions

1 Think about organizations that you deal with on a day-to-day basis where your experience of their ethics as a customer does not match their stated values. What might contribute to that?

2 What benefits do you think organizations can gain from building their ethical considerations into how they think about information management?

3 In the same way as organizations face 'technical debt' today, is it possible that we are also facing 'ethical debt' in the fallout from decisions taken about the adoption of new technologies without appropriate consideration of ethical issues? If so, who pays that ethical debt?

Note

1 Of course, Socrates goes on to describe what happens when the philosopher returns to the cave and cannot see in the dark. The other prisoners interpret this as meaning the world outside the cave is dangerous and they kill anyone who tries to drag them out of the cave into the light. Those of you who have worked on data privacy issues in big data may be all too familiar with this scenario.

Further reading

Object Management Group (2003) [accessed 5 August 2017] The Zachman Framework and the OMG's Model Driven Architecture [Online] http://www.omg.org/mda/mda_files/09-03-wP_Mapping_MDA_to_Zachman_Framework1.pdf

References

Bergen, M (2016) [accessed 5 August 2017] Here's What Steve Jobs Had To Say About Apple and Privacy in 2010 [Online] https://www.recode.net/2016/2/21/11588068/heres-what-steve-jobs-had-to-say-about-apple-and-privacy-in-2010

Collins English Dictionary (n.d.) [accessed 5 August 2017] Ontology [Online] https://www.collinsdictionary.com/dictionary/english/ontology

Collins English Dictionary (n.d.) [accessed 5 August 2017] Taxonomy [Online] https://www.collinsdictionary.com/dictionary/english/taxonomy

DAMA International (2017) Data architecture, *DAMA Data Management Body of Knowledge*, 2nd edn, ed LS Coleman, D Henderson and S Earley, Technics Publications, New Jersey

Deloitte (2014) *Tone at the Top: The first ingredient in a a world-class ethics and compliance program*, Deloitte

Deming, WE (1986) *Out of the Crisis*, MIT Press, Boston

Glance, D (2017) [accessed 5 August 2017] Apple's New Mobile AI Chip Could Create a New Level of Intelligence [Online] https://phys.org/news/2017-05-apple-mobile-ai-chip-intelligence.html

Gruber, T (1992) [accessed 5 August 2017] What is an Ontology [Online] http://www-ksl.stanford.edu/kst/what-is-an-ontology.html

Gruber, T (2007) [accessed 5 August 2017] Ontology [Online] http://tomgruber.org/writing/ontology-definition-2007.htm

Hay, D (1997) [accessed 5 August 2017] The Zachman Framework: An Introduction [Online] http://tdan.com/the-zachman-framework-an-introduction/4140

Holt, J (2017) China VPN Ban: What Happened To Apple's Moral Backbone? [Online] http://fortune.com/2017/08/08/apple-china-iphone-vpn-censorship-ban/

Lee, D (2014) [accessed 5 August 2017] Samaritans Pulls 'Suicide Watch' Radar App [Online] http://www.bbc.com/news/technology-29962199

Marrins, K (2014) [accessed 5 August 2017] Samaritans Radar: 'Charity Deserves Round of Applause For Putting Mission Front and Centre' [Online] https://www.theguardian.com/voluntary-sector-network/2014/nov/03/samaritans-radar-twitter-mission-charity

Molina, B (2017) [accessed 5 August 2017] Apple Pulls VPN Apps From China As Government Clamps Down On Internet Access [Online] https://www.usatoday.com/story/tech/talkingtech/2017/07/31/apple-pulls-vpn-apps-china/524798001/

O'Keefe, K and O Brien, D (2016) [accessed 5 August 2017] New Paradigm Or Ethics Washing – An Analysis of Facebook's Ethics Report [Online] https://castlebridge.ie/system/files/private/whitepapers/new_paradigm_ethics_0.pdf

Panzarino, M (2015) [accessed 5 August 2017] Apple's Tim Cook Delivers Blistering Speech On Encryption, Privacy [Online] https://techcrunch.com/2015/06/02/apples-tim-cook-delivers-blistering-speech-on-encryption-privacy

Phipps, S (2014) [accessed 5 August 2017] Facebook's Big Problem: Ethical Blindness [Online] http://www.infoworld.com/article/2608257/techology-business/facebook-s-big-problem--ethical-blindness.html

Plato (2017) *Republic*, Amazon Classics, Athens

Queally, J and Bennett, B (2016) [accessed 5 August 2017] Apple Opposes Order To Help FBI Unlock Phone Belonging To San Bernardino Shooter [Online] http://www.latimes.com/local/lanow/la-me-in-fbi-apple-san-bernardino-phone-20160216-story.html

Reville, N (2017) [accessed 7 August 2017] The Real Reason Shopify Refuses to Adopt a Hate Speech Policy [Online] https://medium.com/@nreville/the-real-reason-shopify-refuses-to-adopt-a-hate-speech-policy

Sturges, P (2009) Information ethics in the twenty-first century, *Australian Academic & Research Libraries*, 40 (4), pp 241–51

TeenSafe (2016) [accessed 7 August 2017] Facebook Targets Teens With the New Lifestages Feature [Online] https://www.teensafe.com/blog/facebook-targets-teens-new-lifestages-feature/

Tepper, F (2017) [accessed 1 August 2017] Here's Tim Cook's Explanation On Why Some VPN Apps Were Pulled In China [Online] https://techcrunch.com/2017/08/01/heres-tim-cooks-explanation-on-why-some-vpn-apps-were-pulled-in-china

Zachman, JA (1996) [accessed 5 August 2017] Enterprise Architecture: The Issue of the Century [Online] https://enterprisearchitecture.dk/links/files/EA_The_Issue_of_the_Century.pdf

Introducing the Ethical Enterprise Information Management (E2IM) framework

What will we cover in this chapter?

In this chapter we explore with you an approach that we have developed that builds (yet again) on existing frameworks and practices in information management.

By the end of this chapter:

- You will develop an understanding of conceptual models for information strategy.
- You will develop an understanding of how the expectations of stakeholders are essential to determining the quality of the outputs from any information management process.
- You will develop an understanding of the external stakeholder's ethical perspective as the benchmark for your organization's ethical conduct.
- You will have a reference model for ethical enterprise information management that you can use to identify why your organization might have ethical issues in information management, and what you might do about it.

In this chapter, and those that follow, you will see how aligning the adoption of an ethical frame for information management that is grounded in and aligned with established information management disciplines and practices can help, if not to reduce complexity, then at least to reduce the different flavours of complexity you are having to deal with when trying to manage information in an ethical manner.

Building a model for ethical enterprise information management

In Chapter 6 we presented the Zachman framework for enterprise architecture as a tool for framing discussion around ethical concepts in organizations, building on the oft-neglected 'Motivation' column of that framework. A key lesson we need to take from Zachman's approach to looking at how the ontology of enterprise information needs to be managed is that we are dealing with complex systems that need to be consciously engineered to give us the desired results. When we consider the implementation of ethical principles in organizations, the complexity of technology implementation is compounded further by the complexity of defining, communicating and embedding ethical values in an organizational framework. This challenge goes beyond the challenges of determining what is the dominant normative theory for ethics that is being adopted in the organization, or the questions of how we categorize our ethical constructs in the context of an enterprise ontology, and gets to the nitty-gritty complexity of how the organization can ensure alignment between its headline ethical values and the actual experience of the customer and society.

Seeking simplicity – a generic framework for information management

The author and playwright Clare Boothe Brokaw wrote that 'the height of sophistication is simplicity' (Boothe Brokaw, 1931).[1] In a similar vein, we hope through this chapter to share with you a simple yet sophisticated model for discussing the complexity of integrating and implanting ethical concepts into information management practices.

The Ethical Enterprise Information Management (E2IM) model you will explore in this chapter has been developed by the authors in our consulting practice. It is intended to provide a holistic strategic framework within which the role and contribution of other information management disciplines to the execution of effective ethical information management can be identified and managed. It is built around a generic framework for information management first proposed by Professor Rik Maes at the University of Amsterdam in the late 1990s. This model has its roots in prior research on strategic alignment of information technology conducted by Henderson and Venkatraman earlier in the 1990s. In our consulting work in Castlebridge, we have extended the model to describe the interplay of ethics. But to understand the various ethical perspectives that can exist in an organization, we must first help you understand why so many IT projects fail to deliver their expected benefits.

The alignment problem

In their research, Henderson and Venkatraman advocated a four-box grid model to represent the alignment of business and IT functions in an organization, addressing the questions of strategic fit and functional integration between business and IT in the context of the overall strategy of the organization (see Figure 7.1). This framework advocated the alignment of business and IT functions along two basic axes. The vertical axis represented the 'strategic fit' between the organizational processes and procedures with the defined business strategy, and the equivalent fit between IT systems and functions with a defined IT strategy. The horizontal axis represents the 'functional alignment' between the business strategy and the technology strategy,

Figure 7.1   A simple model for information strategy

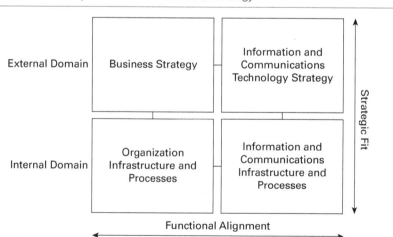

SOURCE adapted from Henderson and Venkatraman

and the alignment between business functions and the technology that is being implemented to support and enable the execution of those processes.

This model is seductive in its simplicity, but it misses a critical element of the information-driven organization, even in the late 1990s. It conflated information with the underlying technology that is used to process and manage it. It also oversimplifies the 'internal domain' of the organization by combining the infrastructure for delivery (organization structures, technology infrastructure, etc) with the processes being executed for delivery of outcomes. This contributed to the failure of IT projects to meet business objectives, as the nuance and importance of information flows and the management of information was often lost.

Professor Maes et al (2000) proposed an alternative model, commonly referred to as the Amsterdam Information Model, that extends both the vertical strategic fit axis and the horizontal functional axis to reflect these gaps. This gives a nine-box model within which is the relationship between the various domains within the organization. The key evolution in this model is the explicit recognition of the need to strategically manage and govern information as a distinct concept, from technology systems as well as an elaboration of the organization domains that need to be considered, to include the planning of the business management structures, information architecture and technology architecture that need to be implemented in an organization to ensure consistent delivery against the defined business and information strategies. The DAMA DMBOK second edition contains a more in-depth discussion of the Amsterdam Information Model (DAMA International, 2017).

Much like the Zachman framework, the Amsterdam model provides a framework for you to consider the connectedness of things in the organization in both the vertical and horizontal planes. It also allows you to consider the implications for and impacts on one part of the model resulting from a strength or weakness in the other. For example, if your business strategy and governance requires compliance with financial accounting and taxation laws but the IT services your staff use on a day-to-day basis were losing, miscalculating or misclassifying transactions, the operation of that IT service would impact on the assumptions and planning about information in the structure of the organization, leading to a failure to meet business strategy and governance goals. Likewise, if your business organization structures are not properly supported by your technology architecture, through segregation of duties and an information architecture that supports data segregation and role-based access to data, it would be difficult across the board to ensure effective governance of information security and data privacy at the operational level.

However, while the nine-box model is more representative of the painful realities of the organization than previous models, in our consulting work in information governance and information quality we have found that it lacks a necessary focus on the stakeholder, be they internal stakeholders (downstream information consumers in the organization) or external stakeholders (customers, citizens, external partners). This sometimes leaves you struggling to answer the 'so what?' question when you try to use a framework like the Amsterdam model to explain what is going on in your organization, particularly when bad things are happening to people because of your organization's handling of their data. As a result, in 2012 we started to extend the Amsterdam model to formally recognize the 'so what?' question in the context of the outcomes that are experienced by stakeholders because of the operation of the business, information and technology functions internal in the organization (Figure 7.2).

By expanding from the original simple four-box model proposed by Henderson and Venkatraman, through the Amsterdam Information Model proposed by Maes et al, and by explicitly recognizing the importance of the stakeholder's perception of the outcomes that they experience as a result of the processing of personal data, you can begin to discuss the impact and implications of business strategy, information architecture, or technology implementation on the experience of the stakeholder. It is important to note that their experience is both in terms of the process outcome (did the process they were engaged in proceed in the manner they were expecting?) and the information outcome (did the information meet their expectation? Was it retained for longer than they would expect? Was it processed in a location that the stakeholder might not have been expecting?).

The connecting lines in these models are as important as the boxes, as the connecting lines represent the alignment between the different perspectives on the organization's information management objectives. As Maes points out, this alignment is a source of tension, with misalignment giving rise to either organization failure or creative tension and innovation. The challenge that organizations face is to manage that tension in a way that mitigates risk, which the International Organization for Standardization (ISO) defines as the 'effect of uncertainty on outcomes'. Ultimately, the stakeholder (usually) does not care how the 'magic' happens in the context of any information processing activity. Your concern is that the correct process outcome is achieved and that the right thing happens as expected.

When you order a book from Amazon, do you expect to be given insights into the business strategy, operational architecture and technical data-processing steps that your data goes through to turn your request for a book

Figure 7.2 The Castlebridge Model

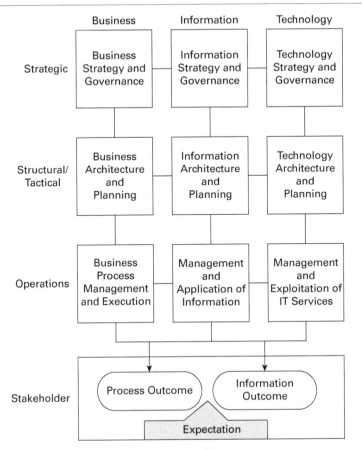

SOURCE adapted from the Amsterdam Information Model

into a delivered item? No. Your concern is with getting the right book, at the right time at the right price, and in the right condition. Of course, failures in the alignment of strategy, structure and operations can lead to delays in shipping, shipping to the wrong address, shipping of the wrong item, or charging of the wrong amount.

While executing ethical information management is not quite the same as ordering the latest book on ethical information management from Amazon, the need to ensure appropriate alignment strategically and functionally in the execution of information management is equally important to ensure that the outcomes meet the expectations of the stakeholders. It is this uncertainty as to the ethical nature of the *outcomes* of information processing that we concern ourselves with for the remainder of this chapter.

Engineering the ethical links

In order to engineer the ethical links in the organization's information management framework we need to consider the practical issues of how codes of ethics and codes of conduct are defined and communicated in the organization. This is usually done through the 'tone at the top' from the organization's leadership (as discussed in Chapter 3). The practical application of an ethical framework in the context of modern information management will need to consider organizational values, processes and development of technology in the context of fundamental ethical principles such as human rights and dignity. This extends beyond an agreed-upon 'code of practice' into ensuring communication of values across an organization, and governance of processes and behaviour. That process requires both horizontal and vertical alignment to ensure values are communicated and implemented consistently.

Without an ethical 'tone' set from the top and full integration of ethical values across an organization and into the planning and design phases of the life cycle, a code of practice may run the risk of ending up a dead and useless 'strategy' document that bears little relation to an organization's strategic practice, or wind up delivering structures that drive 'tick box' compliance to a minimal standard that does not uphold ethical information management practices. These scenarios may result in unexpected adverse consequences.

Therefore, in the context of ethical information management we again see the need to:

- address the strategic, structural and operational layers;
- ensure alignment between business functions, information management and technology implementation;
- consider the perspective of the stakeholder and the outcomes they experience arising from the processing of information.

An organization's priorities may or may not align well with the overall ethical priorities expected by the culture the organization interacts with. This is the ethical expectation of the external stakeholder in the macro context. Organizational or corporate social responsibility is a factor in building trust with the public, and trust is often a vital component of an organization's reputation. An organization that does not clearly uphold the rights of its customers, or align with their ethical expectations, runs a large reputational risk that may affect not just the organization itself but the sector it is in. A telling example of this is the focus that is being brought to bear on online advertising and social media in the wake of allegations of interference by foreign powers in elections and referenda in the United States, the UK and other countries. While the jury might be out on the impact of psychometrical targeting by companies such as Cambridge Analytica, at the time of writing the evidence of large-scale advertising purchases by hostile countries that fed the 'filter bubble' effect in various global elections is unfolding day by day (Frier, 2017; Syal, 2017).

A risk-based approach may be used to help define a proactive, principles-based strategy to work towards outcomes that align with a rights-based ethical framework. Peter Young argues that ethics may be considered a risk issue and a management issue, noting that high-profile scandals point out the 'practical consequences of unethical conduct' and stating that 'organization leaders who espouse a belief that expectations for ethical behaviour have become part of the "risk environment" for top management. So, arguably, both stakeholders and managers view "ethical risk" management as important' (Young, 2004). The ethical dimensions of business are of concern to an organization's customers and stakeholders. However, the internal and external understandings of an organization's ethics may not align. It is important to consider both the internal goals and values of an organization and the external values and expectations of the greater society.

In looking at the morals manifest in business cultures, Steven P Feldman observes that organizations that place their primary priorities on competition and increasing shareholder values often have difficulty integrating their 'competitive values' or a focus on maximizing profit with the 'moral values' of the greater community. Most organizations with strong ethical values had a strong moral vision at executive level. Companies with a 'clear moral vision' integrated an ethical framework that defined the organization's cultures and priorities and directed action, incorporating these values throughout all facets of the organization and extending them to interaction with the larger community (Feldman, 2007). A siloed approach tends to be problematic. As Feldman says, 'The lack of cultural integration between competitive values and moral values plagues many companies' (Feldman, 2007).

The results of such a lack of 'cultural integration' of organizational values and priorities have been seen recently in the scandal surrounding Volkswagen's use of defeat devices, which we have referenced previously. The illegality of using defeat devices to evade environmental regulatory standards is one sign of a disjunct between organizational and societal priorities, but the loss of trust in the organization that has followed shows that the mismatch between the values and ethical standards of the organization extends beyond the letter of the law. It is worth noting that the effects of the scandal are not limited to the organization itself. The consequences of the scandal have affected other automobile manufacturers, destroyed the resale value of diesel cars (Rogers, 2015) and, at the time of writing, have resulted in at least one person going to prison (Shepardson and White, 2017).

An organization needs to understand its own values and priorities so they can communicate them and determine 'right action' or desired behaviour within the organization. To ensure outcomes that are considered desirable from the standpoint of a customer or the larger community, it is also necessary for you to understand how the organization's ethics align with the larger community or societal ethics and expectations. These are the expectations of the external stakeholders of the outcomes they will experience as a result of the management and processing of information by your organization. The following steps are necessary to clearly determine and communicate the ethical framework for your organization:

1 Identify the priorities of the organization and desired behaviour in the organization.

2 Identify how the organizational ethic or priorities align with the larger societal ethical expectations.

3 Determine the desired outcomes and desired behaviour.

4 Ensure you have the tools to promote that outcome.

The tools in this case may include standards to determine the appropriateness of an action or procedure, evaluation of the risks of adverse outcomes (including the possibilities of unintended outcomes), and a system of rights and accountabilities to ensure alignment of decisions and actions with priorities and ethical principles. Outcomes and the alignment of outcomes with customer expectations may also act as a sort of large-scale KPI for the function of the ethical framework.

To ensure effective alignment of information ethics, the ethical framework of an organization needs to be communicated across silos in the organization as part of the core values of your organization, rather than simply being a line item on a management agenda. The communication of values must be strategically aligned in the business vertical, but also needs to be aligned horizontally so that the information-strategy vertical and technology vertical are implemented in a manner consistent with the ethical values of the organization. Where there is a disconnect, a failure to ensure appropriate alignment, it is inevitable that the stakeholders of the organization will experience outcomes that might not meet their ethical expectations.

One way in which a lack of cultural integration of priorities into the organization may be observed is a 'tick box' approach to compliance. In general, a focus on regulatory compliance (a business-strategy decision) may result in a bare-minimum response and a reactionary approach rather than a proactive, strategic use of governance to ensure optimal ethical outcomes for your customers and stakeholders. However, a similar approach to compliance might also be the result of where the organization's ethical framework solely prioritizes increasing monetary value for shareholders as an outcome. In this case, the organization's desired outcomes may come into conflict with the expectations of the larger community that the organization is part of.

This conflict of priorities within an organization is not unique to questions of data privacy and other information governance and compliance initiatives, but it is an age-old conflict in the application of ethics in organizations and society. The resolution of this conflict requires careful and diligent management of behavioural change to align organizational and societal ethics, and indeed to align the ethic of the individual actor to the desired value system. The alignment between the horizontal functional focus of the organization, and the alignment of strategic priorities and objectives at all levels in the organization, requires considered planning and engineering of the ethical information management culture and environment in your organization.

Ultimately, the technology your organization implements is ethically neutral. The application of technology in support of business and information imperatives is an essential element to ensure that ethical standards are met. However, the specification for that technology, the use of that technology, the operation of controls, the communication of requirements, and the identification of and assessment of risks associated with technology require human actors to make ethical choices.

Volkswagen's engines misreported emissions in regulatory checks. They did so because the engine management software was designed to detect regulatory checking and to modify the engine performance characteristics for the duration of that test. That software behaviour was specified by people who defined the requirements for systems; it was coded by people who programmed the systems; it was accepted as desired and acceptable by people who wrote and executed software quality tests for those systems. External reports indicating that there was cause for concern were ignored by people.

A series of ethical choices affected the ultimate delivery of an expected outcome to society (cleaner engines and lower emissions). These ethical choices affected the strategy for and governance of key information in the context of Volkswagen's engine management systems. The pursuit of market growth drove a series of choices that has served ultimately to undermine shareholder value in Volkswagen. It has ultimately damaged trust in the German automotive industry, tainted other car manufacturers (regardless of their use of similar cheats), and raised questions over the effectiveness of government regulation in a number of jurisdictions.

This presents us with a clear conflict between the ethical framework of the organization and the ethical framework of society that has resulted in a series of outcomes which fail to meet the expectations of society. The challenge, and opportunity, arises from the need to understand how to take the abstract concepts of ethics and implement them in a strategic framework for information management, such that informed and effective choices can be made for the governance of information that acknowledges, supports and enables the delivery of ethical outcomes.

Engineering ethical alignment

Decision points and actions at all levels of the organization are coloured by and influenced by the organization's ethical or moral priorities. However, at the outcomes level, the organization comes in close contact with the ethical framework of the larger society. On one hand, the organization's attitudes towards the 'customer' are coloured by the organization's ethical framework. On the other, the expectations of what is considered a quality outcome (process outcome or information outcome) by external 'customers' are shaped by the larger socioethical framework. A significant disjunct between social ethic and organizational ethic is likely to cause unsatisfactory outcomes and responses.

Figure 7.3 shows a conceptual model for information management functions in the context of two nested ethical perspectives – the 'ethic of society' and the 'ethic of the organization'. There is a third, the 'ethic of the individual'. We address this aspect in Chapter 9 in the context of data governance for ethical information management, but in the interests of simplicity we do not represent it in the E2IM framework diagrams. Suffice to say that it is in an organization's best interests to recruit and retain staff who best align with and exemplify the ethical values the organization espouses, and that society expects.

Figure 7.3 Conceptual model of information management functions in the context of ethical frameworks

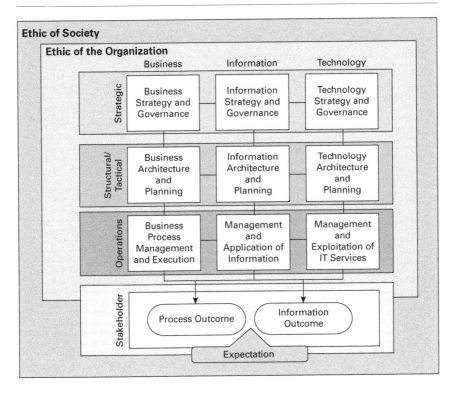

This model is built around our extension of the nine-cell Amsterdam Information Model discussed earlier in this chapter. In our consulting work, Castlebridge extend this model to include the 'Customer Perspective', which constitutes an expectation (or set of expectations) of how the information and process management capabilities of an organization will deliver desirable and expected outcomes for them (information outcomes and process outcomes) (Figure 7.4). The quality of the overall system of information management (the original nine-box model) is defined by how well the information and process outcomes produced by it meets or exceeds the expectations of the customer, in the form of an individual customer or as embodied by society as a whole.

The influence and roles of ethical frameworks on the perceived quality of the system of information management arise in two distinct ways:

1 The ethic of society influences strategic and tactical governance and planning in an organization through the definition and enforcement of laws and regulations, and the development of standards and codes of practice

Figure 7.4 The Castlebridge Ethical Enterprise Information Management (E2IM) model

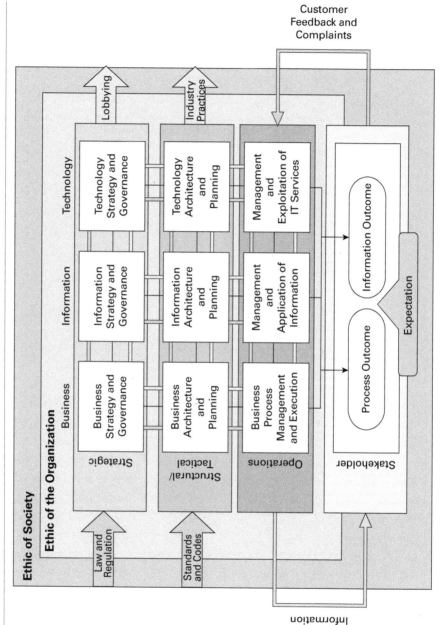

to support the implementation of both legislative requirements and wider concepts of 'good practice'. Customer feedback and complaints (the 'voice of the customer' in quality management terms) drive changes in organization business practices, information management capabilities, and technology components.

2 The ethic of the organization can influence society through lobbying at a strategic level, contribution to establishing what 'good practices' are through benchmarking and contribution to standards working groups, and through education of the customer and the wider market as to the benefits of products or the societal value of the proposed information processing.

Within the organization, the alignment of and execution of business, information and technology functions is generally achieved through the operation of processes, policies, controls and communication within and across organization verticals. This is illustrated in the diagram by the narrow vertical lines, as before. These represent the *documented* governance structures and procedures for ensuring and assuring alignment. However, the effectiveness of these lines of communication and governance can be heavily influenced by the ethic of society and the ethic of the organization, represented by the horizontal lines running parallel to the formal structures.

Where an organization is strongly aligned with the ethic of society, then issues with, questions about and challenges to proposed strategies, methods and procedures for processing information that are at odds with that ethic will be more likely to be communicated and addressed to ensure an overall system of information management that will be capable of better meeting the expectations of customers in that society. On the other hand, if the ethic of the organization is the dominant cultural driver in the organization, we often find such challenges greeted with resistance, attempts to downplay or ignore the risks, or at times an almost bullying approach to obtaining and processing data even to the point of breaching applicable laws and guidance standards.

In short: the decisions an organization takes regarding the implementation of an information architecture or an information governance framework are directly impacted by the manner in which the organization aligns and emphasizes its internal ethical framework with the ethical framework and expectations of society. The 'tone at the top' and the spirit of execution in the middle are essential to the effective implementation of an aligned governance model for effective ethical information management. Where the ethic of the organization runs counter to the ethic of society, or where the ethic of society has yet to fully appreciate the implications of a data-processing activity, we often find ourselves at the mercy of the ethic of the individual. This, in turn, is often subject to peer pressure or conflicts of priority and of objective.

Steven Feldman has described the split personality of business ethics in management as follows, 'On one hand, they [managers] can develop a single-minded pursuit of profit that sometimes has difficulty even bridling itself at the boundaries of the law; on the other hand, business managers are socialized in communities where virtues of honesty, fairness and trustworthiness are held in high regard' (Feldman, 2007).

Unfortunately, this dichotomy of emphasis is not unique to commercial organizations. The single-minded pursuit of one perspective of value can ultimately lead to actions that run counter to commonly agreed ethical values. It is this dichotomy that leads to charities selling or renting access to their donor databases to list brokers without a lawful basis (because it helps make more money for the delivery of service), to government departments demanding bulk data sharing without a clear legal basis and other necessary controls, and to researchers chafing against the constraints that must be placed on their use of and exploitation of data to mitigate against unintended consequences of otherwise valid research goals.

As concern about the ethical and societal impacts of data and data processing grow, we are seeing an increase in organizations such as Facebook beginning to invest in governance structures and control systems to counter 'fake news' and to introduce additional ethical and privacy controls into their business models (Culver, 2017). These are being introduced in response to feedback from customers and from society that the outcomes that are being delivered are suboptimal and undesired. What remains to be seen, however, is whether these changes are merely initiatives affecting the formal 'black line' controls within the organization or whether there is a meaningful realignment of the business, information and technology dimensions of the organization to address the core issues that arise.

The initial resistance of Mark Zuckerberg to accept the potential for Facebook to have influenced the outcome of elections would appear to suggest there may be a disconnect between the ethic of the organization and the ethic of society at the strategic level that could impede meaningful change. At the time of writing, Facebook is scheduled to appear before a Senate Committee hearing (an example of the 'law and regulation' influence of the ethic of society) in November 2017. Media reports suggest that senior executives will not be present, but instead will be attending an investor conference call (Shinal, 2017). This might be considered an example of the shareholder theory normative model of ethics, as the ethic of the organization triumphing over a stakeholder theory or social justice ethical frame, and it does not bode well for the sustainability of changes in ethical practices or thinking in the organization. We hope that, by the time you are reading this, history records a different outcome.

However, in an organization that maintains a balance of priorities that align with the socioethical framework, what is understood to be a quality outcome by the organization should also align with societal expectations. The challenge lies in addressing ethical alignment in the philosophies and strategies for information management in organizations. This requires both an emphasis on introspective re-evaluation of ethics by the organization, as well as an approach to educating and communicating with society about the ethical frame being applied in the organization to the proposed processing. In cases where there is a significant disjunct between the two ethical frames outlined, it also requires a clear articulation to society (the customers) as to how the proposed processing is to the benefit of society, even if it requires an evolution of the ethic of society to permit the processing.

In this way, the expectation of information and process outcomes, and the perceived and experienced quality of the outcomes delivered by the system for information management in the organization, can be more appropriately established and aligned in a way that not only supports a balancing of at least two potentially competing ethical perspectives but may contribute to an improved quality of ethical practices in relation to information in organizations and society alike.

The basic principles of human rights, human dignity and the concepts of Kant's 'categorical imperative' (treating the human individual as an end, not just a means) might be used as foundational checkpoints to test outcomes against expectations of quality in an ethical framework.

Testing outcomes against first principles – the measure of ethical effect

You can apply a two-stage examination of the outcomes against first principles, balancing the outcomes against four ethical questions regarding the preservation or enhancement of human rights. First, you might ask whether the outcome might contribute positively to 'the good', or positive preservation of human rights:

1 Does it preserve human dignity? Does it enhance human dignity?
2 Does it preserve the autonomy of the human?

3 Is the processing necessary and proportionate?

4 Does it uphold the common good?

The second stage asks: does the outcome violate any of these points?

This test seeks a positive outcome as a determiner of ethical action. Where the positive contribution to the social good is not the priority, it balances the priorities against the social ethic of the necessity of preserving human rights. An action with an outcome that violates these rights may be expected to come into conflict with the societal ethic that regards human rights as a fundamental priority.

As modern information management capabilities may process, combine or link, and make available vast amounts of information, it is important to consider the outcomes resulting from data processing that are not the focus or intended outcome. This test will need to consider not just the intended outcome but other anticipated possible outcomes.

Example test of outcomes against first principles

A few brief example scenarios may show how real-world processes and outcomes might be tested against first principles. These are rough illustrations rather than in-depth analyses:

Scenario 1: health identifiers A public-health-services body is planning to implement universal health identifiers for all individuals who use the health services. They foresee many benefits to the implementation, including increased accuracy in prescriptions, a 'single view of patient', and possible cost savings through increased efficiency:

> *Question 1: Does it preserve human dignity? Does it enhance human dignity?*

A properly implemented individual health identifier has the potential to preserve and enhance human dignity; accurate identification of patient and procedure required for the patient can mean the difference between an oral exam and a rectal exam. Reducing the chances of procedural error in delivering medical treatment would not just preserve but enhance the dignity and well-being of the individual.

> *Question 2: Does it preserve the autonomy of the human?*

The question of autonomy raises issues of free and informed consent, which are extremely important for ethical medical practice. The existence of a health identifier might not necessarily adversely affect the autonomy of the patient, but people may object to having their medical information combined in a way that provides an overarching view of what is often extremely sensitive information.

It will also be necessary to consider who is to be allowed access to patient information, and what controls are in place to ensure decision rights are restricted. Control measures will have to be in place to ensure that information management is centred on the individual and ensures their autonomy as active 'choosers' is preserved.

Great care will need to be taken to ensure that the design and implementation of the health identifier preserves the individuals' privacy and their rights to autonomous action as 'choosers'.

Question 3: Is it necessary and proportionate?

If the organization wishes mandatory use of health identifiers across the board, this processing of personal data will have to be justified as necessary and proportionate.

Question 4: Does it uphold the common good?

It could be argued that the identifier will increase accuracy in reporting and statistics, providing necessary information to identify which services are needed most and increase the ability to provide needed services to the public.

This will have to be balanced against the privacy aspects and the proportionality and necessity of processing.

Scenario 2: applications of life-logging technology for Alzheimer's patients

An organization is developing advanced life-logging capabilities to aid people suffering from conditions affecting their memory and cognitive processes. Day-to-day actions and events are recorded to serve as a reviewable record of events – acting, in effect, as a prosthetic memory:

Question 1: Does it preserve human dignity? Does it enhance human dignity?

As this application of technological advancements might possibly do a great deal to ease the distress of a person suffering from conditions such as Alzheimer's disease, it could very much enhance the dignity of the person.

Question 2: Does it preserve the autonomy of the human?

The planned capabilities of the technology would help to preserve the autonomy of the device wearer. However, the life-logging technology would by its nature record the interactions of the device wearer with other people, capturing their personal data as well. Controls would need to be implemented to take their autonomy into account, including the possibility of choosing not to have their data processed.

Question 3: Is it necessary and proportionate?

In the context of the device wearer, the processing would likely be necessary and proportionate. However, the question of necessary and proportional processing also arises in the context of the other people the device wearer comes into contact with. Measures should be taken to ensure that processing of the personal information of these people is minimized, particularly if there are no measures in place to ensure free and informed consent.

Question 4: Does it uphold the common good?

This application of technology is primarily focused on the enhancement of individuals' dignity, but it could also be argued that its availability would also be of more general benefit to communities as a whole. Family and friends of a person affected by Alzheimer's disease might also benefit from its use. Developments in care to aid members of a community are likely to improve the community as a whole.

Scenario 3: use of analytics to create a granular profile for targeted messaging

An organization uses algorithmic analysis of the patterns of social media 'likes' to create granular profiles of anonymized users, identifying information such as age, gender, ethnicity, socioeconomic status and sexual orientation. These profiles are to be used to provide targeted messaging for marketing or political purposes to identified users who match the granular profile:

Question 1: Does it preserve human dignity? Does it enhance human dignity?

These capabilities themselves may not necessarily violate human dignity. However, this depends on the message delivered. Controls would be required to ensure that the uses of this information-processing capability do not violate human dignity.

Question 2: Does it preserve the autonomy of the human?

Although the initial data captured for processing is anonymized, the resulting outcome of the aggregation and analysis is essentially identification of individuals, processing sensitive personal information. This is done without the possibility of meaningful consent on the part of the individual. Autonomy is not preserved.

Question 3: Is it necessary and proportionate?

It would be difficult to argue that this processing is necessary and proportionate. There may be a societal necessity to enable this type of targeted communication, but it must be balanced against the individual's right to be left alone.

Controls would be necessary to justify and ensure the necessity and proportionality of the information processing.

Question 4: Does it uphold the common good?

As with the question of human dignity, the technological capability is neutral. It would entirely depend on the use to which it was put.

The analysis of utility of ethical impact

The outcomes of different actions naturally vary greatly from small effects to extremely large impacts on quality of life. Possible consequences of an action or option can vary from annoyance to fatal. A pragmatic, utilitarian way to measure this may be to apply a basic risk and impact analysis on the actions planned, determining likely consequences of an activity, the severity of impact these consequences might have, and whether there are any controls in place (such as legal regulations) to mitigate this. Two questions for you to ask at this stage are:

1 Are there societal controls in place to ensure human dignity is upheld in this case?

2 What organizational or technical controls can we put in place to ensure human dignity is upheld?

The question of controls includes both external controls such as regulations and internal controls to ensure actions are limited to avoid violating rights.

These controls may be as simple as ensuring that individuals are made aware of the purposes of processing, the basis of processing, and the identity of entities or categories of entities that data may be shared with. The importance of this principle in EU Data Protection law has recently been reinforced by the Bara case in the European Court of Justice (Court of Justice of the European Union, 2015). Dignity may not require consent to be obtained (in Bara the Romanian government agencies had a statutory basis for their data sharing), but it does require that there be an awareness of the nature of the proposed processing.

Table 7.1 represents a possible simple risk-impact analysis focused on the impact of proposed actions on privacy and human dignity and some possible controls to mitigate the risk of violating rights.

Table 7.1 Ethical risk-impact analysis matrix

Action/Decision	Possible Consequences	Probability	Impact	Controls
Mandate mobile phones of minors have 'net nanny' software installed so that parents can 'protect' children	• Loss of sense of autonomy on the part of young people • False positives on activity • Loss of trust • Vulnerabilities in software may expose minors to risk	High	Medium	• Privacy Impact Assessment • Education and training of parent and child • Limit possible surveillance activities (reduce functionality) • Develop app using secure coding principles and standards
Retain data regarding the sexual life of customers instead of securely deleting	Possible exposure of highly sensitive personal information, causing distress, impacts to reputation, social position	Medium	Medium to high	External control: • Data Protection Regulations mandate that data is retained no longer than necessary Internal controls: • Privacy Impact Assessment • Define retention periods • Encrypt data
On retiring of a legacy telecom programme, send an automated message to customers who were previously subscribed to the programme, informing them that they have opted out of the programme	Confusion and distress of customers who are led to believe there is unauthorized activity on their account	High	Low	Internal control: suppress messages to customers who had changed programmes before a particular date
Analyse internet search results to determine interests of individual for advertising purposes	Perception of surveillance has chilling effect on willingness to search for knowledge, intellectual freedom	High	Medium	• Anonymize data • Create large-enough clusters of data to mitigate direct targeting of individuals • Educate users about ad blockers

This type of analysis is similar to a traditional risk analysis in which the probability and impact of the consequences of an action can be identified and assessed, and the relevant controls to mitigate and rebalance that risk are identified. In the context of privacy-impacting processing, this type of analysis is a key component of a Privacy Impact Assessment, going beyond basic 'tick box' checks against statutory requirements. Instead it ensures a focus on first principles of ethical behaviour, combined with regulatory requirements and the influence of other externally defined standards.

In cases that touch upon fundamental human rights, the risk appetite of an organization should be low. This requires that the organization have a clear understanding of the balance and trade-offs between their goals, as expressed through the ethical framework of the organization, and the expectations of their customers, as expressed through the ethical framework of society. This highlights the importance of impact analyses such as Privacy Impact Assessments, and the need to anticipate in planning and design which areas may impinge upon human rights and ensure controls are in place to mitigate risk and uphold human dignity.

Ethics and big data

In Chapter 1 we introduced the European Data Protection Supervisor (EDPS) in the context of the regulatory focus on information ethics in Europe. In Chapter 1 we examined some of the core concepts the EDPS was promoting, from the perspective of the ethical models that they seemed to be aligning with. In the paper 'Towards a New Digital Ethics' (EDPS, 2015) the EDPS has thrown a clear focus on ethics and human dignity into the overall discussion of data protection and privacy.

The EDPS opinion identifies four key themes through which human dignity can be preserved through ethical practices in 'big data' (Figure 7.5). The framework we have outlined in this paper aligns with these themes and provides a model for the practical implementation of strategic, tactical and operational governance models for information in organizations. The E2IM framework provides a basis to understand and implement the principles that the EDPS has set out in the opinion on ethics in big data.

Future-oriented rules and enforcement

In our framework, legal and regulatory rules are the input of society into the ethical framework of the organization. This input happens at the strategic

Figure 7.5   The EDPS vision for ethics and dignity of individual in 'big data' (adapted)

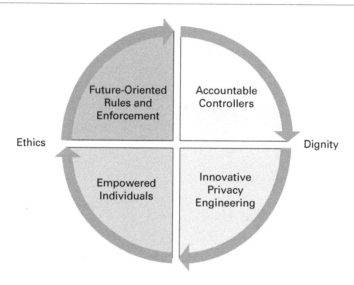

level to influence the strategic and governance decisions for business, information and technology.

Once the voice of society is heard through externally imposed rules, these need to be internalized into the ethical framework of the organization, cascading down from strategic to operational decision makers, and aligning across the three fundamental activity domains of the organization (business, information and technology).

The organization can seek to influence rules at the strategic level through lobbying activities, which would include traditional lobbying of legislators but would also include education of wider society about the nature and scope of proposed processing and the trade-offs and benefits.

Regulatory rules need to be explicit enough to be meaningful and enforceable but not so prescriptive as to prevent their evolution in response to changes in the potential application of emerging capabilities in technology or to changes in the wider ethical framework of society.

Of course, without effective and visible enforcement, particularly in a form that has consequences at the strategic level in the organization, there will be inevitable misalignment of objectives and governance within the organization. This enforcement needs to be meaningful to counteract the conflicts of priorities identified by Feldman and others, which we discussed earlier.

It is tempting to believe that the influence of the 'court of public opinion' would play a role here. However, this societal penalty may only be as long-lived as the news cycle, hence we do not include it at this level in our framework. Financial and criminal sanctions against organizations and individuals help personalize the need to align the ethic of the organization with the ethic of society.

Ultimately, both brand pressures and other sanctions will provide a 'carrot and stick' in the context of enforcement as the 'customer expectation' of information or process outcomes might be sufficiently negative as to dissuade people from buying a product, using a service, or sharing full and truthful information with a government agency.

Accountable controllers

The EDPS tells us that: 'Accountability requires putting in place internal policies and control systems that ensure compliance and provide relevant evidence in particular to independent supervisory authorities' (European Data Protection Supervisor, 2015). This requires formal planning for the implementation of and execution of defined systems of governance for business functions, information assets, and technology platforms. In particular, the ability to generate and produce consistently reliable evidence for the operation of controls over the processing of data is essential.

The EDPS has argued for more responsible initiative on the part of businesses. These we identify as 'standard practices' that might emerge from within an organization and which might be held up as being of benefit to their wider industry or to society (we refrain from using the term 'best practice' as this implies no scope for continuous improvement). The EDPS also identifies guidance from data protection authorities, codes of conduct, certifications and other mechanisms to support accountable behaviours in the organization.

Another sub-theme in the EDPS commentary on 'accountable controllers' is the importance of proactivity and transparency of processing in ensuring robust trust. Our framework represents this through the explicit focus on the customer's expectations of information and process outcomes and the customer feedback loop.

Empowered individuals

The EDPS opinion discusses the need to recognize that individuals are empowered, but also to provide the ability for individuals to exercise power and control over their data and how it is to be used. They discuss the concepts of pro-sumers, consent and data ownership. These reflect the interplay between the individual as an actor in society and the organization.

This societal expectation of the types of process and information outcome that an organization should deliver, and the ability of the organization to meet these expectations, defines the overall quality of the system of information management in an organization to support human dignity through the application of ethical principles and practices.

Educating the customer about the uses of data, and avoiding the pitfalls of assuming – without appropriate explanation, lawful basis or consent – ownership of someone else's data that is linked to their individual personality, is one approach to empowering individuals. Providing mechanisms for individuals and society to provide feedback on how data is being processed, and the impact on human dignity, is another.

However, for these mechanisms to be effective in practice, the organization needs to ensure appropriate alignment and governance of the business, information, and technology functions that contribute to the delivery of the expected information and process outcomes. Part of that governance is an ability to respond to and adapt governance controls to feedback from society, whether it is represented by an individual, a civic society organization or a regulator.

Ultimately, as the EDPS points out, in the balancing act between personal data privacy and other concerns such as public interest and the rights of others, human dignity is a constant that must be respected at all times. This right is best supported through mechanisms for governance of information, which allow the 'voice of the customer' to be heard and their dignity to be recognized.

Privacy-conscious engineering

Giovanni Buttarelli, the current European Data Protection Supervisor, tells us that:

> Human innovation has always been the product of activities by specific social groups and specific contexts, usually reflecting the societal norms of the time. However technological design decisions should not dictate our societal interactions and the structure of our communities, but rather should support our values and fundamental rights. (European Data Protection Supervisor, 2015)

Buttarelli describes many mechanisms and approaches by which this balancing of technology design against societal interactions and fundamental rights can be achieved – techniques such as metadata to tag records with their data protection requirements, data aggregation and empowerment of individuals through anonymity.

A 'first principles'-based approach building on an assessment of the proposed outcomes against their ability to support human dignity, and their alignment with fundamental concepts in ethical philosophy, is a key first step that you should take to implementing ethical information management practices. To incorporate these into effective day-to-day operative governance frameworks, you need to focus not just on technology but on the 'business' processes, functions and objectives that you intend such technologies to support and enable. Hence the importance of the E2IM framework in ensuring effective alignment of perspectives, strategies and practices.

This 'principles first' approach must, by its very nature, be based on an assessment of the proposed outcomes for society and the desired outcomes of the individuals on whose behalf you are processing this data. From there, your organization must engineer both your technology and the organizational ethics to ensure appropriate attention and respect is paid to ethical concerns such as privacy in a holistic governance environment, rather than this being a hasty afterthought.

Conclusion

The vital importance of an ethics framework to govern the development and use of new technologies has been recognized again and again. New developments in information management tools and capabilities shine new light on the need to take steps to actively engage in determining a framework that ensures rights are upheld.

A framework for ethical information management practices will need to look to the future to ensure processes are designed with regard to respect for human dignity and fundamental rights such as privacy and data protection. Communication of these values and ethics in an organization must be cross-functional and extend across silos, and will need to be supported by a governance framework that ensures accountability. Following good information governance practices and ensuring ethical requirements are considered at the beginning stages of the information life cycle will help to ensure that new developments in information processes and technologies enhance the dignity and empowerment of the person.

In discussing the need for an ethical framework for modern information management tools, it is useful to ground yourself in first principles and to look back to lessons learnt in other areas and disciplines. Technology itself is neutral; our use of technology must be ethical. The fundamental requirement in any design or plan to use technology in a novel way is to ensure that the outcomes of the new use do not result in violations of human dignity, whether by design in which the individual is seen as a means rather than an end, or by unintended consequences of a well-intended process. Rather, from initial planning and design, the ethical values of upholding human dignity must be integrated and communicated as a vital consideration in the design and implementation of new technology and processes. A principles-based, outcomes-focused framework may provide tools to determine priorities in the contexts of organizational and societal values in order to identify and mitigate the risks of adverse outcomes.

CASE STUDY Rape crisis centres and a government agency

The Rape Crisis Network Ireland is a non-governmental organization (NGO) in Ireland that provides crisis support to victims of sexual assault. In 2017 they were asked by an Irish government agency that funds their activities to provide detailed information on users of their services. An online questionnaire was distributed that asked for very granular information, including seeking numerical breakdowns of service users by a range of criteria that would enable an individual to be singled out from the data.

The Rape Crisis Network Ireland refused to provide granular information of this nature on the basis that it could infringe on the data privacy rights of these individuals as the state agency in question had the potential ability to identify individuals by cross-referencing with other data, and in any event the data could indirectly identify people.

The state agency informed the Rape Crisis Network Ireland that their funding would be cut if they did not comply with the request to submit survey responses either online or via a hard-copy form. They were also advised by the state agency that they were to assume consent from the survivors of sexual assault for the processing of particularly sensitive personal data.

The Rape Crisis Network Ireland, in consultation with their legal advisors and specialist data privacy consultants, responded to the survey using the hard-copy forms, but provided answers that were aggregated insofar as was possible to mitigate the risk of data being identifiable (eg rather than asking for specific numbers in a category of service user, they provided a range).

This was deemed unacceptable by the state agency in question and the Rape Crisis Network Ireland organization had its funding cut to a level that impacted the charity's own internal research and data analysis capabilities.

Case study discussion questions

- What ethical issues arise here?
- How would you go about assessing the ethical issues in this case study?
- What normative model of ethics was the rape crisis network applying? Why?
- How might the data gathering and analysis have been done differently?
- What role might the E2IM framework play in helping to assess the issues in this case study and plan for data-gathering activities?

Chapter summary

In this chapter we introduced the E2IM model for Ethical Enterprise Information Management:

- We provided an overview of conceptual models for information strategy.
- We provided a model that explicitly reflects the role of stakeholders in the ethical information management process.
- We explored the application of the E2IM model, including the importance of the feedback loops to ensure alignment between the ethic of society and the ethic of the organization so that there is alignment between both and stakeholder expectations will be met.
- We examined a number of real-world scenarios to demonstrate the application of ethical information management principles.
- We explored how the E2IM model can be used to align with and address the increased regulatory focus on ethical information management, particularly in a European context.

Questions

1 How might the culture of your organization affect the ethical choices that are taken within the overall governance models adopted?

2 How might the concept of 'ethic of society' and 'ethic of organization' and their interplay with formally defined data governance and information

architecture explain some of the failings of organizations to properly apply or reflect ethical values in the delivery of products or services?

3 Is ethical information management a 'one off' activity or should organizations be applying a continuous improvement approach to ensuring alignment of the ethic of the organization with the ethic of society? How might that be achieved?

Note

1 This quote is often misattributed to Leonardo da Vinci.

Further reading

While not directly related to the issues of Information Ethics, the Opinion on Accountability published by the Article 29 Working Party (aka the European Data Protection Board post May 2018) highlights a number of areas that are relevant to the E2IM model.

Article 29 Working Party. 2010. *Opinion 3/2010 on the principle of accountability* http://ec.europa.eu/justice/policies/privacy/docs/wpdocs/2010/wp173_en.pdf

References

Boothe Brokaw, C (1931) *Stuffed Shirts*, Horace Liveright, New York

Court of Justice of the European Union (2015) [accessed 30 September 2017] Case C-201/14 Smaranda Bara and Others v Presedintele Casei Nationale de Asigurari de Sanatate and Others [Online] http://curia.europa.eu/juris/document/document.jsf?text=&docid

Culver, KB (2017) [accessed 20 September 2017] The Ethics of Facebook's Fake News Dilemma [Online] https://observatory.journalism.wisc.edu/2017/02/07/the-ethics-of-facebooks-fake-news-dilemma/

DAMA International (2017) *The Data Management Body of Knowledge*, 2nd edn, Technics Publications, New Jersey

European Data Protection Supervisor (2015) [accessed 20 September 2017] Towards A New Digital Ethics: Data, Dignity, and Technology [Online] https://edps.europa.eu/sites/edp/files/publication/15-09-11_data_ethics_en.pdf

Feldman, SP (2007) Moral business cultures: the keys to creating and maintaining them, *Organizational Dynamics*, **36** (2), pp 156–70

Frier, S (2017) [accessed 20 September 2017] Facebook Plans Big Overhaul of Political Ads After Criticism [Online] https://www.bloomberg.com/news/articles/2017-09-21/facebook-says-it-will-release-russian-election-ads-to-congress

Henderson, J and Venkatraman, N (1993) Strategic alignment: leveraging information technology for transforming organizations, *IBM Systems Journal*, **32** (1), pp 472–84

Maes, R, Rijsenbrij, D, Truijens, O and Goedvolk, H (2000) Redefining business alignment through a unified framework, white paper, Universiteit van Amsterdam, Cap Gemini Institute

Rogers, C (2015) [accessed 20 September 2017] Kelley Blue Book: Volkswagen Diesel Car Values Decline 13% [Online] https://www.wsj.com/articles/kelley-blue-book-volkswagen-diesel-car-values-decline-13-1444147701

Shepardson, D and White, J (2017) [accessed 20 September 2017] VW Engineer Sentenced To 40-Month Prison Term In Diesel Case [Online] https://www.reuters.com/article/us-volkswagen-emissions-sentencing/vw-engineer-sentenced-to-40-month-prison-term-in-diesel-case-idUSKCN1B51YPonths-prison-role-diesel-scandal/602584001/

Shinal, J (2017) [accessed 5 October 2017] [Online] https://www.cnbc.com/2017/10/04/zuckerberg-sandberg-not-likely-to-testify-before-congress-source.html

Syal, R (2017) [accessed 21 November 2017] 'Fake News' Inquiry Asks Facebook to Check For Russian Influence in UK [Online] https://www.theguardian.com/technology/2017/oct/24/fake-news-inquiry-asks-facebook-check-russian-influence-uk-mark-zuckerberg?CMP=twt_a-technology_b-gdntech

Young, P (2004) Ethics and risk management: building a framework, *Risk Management*, **6** (3), pp 23–24

Information ethics as an information quality system

08

What will we cover in this chapter?

Quality is often defined as 'consistently meeting or exceeding customer expectations'. In the Castlebridge framework we discussed in Chapter 7, the 'customer' is identified as an affected stakeholder and could be an external customer using the goods and services of your organization, or an internal customer using information that your organization has obtained, or some other member of society who is affected by the process or information outcomes that are delivered by the organization.

In this chapter we will:

- Examine the concept of information ethics as an information quality system.
- Identify the role of normative business ethics in the delivery of quality or quality outcomes.
- Explore a methodology for information quality assessment.
- Explore the parallels between information quality management and ethical information management.
- Identify how information quality management principles and techniques can be applied to support ethical information management objectives.

Ethics as a quality system

In an article in the *Electronic Journal of Business Ethics and Organization Studies*, Larry Pace defined quality as 'doing the right thing the right way the first time every time' (Pace, 1999). Depending on your preferred source attribution, either W Edwards Deming or Henry Ford told us that 'Quality means doing it right when no one is looking.' As Pace points out in his article, these definitions of quality immediately begin to draw our thinking to ethical questions. What is the right thing? Who gets to decide what is right?

Ultimately, quality is an inherently ethical concept, and it could be argued that many of the challenges you can face when trying to implement information quality management principles in an organization have their root in the dominant normative business ethic in the organization. Organizations that are dominated by a shareholder value ethic may be resistant to quality practices that require short-term costs. Indeed, W Edwards Deming, in his seminal book *Out of the Crisis*, identified 'emphasis on short-term profits' as one of the 'Seven Deadly Diseases of Management', along with running an organization on visible numbers alone (Deming, 1986).

This focus on short-termism could even be a key root cause of some of the failures of quality management in Western organizations, where the tools of quality management are often applied pragmatically to cost reduction or improvement of productivity to improve the bottom line in the organization. While these goals are present in Japanese and Asian approaches to quality management, the cultural approaches to quality adopted in these countries tend to be more humanistic and holistic in their approach. Quality is considered an explicitly ethical value. In the words of Larry Pace, the Japanese in particular 'approach quality from the perspective of human happiness' (Pace, 1999).

A quality systems approach to information ethics is essentially consequentialist. At a deeply practical level, you need to consider what the outcomes of actions will be, and whether those outcomes match expectations, and have some ability to respond when the outcomes do not match expectations. As you learnt when we discussed the E2IM model in Chapter 7, those expectations are both the expectations of individual stakeholders and the wider expectations of society as to what is 'right' (see Figure 7.4). In the recent criticism and concern around social media platforms such as Facebook and Twitter, whether it is the potential for them to be used to subvert democratic processes or the proliferation of hate speech and bullying of vulnerable individuals, we see this consequentialist drama playing out. The same is happening in the context of online behavioural advertising and the associated data analytics processes. The technologies and the platforms that have evolved have resulted in information and process outcomes that society, as a collective whole, feel does not match their ethical expectations. This is triggering disruption in the industry and pushing the end customer to modify their use (Griffith, 2016) or abandon social platforms entirely (Haque, 2016). One group of researchers has predicted that, just as Facebook spread like a viral outbreak, its decline will be equally as abrupt as users stop interacting (Cannarella and Spechler, 2014).

This story is familiar to students of the evolution of the quality movement. The potted history is that in the post-Second World War era, pioneers such as W Edwards Deming and Joseph Juran were brought to Japan to assist in rebuilding the country and its economy by teaching quality management principles, which were famously adopted and built on by companies such as Toyota. These principles had been applied in the West during wartime, but post-war the giants of the US auto industry failed to sustain the focus on quality and efficiency, in factors such as reliability and fuel economy. The fuel crisis of the 1970s made consumers (particularly younger and less affluent consumers) more aware of the cost of non-quality in their cars and led to a shift in buying patterns to cars that were easier and cheaper to run and maintain (for a discussion of this see Beckford, 2002). We have seen similar shifts since the late 1990s as Japanese car manufacturers have pioneered the development of hybrid engines and other alternatives to fossil fuels.

Umair Haque flagged this issue for social media platforms in 2016 when he wrote in the *Harvard Business Review* (Haque, 2016) that 'learning to produce high- versus settling for low-quality interactions is one of the great challenges of competence for institutions today'. Thirty-one years earlier, Kaoru Ishikawa, the pioneer of quality management in Japan, summarized the ethical dimension of quality in a way that should resonate profoundly in today's information age (Ishikawa, 1985): 'In management, the first concern of the company is the happiness of people who are connected with it. If the people do not feel happy and cannot be made happy, that company does not deserve to exist.'

We have many ways to define what is 'good', whether we are asking what is 'quality' or what is 'ethical'. Compliance to legislation is a bare minimum for outcomes to match societal expectation. This corresponds to the shareholder value normative model of ethics that you learnt about earlier in this book. Essentially, this model of quality is whether you or your organization have been caught doing something illegal. The level of 'good' in this context is often measured by the level of potential penalty or the severity of impact on the organization that might arise from any associated negative publicity.

The organizational ethic of ensuring you do not do business with firms who engage in slavery to deliver their goods or services is one example of this ethical value in action. Doing the minimum necessary to comply with data privacy laws would be another example.

An organization that excels, that builds trustworthiness and confidence in its quality of product, exceeds the bare minimum expectations of legal, differentiating itself on its 'quality'. According to Deming, good quality means a predictable degree of uniformity and dependability with a quality standard suited to the customer. This definition requires a standardized approach to understanding what constitutes a desirable outcome for the customer. In an ethical context, this requires a formal balancing of often competing interests, perspectives and rights. As such, it aligns with the stakeholder-theory model of ethics we discussed in an earlier chapter. The organization must consider who its stakeholders are, what their needs and expectations are, and what the ethical priorities of these representatives of society are, and put controls in place to ensure that those desired outcomes are consistently and measurably delivered. In other words, it requires a system of clearly communicated values and accountability. It also requires mechanisms that will allow the organization to measure where stakeholder expectations are not being met and react accordingly, but also to identify when the wrong metrics of stakeholder satisfaction are being used to drive decisions. Self-policing and effective mechanisms for feedback and response become essential when the driver for changes to process and information outcomes is not the action of a regulator or law-enforcement body.

The social justice perspective on ethics aligns with the quality philosophy of exceeding the expectations of customers, not just meeting them. It requires an assessment of 'good' and 'right' based on wider social values and a consideration of the impact of data processing and data management activities on the wider fundamental rights and freedoms that underpin a very well defined and communicated set of internal values within the ethic of the organization, but also within the ethic of the individuals who make up that organization. Just as with organizations that seek to meet expectations above basic legal compliance, organizations that are trying to exceed the expectations of their stakeholders need to ensure that there are mechanisms defined in the organization to measure where expectations are not being met and react accordingly. It is even more important that organizations pursuing a social justice model of ethics have mechanisms to identify when they are using the wrong metrics for feedback or where their perception of social justice is not striking the correct balance and could be delivering undesired process or information outcomes.

Where the ethical standards expressed in the ethic of the organization are aligned with the expectations of stakeholders, as expressed through the ethic of society, the organization will be viewed to be at least meeting a baseline ethical standard in the conduct of the business. Ultimately, the development of ethical standards in organizations and society is intended to reduce the frequency of occurrence of unethical actions through consequences tied to the outcomes produced. Positive outcomes receive positive rewards: increased revenue, increased market share, reduced customer dissatisfaction, improved citizen trust in government processes. Negative outcomes receive negative rewards: loss of business, loss of revenue, distrust of government processes.

In this way, the evolution of ethics in an organization is analogous to the development of quality standards and systems in organizations. In that context, the practical development of ethical information management methods and practices in an organization should be able to draw on established quality management and information quality management practices.

Applying quality management principles to ethical information management

A recurring theme in this book is the principle that the measure of ethics is the actions taken on the basis of an ethical framework. The quality of the outcomes arising from such action might therefore be the sole measure for ethics, from the consequentialist perspective. You have already seen how Kaoru Ishikawa equated the happiness of people connected to a company with the fate of the company. When we consider quality management and information quality, we are often tempted to look to published standards to see what they might tell us about how to apply ethical concepts in a practical context. However, traditionally, standards lack an explicit ethical dimension. As such, organizations often wind up doing things that are perfectly legal but are unethical or potentially unethical, even when following well-established quality management standards such as ISO9001 or ISO9004 (Stimson, 2005).

While there is extensive work under way in recent years across standards bodies such as IEEE and ISO to look at standards for ethics, particularly in information management and the emerging internet of things (IoT) and 'big data' technologies, many of the tools and techniques that you will need to adopt in an ethical information management context can be found in, or adapted from, fundamental principles and practices in quality management and information quality management. In Chapters 1 to 3 you learnt about the 'first principles' perspectives on the philosophy of ethics and how they apply to information management, we will now look at some of these fundamental quality principles and practices.

W Edwards Deming's 14 points and seven diseases

In his seminal book *Out of the Crisis* (Deming, 1986), W Edwards Deming set out what he described as a 'System of Profound Knowledge' for quality management and organizational improvement. As part of that system, he set out 14 points for the transformation of businesses, along with seven 'deadly diseases' of management, which he warned organizations to avoid. While not all of them are directly relevant to the discussion of ethical management, Stimson identifies eight of the 14 principles as being directly relevant to the discussion of ethics and the development of ethical frameworks in organizations. Indeed, Stimson refers to Deming as a source for deriving a 'secular basis for ethical behaviour from the tenets of quality' (Stimson, 2005). Furthermore, when we look at many of the challenges that are facing some of the leading 'born on the internet' businesses, Deming's fundamental principles appear very prescient.

Stimson's assessment of the alignment between Deming's 14 points for transformation looked at their relationship to business ethics and identified eight principles that were directly relatable to the broader topic of ethics. In the context of information ethics, and with the benefit of our model set out in Chapter 7, Deming's principles provide a broader base for ethical information management than that identified for ethics in general. We summarize this in Table 8.1.

Deming also wrote about what he termed the '7 deadly diseases of management'. Each of these impact on quality, but they also have an impact on the ethical management of the organization and information ethics in particular. Table 8.2 summarizes this perspective.

The Plan-Do-Study-Act cycle

One of the fundamental techniques that was pioneered by Deming in the field of quality management was the Plan-Do-Study-Act (PDSA) cycle (Figure 8.1). This is often referred to as the Deming cycle but is more correctly attributed to Deming's mentor, Walter Shewhart. This cycle is often mislabelled as the Plan-Do-Check-Act cycle and it is important to note

Table 8.1 Deming's 14 points for transformation mapped to ethics

	Deming's Original Principle	Stimson	O'Keefe/ O Brien	Comment
1	Create constancy of purpose		•	It is difficult to embed ethical principles at the front line if your organization's values change frequently
2	Adopt the new philosophy	•		Management need to wake up to the importance not just of quality data but of ethical data management practices
3	Cease dependence on inspection to achieve quality		•	Deming's point here was that inspection does not improve quality, and the best strategy was to improve processes to reduce variation around the standard
4	End the practice of awarding business based on the price tag		•	In the modern data world, it is cheap to outsource processing to third parties, but the ethical supply chain for data services should be considered
5	Improve constantly and forever		•	Deming's principle addresses continuous improvement of processes to eliminate the causes of error. In an ethical context, this also means continuously evolving the expression of ethical values and the need for organizations to recognize when the ethic of the organization is at odds with the ethic of society
6	Institute training on the job	•		Deming believed well-trained employees are more inclined to do their best. However, he also highlighted that expecting staff to do their best without providing a framework of knowledge would lead to confusion. In the context of information ethics, this is essential to align individual ethic with organization and society

7	Institute leadership	•	Deming called on organizations to develop leadership and leaders to help people do a better job. This was a mandate for empowerment and delegation of stewardship roles through the organization. Ethical leadership is also important – empowering staff to look behind data to understand the information and process outcomes being delivered
8	Drive out fear	•	In the context of ethical information management, staff should be able to speak 'truth to power' and question the business decisions, information models and technical architectures being implemented
9	Break down barriers between departments	•	One of the key challenges we see in organizations is the continued dominance of silo-thinking. Improving communication between departments helps support the evolution of the ethic of the organization and alignment with the ethic of society. It also helps avoid 'groupthink' in relation to ethical issues
10	Eliminate slogans, exhortations and targets causing adversarial relationships	•	Deming's point here was that the organization should avoid 'management by soundbite' that can create adversarial relationships between teams or between the organization and other stakeholders. In addition (and counterintuitively to the 'data-driven' mandate), running the organization based on numerical goals and targets only is not advised. What Deming
11	Eliminate management by numerical goals; substitute leadership	•	meant in this context was that management needed to understand the factors driving the numbers as well as the numbers themselves

(continued)

Table 8.1 (Continued)

	Deming's Original Principle	Stimson	O'Keefe/ O Brien	Comment
12	Remove barriers that rob the worker of their pride in workmanship	•	•	No one likes working for a company that is derided for doing unethical things or producing low-quality products or services. The barriers that can block pride in workmanship can include organizational culture or governance that prevent ethical concerns being raised and discussed. From an ethical perspective this is also a question of how the organization supports and promotes the dignity of their own staff. If there are ethical problems at the front line, the problem rests with the decisions made and processes implemented by management
13	Institute a vigorous programme of education and self-improvement		•	Your staff need to be able and be encouraged to develop their skills and understanding of their role. They should be encouraged to learn new skills and perspectives. As technical education becomes increasingly specialized, it is increasingly important for people working in information management roles to look to other fields for potential solutions to the challenges we increasingly face
14	Put everyone in the company to work to accomplish the transformation		•	Just as with quality, ethical information management is not a job for the 'ethics' department. In the Castlebridge model, the operational front-line staff have a key role to play in the continued execution of ethical practices, but need to be supported by their peers elsewhere in the organization

Table 8.2 Deming's 7 deadly diseases – the information ethics perspective

	Deming's Description	Relevant to Ethics	The Information Ethics Perspective
1	Lack of constancy of purpose	•	If the organization's mission and values keep changing, it becomes difficult to sustain an organization ethic, so the organization defaults to the ethics of individual actors 'doing their best'
2	Emphasis on short-term profits	•	Focusing on short-term profits and profit targets is a function of the shareholder-theory model of ethics. When the organization is focused on the next quarter's bottom line, the risk of ethical issues in innovation or information processing being ignored or not considered increases. Likewise, where performance rating/merit rating processes create pressures on ethical behaviour, as the delivered outputs of processes are almost entirely the function of the processes and systems implemented
3	Evaluation of performance, merit rating, annual review	•	
4	Mobility of top management	•	From quality and ethics perspective, the mobility of top management creates issues because senior managers often are not around long enough to deal with the consequences of initiatives. On the other hand, top management who 'get' quality or ethics can often move out of organizations when they find themselves unable to affect change or when the ethic of the organization is at odds with the ethic of the individual. It also contributes to managers manipulating data or selectively reporting data to support their personal career progression
5	Running company on visible numbers alone	•	While Deming was a statistician by training, he understood the limits of numbers. He understood that there are often things that cannot be measured but still need to be managed. Deming stressed the need to understand the 'why' of numbers as well as the 'what'. In the context of information ethics, this means avoiding causation and correlation errors and also considering the non-quantifiable aspects of processing activities
6	Excessive medical costs	•	These are the costs arising as a result of the remediation of process and information outcomes. Either people are made ill (stress, medical error, etc) or the organization is sued
7	Excessive legal costs	•	

Figure 8.1   The PDSA cycle

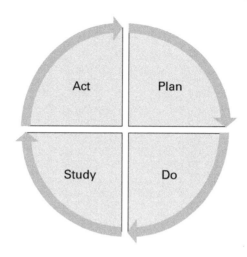

that Deming stressed the importance of studying results rather than merely checking, and actively disavowed Plan-Do-Check-Act terminology (Moen and Norman, 2010). Much like the ethical principles you have read about earlier in this book, the PDSA cycle is the result of an evolution of thinking in scientific method principles going back to Galileo.

Deming's view was that checking rather than studying focused attention on simple success or failure or implementation, rather than understanding why the implementation succeeded or failed and developing the capability to revise expectations or revise the proposed model for action. This analysis component is essential in the context of ethical information management as it is through this reflection that you develop quantitative and qualitative understanding of how their processing and use of information delivers desirable information outcomes and process outcomes for stakeholders. It is also through this process that gaps between the ethic of the organization and the ethic of society can be understood and strategies developed to ensure appropriate alignment.

The PDSA cycle forms part of what Deming described as a 'Model for Improvement'. It is an analysis method that helps answer the following questions:

- What are we trying to accomplish? (What is our plan?)

- How will we know that a change is an improvement? (Do a pilot, study results.)

- What change can we make that will result in an improvement? (Study results, act on results.)

In the context of ethical information management, these questions form part of the basic questions we need to ask of any information-processing or information-technology adoption, a topic we will return to in a later chapter.

Understanding the PDSA cycle

The PDSA cycle is an important tool in the quality systems toolbox, and it is likewise an important weapon in the arsenal of the information ethicist. As such, it is important that you understand the core principles of this deceptively simple tool.

Plan In this phase of the cycle you need to define what your objectives are. What is it you are hoping to achieve through the new process or processing activity? This is the phase when the proposed information-processing activities are planned and the criteria for determining successful execution of the processes are identified. At this stage in the process you should be able to make some predictions as to the nature of outcomes from the processing. It is also at this stage, in Deming's view, that you need to consider who is to do what during the execution of the processing.

If you are familiar with the principles of Privacy by Design or have conducted Privacy Impact Assessment methods, you will recognize some distinct similarities between what Deming considered to be essential elements of the planning phase for the management of quality in organizations and the things that you need to be considering when assessing whether the processing of data about people infringes on their 'right to be left alone', or whether the processing activities as proposed strike an appropriate balance between the rights of the individual and the objectives of the organization. Deming stressed the importance of identifying the who, what, when, where and how of the proposed process at this stage. You will recall that these are the key interrogatives that form the vertical dimensions of the Zachman framework, which we discussed in Chapter 6.

You will recall that the Zachman framework also includes a 'Motivation' column, corresponding to the fundamental question of why a function is being performed and why particular data is being used for that purpose. While not explicitly referenced in the PDSA cycle, as it is commonly taught and understood, Deming implicitly referenced the importance of considering the 'Why' questions. In *Out of the Crisis* (Deming, 1986) he posed the questions set out in Table 8.3.

Do In the 'Do' phase of the PDSA cycle you start to execute your plan and carry out your processing activities. You identify and document problems or

Table 8.3 Deming's 'Motivation for Quality' questions – mapped to information ethics

Deming's Question	The 'Why' Corollary in Information Ethics
What would be the effect if your organization stopped producing its products and services?	What is the value or purpose that is served by the information processing activity? What would happen if you stopped (or didn't start)? Why are you doing this?
How do your errors affect your immediate customers?	Why should you prevent errors and ensure the right process/information outcomes are delivered? What is the impact on the individual?
How far beyond your immediate customer can you trace the effect of what you do?	Why would your errors or successes impact on others? Why is that important?
What would happen to you if your suppliers did not do their job?	Why is the lineage of data important and why would defects in that information supply chain matter to your organization and/or the people whose data you are processing?

unexpected outcomes. Crucially, you need to start gathering some data about how well things are going (or not). Deming recommended doing small-scale or pilot projects. In the context of information management and information ethics, this might be achieved most cost-effectively by whiteboarding the process, engaging in focus groups with stakeholders, or implementing the process on a small scale.

An example of this is how social media platforms sometimes roll out changes to features, algorithms, or presentation of information in smaller markets. This lets them test the implications and impacts of their changes to see how they will be accepted (or not) by users, and whether they will deliver on the other objectives of the company. For example, Facebook often trials changes to its news feed in discrete markets to see what the impact might be. In October 2017 they trialled a change to news feeds in six countries, which saw non-promoted posts moved out of the main news feed into a secondary feed. Posts from family, friends and paid-for promoted posts remained in the main news feed. The impact on users has been a dramatic drop in engagement with Facebook pages of up to 80 per cent (Glenday, 2017; Hern, 2017).

Study 'Study the results. Do they correspond with hopes and expectations? If not, what went wrong? Maybe we tricked ourselves in the first place and should make a fresh start' (Deming, 1994). In this simple paragraph, Deming encapsulated what we need to do, and why simply 'checking' is not enough. You need to analyse the data you have about the processing activities and identify what has happened. This needs to be compared to the predictions and assumptions made during the 'Plan' phase. Importantly, it needs to be summarized to document what has been learnt and identify the process and information outcomes that have resulted from your activities.

In an information ethics context, you might want to consider whether anyone raised unforeseen scenarios as you rolled out your new systems and processes. Did you get complaints or negative feedback? (Remember, in the E2IM framework complaints and feedback to the operational level of the organization are important signals that the ethic of the organization and the ethic of society might be misaligned and the information and/or process outcomes you are delivering are meeting expectations.)

In the Facebook example above, studying the impact on the reach of non-promoted sharing may illustrate that there is a negative for organizations that have built their models on free content distribution through Facebook, as opposed to paid-for content. Cynics might suggest that this meets Facebook's objective of increasing their paid-for advertising revenues. However, further study of the processing and potential outcomes might reveal that this has a social benefit in curtailing the 'fake news' epidemic that has dogged the organization through 2017. Changes made by Facebook to the Newsfeed algorithm in October 2017 appear to have addressed content published by organizations differently to previous changes in this processing.

Act If the sole medium of expression for ethics is action, to paraphrase Jane Addams, then this phase of the PDSA cycle is perhaps the most pertinent. Deming sets out three options that you have at this point in the cycle (Deming, 1994):

- adopt the change;
- abandon the change;
- go around again, changing some of the input variables.

These decisions will be informed by the analysis in the 'Study' phase of the cycle. But that analysis will require you to have made some predictions about what the outcomes should be and whether they will be acceptable to your customer or other stakeholders.

The Satori Project

In recent years the European Union has funded a long-running study of ethics in the broader context of research and innovation called the Satori Project (Reijers et al, 2016). As part of their framework for creating Ethics Impact Assessments, the Satori Project has looked at various approaches and methods of conducting ethical impact assessments. In their framework output on ethics assessment procedures, they highlight the use of a Plan-Do-Check-Act cycle (Satori, n.d.).

This work is a valuable contribution to the development of ethical information management practices, but it falls into the trap of interpreting 'Check' as a check on the performance of the process rather than an assessment of whether the proposed processing activity has delivered the predicted or expected results in the context of an information or process outcome that meets the expectation of the ethic of society. As we have discussed, Deming was clear that his cycle did not involve a 'Check' of how well a process has run but instead called for a 'Study' of outcomes against the original objectives of the proposed change or development. While it is an important aspect of continuous improvement to verify the output of the Ethical Impact Assessment process against the desired results, it is equally if not more important to ensure that, as a result of following any process for assessing the ethical impacts of information processing, the actual information and process outcomes experienced by the people interacting with your process, product or service meet their expectations.

Mapping Deming's principles to an information ethics case study

In *Out of the Crisis*, Deming famously said that 'In God we trust, everyone else must bring data'. While the relationship of Deming's principles to information ethics makes intuitive sense when we consider ethics in general as a quality system, it would probably be helpful for you if we could relate it to a topical (at the time of writing) case study. Charlie Warzel's October 2017 Buzzfeed article How People Inside Facebook Are Reacting To The Company's Election Crisis (Warzel, 2017), on the reaction of staff inside Facebook to the coverage of the social network's role, is instructive in this regard as it addresses a number of the points we have discussed earlier in this chapter.

'Many employees feel like they are part of an unjust narrative that has spiralled out of control' According to Warzel, inside Facebook 'many in the company's rank and file are frustrated. They view the events of the previous month and those that preceded it as 'part of an unjust narrative that has spiralled out of control, unchecked'. Facebook staff reportedly feel the company is being scapegoated for a range of other factors that may have influenced the US presidential election in 2016, and potentially other votes around the world. However, as Warzel describes it: 'as the drumbeat of damning reports continues, the frustration and fundamental disconnect between Facebook's stewards and those wary of its growing influence grow larger still' (Warzel, 2017).

This describes a clear disconnect between the ethic of society and the ethic of the organization that raises fundamental questions around the ethical management of information and data. Also, it is symptomatic of a culture of fear (a fear of 'speaking truth to power' about the culture and structures of the organization and the impact of the process and information outcomes delivered) and highlights a culture of slogans, exhortations and targets that have become ingrained in the organization to the extent that external criticism is considered by some in an adversarial way.

'Things are organized quantitively at Facebook' In Warzel's (2017) article he interviews a former Facebook engineer who describes the quantitative culture of the organization. The company was more concerned about the volume of links that users were sharing rather than the content that was being shared. The focus was quantitative rather than qualitative data. The quantitative data was easy to measure. Not only that, but the performance management and reward structures in Facebook are linked to those metrics. Considering the content that was being shared 'simply wasn't one of their business objectives'.

Here we see two of Deming's 14 Points and at least one of the 7 Diseases at play, creating an environment in which the organization did not question the key metric, and did not consider the interplay between the sharing of data and the well-documented 'filter bubble' phenomenon that the platform's algorithmic processes contributed to, leading to an increased proliferation of partisan content. As Warzel describes it, 'the platform's design pushes its users into echo chambers filled with only the news and information they already want, rather than the potentially unpopular information they might need' (Warzel, 2017).

Missed opportunities? According to Warzel's article, in 2015 a Facebook engineer noticed something odd in Facebook's data about link sharing. The top 25 results included a small number of sites that were essentially aggregators for hyper-partisan content but appeared to be among the most widely read websites on the site. The engineer shared this information in an internal discussion forum, but for a quantitatively data-driven company, Facebook seemed to be unable to appreciate the potential for this to have been a 'special cause' of defect in their processes and in the process and information outcomes that the people using their platform were experiencing.

Within the PDSA cycle, Facebook seems to have missed an opportunity to study what was happening and to understand whether this data represented an outlier, an error in the data, or a special cause of defect. For example, the application of a simple 'Five Whys' analysis might have helped direct further quantitative analysis of the sharing to determine why these aggregator sites were so prominent in the top 25 shared sites. One hypothesis that might have been tested would be if the sharing of content on Facebook followed a normal statistical distribution in terms of the type of content being shared, and if this pattern of sharing was outside the expected statistical distribution. This type of analysis could also have looked at why content, described by one former senior employee as 'liberal media stuff', wasn't shared or read, which suggests there was an awareness in Facebook that their content sharing was not following a normal statistical distribution – and which might have been an alert that the filter bubbles Facebook creates were becoming biased towards political and social narratives.

According to Alex Kantrowitz, while it 'was likely never the company's intent to create a system that encouraged people to hear only what they wanted – whether or not it was true – Facebook didn't get here by accident' (Kantrowitz, 2016). The haste with which the platform moved to implement a link-sharing button in their mobile feed in 2012 set in motion a chain of data decisions that may have resulted in the exacerbation of fake news and filter bubbles. The changes to sharing functionality let people share quickly on mobile, without much thought. But, as Kantrowitz points out, on mobile people are less likely to take the time to provide comments on their shares that provide context. This metadata about the motive for the share or any 'editorial' comment by the sharer was potentially lost.

Create constancy of purpose Add to this a shift in strategy coupled with a shift in Facebook's purpose, as expressed by Mark Zuckerberg to be a 'personalized newspaper for every person in the world' (Kantrowitz, 2016). Being data driven, Facebook introduced 'quality improving' measures that Kantrowitz describes as 'well-intentioned but fundamentally flawed' as they served to reinforce filter bubbles and confirmation bias by not showing people stories that the algorithms said they would disagree with. This, again, is another example of Facebook managing by visible numbers to drive up another key metric – the amount of time a user spends on Facebook each day.

But is Facebook a newspaper? What is the purpose that Facebook serves, and is it resourced to do that in a way which meets with relevant ethical standards? In traditional newspapers, sources who regularly provide false stories find themselves dismissed by editors. There are mechanisms by which points of view that are contrary to the editorial line of the newspaper can be reflected. There are other news sources. However, Facebook has become a primary source of current-affairs content for many people, but has yet to tackle the filter-bubble problem.

Warzel (2017) also highlights this problem when he writes that 'those inside the company continue to struggle with what, exactly, the company is, and what it is responsible for'. Within the ethic of the organization this lack of constancy of purpose poses problems. Within the ethic of society there are growing calls for Facebook, if it is a media company now, to be regulated as such (Ingram, 2017).

Some glimmers of study? In response to the 'fake news' crisis, Facebook has done analysis of how their platform is used, and has begun to introduce changes in its newsfeed algorithms to weed out individuals who are prolific posters (Wagner, 2017). These changes do not affect publishers (ie organizations). According to Facebook, if you post more than 50 times a day, Facebook's algorithms reduce the distribution of those links on the network. This is done without looking at the content in each case, relying instead on a correlation between 'these types of users and spammy/false content'. In effect, Facebook have applied a quota on posting, above which action is taken.

Facebook has had historic problems with ensuring they were managing fake news in an editorial process. While on one hand they want to position themselves as a primary source for news, they have struggled with the editorial challenges of content curation and perceived editorial bias, so in a culture that is quantitatively driven this may be the best proxy metric for validity of content that can be identified in their operating model. It may also be that the recent pilot of algorithm changes to reduce the effect of non-paid-for commercial posts is the response of the ethic of the organization to something that the ethic of society says is a problem.

The open question is whether society accepts advertising dollars as a proxy for veracity and validity of content, or will Facebook have to return to human editors, like the newspapers they had sought to displace? The other question is whether Facebook, in planning these changes, considered the impact on legitimate organizations who distribute content through their platform, or the people who work for them, particularly given the fact that no notice was given of the change. Also, the impact on legitimate grass-roots movements and small businesses who lack the finances to pay for promoted adverts, particularly in developing countries, remains to be seen. The other question is whether Facebook's model for planning and executing changes to their platform fully considers the impacts on stakeholders, and whether Facebook's 'very scale might estrange it from how other people see the world' (Madrigal, 2017).

Special and common causes in Deming's 'System of Profound Knowledge'

Deming identified two categories of defect that could occur in a process. He termed these 'special causes' and 'common causes'. Special causes are things that happen due to unforeseen circumstances or changes in the processes in your organization and are outside your control. Common causes of defect are those things that contribute to defects and errors that are inherent in the processes of your organization and are within the control of management. Deming's advice to management was that they needed to use statistical techniques such as statistical process control to identify special causes and common causes, and prevent the former while reducing the frequency of the latter. This can only be done by addressing the processes that were creating the product.

At the heart of Deming's approach to quality management is the principle that quality is something that is designed into products and the processes that are creating them. Defects detected through inspection have already been created, so mass inspection is not going to stop errors from happening. At best, it will mitigate the impact of defects being released to the customer, but it will not stop errors from happening. Deming was clear: if the process is producing defective products, the problem lies in the means and methods of production and this is where remedial action should be taken.

In the context of the E2IM framework, Deming's guidance on special and common causes and the importance of designing quality into the process means that your organization needs to consider the business, information and technology perspectives of your information management strategy and processes in order to consider how you might avoid special causes of ethical defect or common causes of ethical issues. The key lesson in this context is that it is not the responsibility or accountability of your front-line operational staff when a systemic ethical issue arises (what Deming would term a 'common cause'; what we would term an issue in the 'ethic of the organiza-tion'), rather it is the responsibility of management to address the underlying systemic root causes (in the case of ethical information management, this may include processes, governance, corporate culture and underlying busi-ness models, as well as technologies).

Deming also stressed the importance of what he referred to as a 'Theory of Knowledge' and the understanding of fundamental principles when it came to improving quality. This included understanding when something was a special cause or a common cause: 'Best efforts are essential. Unfortunately, best efforts, people charging this way and that way without guidance of principles, can do a lot of damage' (Deming, 1986: 19).

Failure to properly analyse and address systemic issues that lead to quality problems leads to inefficient, ineffective and often unsustainable approaches to improving quality. While Deming was referring to principles of manage-ment in the first instance, a rereading of his work from an ethics perspective highlights the importance of 'Big P' principles in the organization – the effec-tive development of the ethic of the organization in a way that is aligned with the ethic of society to consistently deliver the information and process outcomes expected by your organization's stakeholders.

Looking again at Facebook and the fake news issue we see an organiza-tion that appears to be addressing the symptoms of special and common causes in its core processes in order to improve the ethical outcomes. However, it remains to be seen if Facebook will tackle the underlying root causes in its processing of data that give rise to these issues and others. In the E2IM framework, this extends to considering the business model and strategy that might be contributing to the problem. It also serves as a key lesson for the rest of us in the context of how we define and develop big data analytics capabilities and AI models. Without taking time to consider the ethical implications of processing and ensuring you consciously engage in ethical design of information management processes, or information-driven processing, you may find yourself firefighting issues with the information or process outcomes you produce.

Defining and measuring 'good' in the context of information quality

Just as with ethics, information quality[1] management requires you to have some mechanism for defining and measuring what 'good' is. It also requires formal processes and methods to plan for, design for, and ensure controls for good-quality information. Of course, just as in debating what is 'ethical',

Table 8.4 Definitions of information quality

Practitioner	Definition of Quality applied to Information and Data
Larry P English	Consistently meeting or exceeding knowledge worker and end-customer expectations (English, 1999)
Dr Thomas C Redman	Data are of high quality if those who use them say so. Usually, high-quality data must be both free of defects and possess features that customers desire (Redman, 2008)
Danette McGilvray	The degree to which information and data can be a trusted source for and/or all required uses. (McGilvray, 2008)

there are a variety of schools of thought on the topic of what quality information is and how best to measure it. Table 8.4 summarizes definitions of 'information quality' from several key writers in the field of information quality management.

All the above authors are strong advocates of a quality systems approach to the management of information in the organization in order to ensure the consistent delivery of the desired information and process outcomes. According to DAMA International: 'Formal data quality management is similar to continuous quality management for other products. It includes managing data through its life cycle by setting standards, building quality into the processes that create, transform and store data, and measuring data against standards' (DAMA International, 2017).

Regardless of which definition of information quality you prefer, all methodologies for the management of information quality require you to measure some aspect of the information to give you an indication of whether the processes in your organization are producing the right quality of information in the right way. Depending on the context of your processing, different aspects of your information will be more important from a quality perspective. This is the intangible information equivalent of checking that the ingredients you are putting in a meal are the right ones for the recipe, are fresh enough and are present in the right quantities. In the same way as an absence of onions from your meringue mix is a good indicator that you have avoided a culinary quality disaster, the context of the processing drives the criticality of certain quality characteristics and the significance of high or low values.

Adapting information quality methods for ethical information management

Information quality management is about more than just measuring the quality characteristics of your data. You need to be sure you are addressing the right issues, and you need to be certain you are tackling the root causes of information quality issues in the organization. There are a multitude of methodologies and best practices identified and documented for information quality management, and reviewing all of them would take a book in its own right. If you are new to the topic and want to learn more, we provide a list of recommended reading for information quality at the end of this chapter. For the purposes of this chapter, we have picked one methodology by our friend and mentor Danette McGilvray to use as an example. However, our comments are generally applicable to other methodologies that build from a quality systems approach to information management.

Within Danette's methodology she sets out a straightforward 10-step iterative approach to managing information quality projects (Figure 8.2). When you break things down into simple, straightforward steps it can really help to get people in your organization engaged with solving the problem or improving the situation. As an iterative approach, people following this process can circle back to previous steps in the process to elaborate on detail or develop a deeper understanding of data quality issues as more information becomes available.

In addition to these steps, Danette also describes a holistic framework for information quality that mirrors many of the interrogatives from the Zachman framework we discussed in Chapter 7 (the 'who, how, what, where and when' of the information processing in the organization). This highlights the importance of understanding the overall environment in which the information is being processed and used, so that you can tackle quality problems.

McGilvray provides some useful definitions of information quality metrics (she uses the term 'data quality dimensions') that organizations might apply. When describing her data quality dimensions, Danette categorizes data quality metrics based on how they might generally be assessed, measured or managed. This reflects the fact that different dimensions, and the specific granular metrics that they include, can require different tools, techniques and processes to measure and manage.

The data quality dimensions are outlined in Table 8.5.

(Note, Table 8.5 does not include the full list of data quality characteristics identified by Danette McGilvray, and we recommend that if you want

Figure 8.2 Danette McGilvray's 10 Steps to Quality Data and Trusted Information™ Process

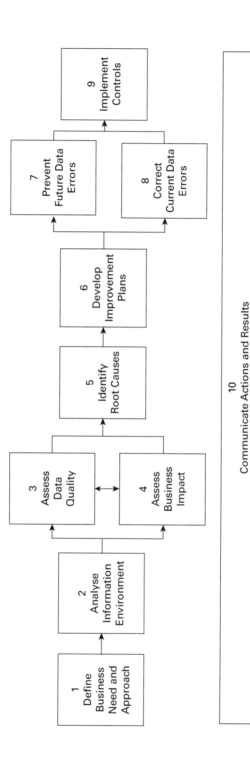

Table 8.5 Example data quality dimensions from Danette McGilvray

Data Quality Dimension (McGilvray)	Definition (McGilvray)	Comment (Authors)
Data Specification	A measure of the existence, completeness, quality and documentation of standards, data models, business rules, metadata and reference data	This dimension addresses the quality of how well the artefacts we would expect to see in the Zachman framework are defined or exist in the organization
Data Integrity Fundamentals	A measure of the existence, validity, structure, content and other basic characteristics of the data	This includes data quality metrics such as completeness, and general conformity to requirements or standards that relate to the data
Duplication	A measure of the unwanted duplication existing within or across systems for a particular field, record or data set	Duplication is a common problem in data quality. From an ethical perspective, tackling duplication can become a problem where staff are incentivized/rewarded for volume of records (eg number of customers)
Perception, Relevance, Trust	A measure of the perception of and confidence in the quality of the data; the importance, value and relevance of the data to business needs	This is a critical metric that has a strong analogue in information ethics
Transactability	A measure of the degree to which data will produce the desired business transaction or outcome	In the context of the E2IM model, this dimension is an important one – how likely is your organization to be able to deliver the required process or information outcomes?
Accuracy	A measure of the correctness of the content of the data (which requires an authoritative source to be defined and accessible)	Accuracy is usually measured either against the real-world thing (accuracy against reality) or against an approved valid surrogate source
Consistency and Synchronization	A measure of the equivalence of information stored or used in various data stores, applications and systems, and the processes for making data equivalent	In the context of the E2IM model, this dimension can be a useful surrogate for the quality of governance and architecture for information in the organization

to learn more about this topic you seek out a copy of McGilvray's book. There are a range of other authors in this field whose published methodologies set out a range of other data quality dimensions and measurable quality characteristics. We have included some in the Further Reading section at the end of this chapter.)

Adapting the Ten-Steps™ for ethics

During our consulting and training work in Castlebridge, we have adapted Danette's process as a tool for supporting data-privacy and information-ethics projects. It is important for you to have a structured approach to engaging in the analysis and discussion of information-ethics issues in your organization. The key challenge you will tend to face is keeping the discussion of ethical issues grounded and to avoid the creation of a 'talking shop' where issues are debated but do not translate into tangible action. It is important you have a simple process to keep activities focused as the translation of ethics into action is the key that organizations tend to struggle with in the accelerating Information Age.

It is important to note that Danette McGilvray's Ten-Steps to Quality Data and Trusted Information™ is not a linear process. The process of executing information and data quality improvement is iterative, and in her book Danette is explicit that you can circle back to earlier steps in the process whenever needed and to reflect iterative elaboration of detail as issues are explored or business needs become clarified (McGilvray, 2008). Building on the iterative nature of the Ten-Steps™ (Table 8.6), the key modifications we have made to Danette's process are to *explicitly* add in feedback loops that direct you to reassess your business need and approach when you encounter ethical issues that are either showstoppers or for which remedies cannot be implemented in a cost-effective manner (Figure 8.3). In this respect, our adaptation applies the iterative principles of the Deming/Shewhart PDSA cycle in a very direct manner in this ethical context.

Developing ethical-information quality dimensions

As discussed earlier, the quality of information is something that can be, to a greater or lesser extent, objectively measured. It is outside the scope of this book to explore all the different quality characteristics you might use to measure the quality of information. For our purposes it is enough that you understand that the quality of information is something that can be measured and managed using a variety of techniques.

Table 8.6 Mapping the 10 steps to E2IM

Key Steps in McGilvray's Ten-Steps™		E2IM Ethical Perspective
Define business need and approach	Define and agree the business need (issue/opportunity/goal) to be addressed, and the approach being taken	From the perspective of the E2IM framework, when you do this you need to consider the information and process outcomes you are seeking to deliver. Where you have to review in response to an ethical issue arising, it is useful to have a clearly defined statement of the purpose for your processing of information and the approach that is being taken
Analyse information environment	Gather, compile and analyse information about the current situation and the information environment and information life cycle	Understanding the information environment is essential in an ethics review context. Apart from the technology environment, it is important to consider and to take time to correctly identify who your stakeholders are and the ethic of society that is communicated through feedback received from these stakeholders
Assess data quality	Evaluate data quality for the data quality dimensions that are applicable to the issue. This provides the basis for determining root causes and improvements/corrections	You need to evaluate the quality of data and data processing from the perspective of the relevant ethical dimensions applicable to the processing
Assess business impact	Determine the impact of poor-quality data on the business. This helps support business-case development for improvements	The key question to address here is whether the processing can be done legally or ethically, and what the impacts would be on the organization of a legal or ethical issue arising
Identify root causes	Identify and prioritize the true root causes of the data quality problems and develop specific recommendations	Identify and prioritize the true root causes of the ethical quality problems identified and develop specific recommendations to address them

(continued)

Table 8.6 *(Continued)*

Key Steps in McGilvray's Ten-Steps™		E2IM Ethical Perspective
Develop improvement plans	Finalize specific recommendations for action to address root causes	Finalize specific recommendations for action to address root causes. From an E2IM perspective, we close a loop here because if the organization is unwilling to invest in addressing the root causes of ethical issues, they will remain 'live' and the organization's leadership will need to take a conscious decision to proceed with processing that has been identified as having ethical issues or legal issues. This may result in future legal liability for the organization or individuals
Prevent future errors	Implement solutions that address root causes data-quality issues	Implement solutions that address root causes of ethical issues
Correct current errors	Implement steps to make appropriate data corrections	Implement steps to remedy legacy ethical issues. This may present challenges for any organization with historic ethical breaches that may give rise to legal liability, but it is arguably worse to allow historic unethical practices to go unreviewed and unresolved. Again, organization leadership has to take a conscious decision on what to do, or not to do, in this context
Implement controls	Monitor and verify improvements implemented and maintain improved results by standardizing, documenting and continuously monitoring successful improvements	Monitor and verify improvements and document decisions taken. Continuously monitor successful ethical improvements to ensure behaviours have changed and outcomes are being consistently delivered
Communicate actions and results	Document and communicate the results of quality tests and improvements made to processes	Document and communicate the results of your ethical assessments, improvements made and the results of those improvements

Figure 8.3 A 10-step framework for ethical information management

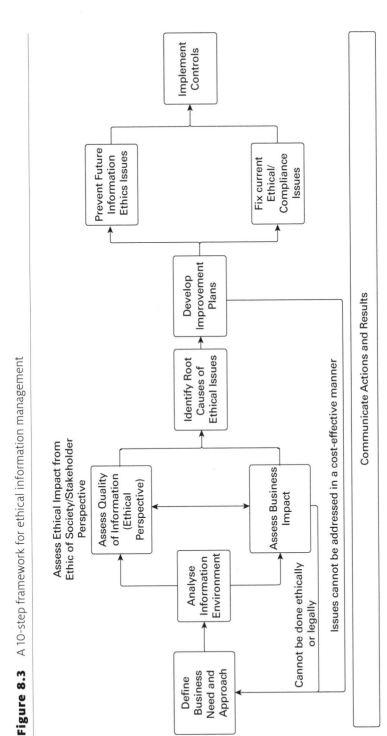

Assess Ethical Impact from
Ethic of Society/Stakeholder
Perspective

Implement
Controls

Prevent Future
Information
Ethics Issues

Fix current
Ethical/
Compliance
Issues

Develop
Improvement
Plans

Identify Root
Causes of
Ethical Issues

Assess Quality
of Information
(Ethical
Perspective)

Assess Business
Impact

Analyse
Information
Environment

Define
Business
Need and
Approach

Cannot be done ethically
or legally

Issues cannot be addressed in a cost-effective manner

Communicate Actions and Results

SOURCE adapted from McGilvray's 10 Steps™

The importance of having a metric of quality is that it allows you to demonstrate the scale of a problem, and to demonstrate improvement arising from remedial actions you might take to improve the quality of information in your organization. It also helps take what can often be abstract concepts and solidify them for discussion. One of the challenges we face when discussing ethical information management is taking the abstract concepts such as Kant's formulation of the categorical imperatives and turning them into something that is quantifiable in the same way, even if only by way of measures that are proxies for ethical concepts.

Some characteristics of ethical data management: outcomes of ethical information management

The E2IM framework stresses the importance of considering the information and process outcomes of any processing activity, and the overarching measure of ethical 'quality' is how well your organization addresses the alignment of the ethic of the organization with the ethic of society. Below we describe some dimensions for the quality of information ethics. These are intended as a guide and are not prescriptive. Just as in the traditional information quality domain, we expect and welcome debate and discussion on these topics.

Utility

A measure of to what extent the information and/or process outcomes will do good in society or will promote happiness. This quality follows directly from Irish philosopher Francis Hutcheson's definition of the principle of utility: 'that action is best, which procures the greatest happiness for the greatest numbers' (Hutcheson, 1726).

This characteristic is very broadly defined but may at the same time be useful for its broadness of definition. This characteristic is one of the dimensions of the Castlebridge utility/invasiveness model discussed in Chapter 10. Some metrics you may look for are stakeholder satisfaction, the degree to which your process or outcome solves a problem, etc. At a more operational and functional level, you can also look at this characteristic as a measure of 'usefulness' to individuals or to society.

Beneficence/non-maleficence

A measure of the extent to which the process or processing promotes well-being, or the extent to which the processing supports physical well-being and the good of society in a way that doesn't cause harm. This is an ethical dimension we inherit from medical ethics. Fundamentally, the primary measure for this characteristic is to avoid causing harm. The harm to be considered may be an impact on other rights and freedoms of individuals.

At a broader and more philosophical level, this characteristic may overlap with utility or may be a counterweight metric. However, it is best regarded as a separate characteristic to allow for recognition of issues as you drill down to more granular levels of analysis. Something may have very high utility but create a significant risk of maleficence in its use, which would need to be balanced in some way. The 'filter bubble' in social media is an example of something that may have utility but carries with it a high degree of maleficence, given its potential to be misused or abused.

Justice/fairness

Justice is a key virtue in virtue ethics, and it is one of the foundational principles in more recent utilitarian normative ethics. It is a clear expected outcome for ethical information management.

In this context, justice and fairness can be defined as a measure of the extent to which your processing results in equal treatment of people or even increased equality. Information outcomes and process outcomes that rank strongly on the dimension of justice/fairness will result in the equal and fair treatment of people, results or distribution of resources. Those that do not will result in some curtailment of equality, some bias against individuals, and some unfairness in the distribution of resources.

This quality characteristic is a key metric that has been identified in questions of algorithmic accountability, as we discussed in Chapter 4, where we observed questions regarding the outcomes of algorithmic decision making disproportionately better or worse for one group or subset of people.

Verity/non-deceptiveness

Verity as a data characteristic relates to the integrity, truthfulness, honesty or accuracy of your representation, construction, or the results of information management.

It is best defined as a measure of how closely your processing activities and use of data match what you had declared your processing to be. Verity/non-deceptiveness is an external corollary to traditional information quality metrics such as McGilvray's internal 'quality of information specification' or 'perception, relevance and trust'.

The emergence of transparency as a key requirement in data privacy laws globally is an example of the importance of this dimension in the context of ethical information management. However, the changes to vehicle engine-testing standards being developed in response to the Volkswagen emissions scandal, along with the sanctions taken against the company and individual managers, also highlights the importance of this as a measurable ethical-quality dimension.

Activities with a low verity/non-deceptiveness score could be labelled corrupt/misleading, which raises issues in the context of the justice/fairness dimension.

Autonomy

Autonomy involves respect for people's self-determination. In the context of dimensions of ethical information management, autonomy is the measure of the extent to which the outcome of your process respects or infringes on people's self-determination or ability to choose an action for themselves.

This measure is influenced by the extent to which people are able to make their wishes known in relation to the processing, whether the design of a system or process is transparent in allowing choice or whether it suppresses true, informed choice. An information imbalance where an individual 'agrees' to something they are not aware of agreeing to does not represent a true choice, which constrains their autonomy and could also be considered a defect in the context of the verity/non-deceptiveness dimension. Likewise, obfuscation through information overload – that makes it harder for people to understand their choices – also can constrain autonomy.

In the broader context, processing that removes the potential for choice from an individual by, for example, not making information about a product, service or other benefit available to them based on the processing of data about them, or which results in constrained choices for that person in the exercise of other rights or freedoms, would also be processing that would impact on autonomy.

This characteristic is incredibly important to consider in creating clear, transparent communication to inform people's decision making and allow them to understand the choices they make, or are made on their behalf, through your processing of information.

Privacy/non-invasiveness

Privacy/non-invasiveness is a measure of the level of intrusion in to the personal life, relationships, correspondence or communications of the individual or a group of individuals as a result of the processing activity or the information outcome or process outcome that is delivered. It is not a measure of compliance with privacy laws, although this may be a factor you might consider in an analysis. One aspect of privacy/non-invasiveness is the level of autonomy or choice that an individual can exercise over the processing of data about them.

For example, the analysis of the metadata of your communications on private chat applications and your public communications on social media may reveal a significant amount about you, your personality, or other aspects of your identity such as sexual orientation. While this might have utility, and may have beneficence, it may still be highly intrusive.

Privacy/non-invasiveness may be a singular dimension at a macro level of analysis, but as you dig deeper into understanding the root causes and underlying ethical issues in the processing of information in the organization you may want to focus your assessments by considering necessity and proportionality of processing of personal data.

Necessity

Necessity is a measure of the extent to which the proposed processing is addressing an issue that, if left unaddressed, may result in harm to or have some other detrimental effect on society or a section of society. This is based on the analysis of the collective body of the EU's Data Privacy Regulators, the Article 29 Working Party, which has been reconstituted since the end of May 2018 as the European Data Protection Board (Article 29 Working Party, 2014).

It is also a measure of the extent to which specific processing is necessary to achieve a stated information or process outcome. In this context it is a corollary of McGilvray's 'Transactability' dimension of data quality. Rather than considering the degree to which the data will produce the desired outcome, 'Necessity' considers whether the desired outcome requires the processing of the information at all.

Proportionality

Proportionality is best defined in this context as a measure of the degree to which the interference in privacy, and the potential infringement or curtailment of other rights, caused by the measure is counterbalanced by the benefit to society or a section of society arising from the objective being pursued.

A key ethical test is to determine if the same objective could be achieved with a more limited impact on individuals and their autonomy.

Impact on human rights and freedoms

Ethical data use will uphold or protect the human rights of individuals, based on Kant's declaration that we should treat people as an ends in and of themselves, not just a means to an end.

This dimension is a measure of the degree to which the proposed processing upholds or protects rights, or curtails or constrains them. There will, inevitably, be balances to be identified between competing rights, and between the competing rights of different stakeholders.

Among the rights to consider in this context is the right to human dignity. The extent to which your management of information contributes to the upholding of this right is, arguably, a fundamental ethical question and a critical quality metric. After all, as Kaoru Ishikawa told us earlier in this chapter: in management, the first concern of the company is the happiness of people who are connected with it. If the people do not feel happy and cannot be made happy, that company does not deserve to exist (Ishikawa, 1985).

We propose these quality characteristics for ethical information management as a starting point for discussion and revision. The corresponding definitions, concepts and principles are long debated, but may still be acted upon. The underpinning principles and concepts are complex, as are humans and their actions and decisions, and the contexts in which people act. There will, inevitably, be overlaps and interconnectedness between the different dimensions. You will probably have noticed that not only do many of these characteristics have multiple layers of definition at different levels but they may be interrelated with each other.

But having a defined set of dimensions of quality in ethical information management, much like a 10-step framework for assessing impacts, provides an essential starting point for discussions. To decide what metrics you can look at, you will need to agree on and communicate a useful definition for context, but you will also need to remember that human problems and solutions are much more complex than mechanical errors or software bugs.

From a quality-control perspective, you must remember that you will not be able to capture all aspects in your metrics. As Deming cautioned, you need to stop managing by the visible numbers and metrics in the organization and study the root causes of ethical issues in your organization's processing of information. Based on that learning, you will then need to align the business, information, and technology strategies and governance of the organization to ensure the right information and process outcomes are delivered consistently.

Chapter summary

In this chapter we introduced the concept of information ethics as a quality system.
   We:

- Examined the concept of information ethics as an information quality system.
- Identified the role of normative business ethics in the delivery of quality or quality outcomes.
- Explored a methodology for information quality assessment.
- Explored the parallels between information quality management and ethical information management.
- Identified how information quality management principles and techniques can be applied to support ethical information management objectives.
- Related ethics and information ethics concepts to the work of W Edwards Deming.
- Mapped an information ethics assessment and improvement approach to a proven information quality management methodology.
- Applied the theory of quality management practices to current real-world scenarios to diagnose the root cause of issues such as 'fake news'.
- The key takeaway from this chapter is that once you begin to consider stakeholders in the definition of your ethical framework for the organization, you very quickly find that quality management principles and practices can be applied to help develop, communicate, measure and manage many aspects of your ethical enterprise information management initiatives.

Questions

1 What does it mean to consider information ethics as a quality systems problem?

2 We are adopting new technologies and technology-driven business models at a rapid pace. What other lessons can we learn from manufacturing

quality and other quality management practices to help avoid ethical cul-de-sacs in new technologies?

3 What proxy metrics for ethical information management behaviours can you identify in your organization?

Note

1 For the purposes of this book we use the terms 'information quality' and 'data quality' synonymously. There are technical and semantic differences between the concepts of information and data and their quality characteristics. Suffice it to say that information is data in a context that allows it to be used to make or inform decisions.

Further reading

Beckford, J (2002) *Quality: A Critical Introduction*, 2nd edn, Routledge, London

Deming, WE and Orsini, JN (2013) *The Essential Deming: Leadership principles from the father of quality management*, McGraw-Hill, New York

Halis, M, Akova, O and Tagraf, H (2007) The relationship between ethics and quality: conflicts and common ground, *Serbian Journal of Management*, 2 (2), pp 127–45

Ishikawa, K (1985) *What Is Total Quality Control? The Japanese Way*, Prentice-Hall, New Jersey

Redman, TC (2000) *Data Quality: A Field Guide*, Digital Press, Boston

Walton, M (1988) *The Deming Management Method*, Perigee, New York

References

Article 29 Working Party, 2014 [accessed 25 October 2017] Opinion 01/2014 On the Application of Necessity and Proportionality Concepts and Data Protection Within the Law Enforcement Sector [Online] http://ec.europa.eu/justice/data-protection/article-29/documentation/opinion-recommendation/files/2014/wp211_en.pdf

Beckford, J (2002) *Quality: A Critical Introduction*, 2nd edn, Routledge, London

Cannarella, J and Spechler, JA (2014) [accessed 30 September 2017] Epidemiological Modeling of Online Social Network Dynamics [Online] https://arxiv.org/pdf/1401.4208v1.pdf

DAMA International (2017) *DAMA DM-BOK: Data Management Body of Knowledge*, 2nd edn, Technics Publications, New Jersey

Deming, WE (1986) *Out of the Crisis*, Cambridge University Press, Boston

Deming, WE (1994) *The New Economics*, 2nd edn, MIT Press, Cambridge MA

English, LP (1999) *Improving Data Warehouse and Business Information Quality*, Wiley, New York

Glenday, J (2017) [accessed 24 October 2017] Facebook Signals End To News Feed Reach For Non-Promoted Posts [Online] http://www.thedrum.com/news/2017/10/24/facebook-signals-end-news-feed-reach-non-promoted-posts

Griffith, E (2016) [accessed 30 September 2017] Facebook Users Are Sharing Fewer Personal Updates and It's a Big Problem [Online] http://fortune.com/2016/04/07/facebook-sharing-decline/

Haque, U (2016) [accessed 30 September 2017] The Reason Twitter's Losing Active Users [Online] https://hbr.org/2016/02/the-reason-twitters-losing-active-users

Hern, A (2017) [accessed 23 October 2017] Facebook Moving Non-Promoted Posts Out of News Feed in Trial [Online] https://www.theguardian.com/technology/2017/oct/23/facebook-non-promoted-posts-news-feed-new-trial-publishers

Hutcheson, F (1726) *An Inquiry into the Original of Our Ideas of Beauty and Virtue*, Dublin

Ingram, M (2017) [accessed 10 October 2017] Facebook and Google Need to Be Regulated, Says British News Industry [Online] http://fortune.com/2017/03/09/facebook-google-regulated/

Ishikawa, K (1985) *What is Total Quality Control? The Japanese Way*, Prentice-Hall, New Jersey

Kantrowitz, A (2016) [accessed 1 October 2017] How the 2016 Election Blew Up in Facebook's Face [Online] https://www.buzzfeed.com/alexkantrowitz/2016-election-blew-up-in-facebooks-face

Madrigal, A (2017) [accessed 24 October 2017] When the Facebook Traffic Goes Away [Online] https://www.theatlantic.com/technology/archive/2017/10/when-the-facebook-traffic-goes-away/543828/

McGilvray, D (2008) *Executing Data Quality Projects: Ten steps to quality data and trusted information*, Morgan Kauffman, Boston

Moen, RD and Norman, CL (2010) Circling back: clearing up myths about the Deming Cycle and seeing how it keeps evolving, *Quality Progress*, November, pp 22–28

Pace, LA (1999) [accessed 15 October 2017] The Ethical Implications of Quality, *Electronic Journal of Business Ethics and Organization Studies,* **4** (1) [Online] https://jyx.jyu.fi/dspace/handle/123456789/25323

Redman, DTC (2008) *Data Driven: Profiting from your most important business asset*, Harvard Business Review, Boston

Reijers, W et al (2016) [accessed 15 October 2017] A Common Framework for Ethical Impact Assessment [Online] http://satoriproject.eu/media/D4.1_Annex_1_EIA_Proposal.pdf

SATORI, n.d. [accessed 30 September 2017] Section 4: Ethics Assessment Procedures [Online] http://satoriproject.eu/framework/section-4-ethics-assessment-procedures/

Stimson, WA (2005) A Deming inspired management code of ethics, *Quality Progress*, February

Wagner, K (2017) [accessed 30 June 2017] Facebook Found a New Way to Identify Spam and False News Articles in Your News Feed [Online] https://www.recode.net/2017/6/30/15896544/facebook-fake-news-feed-algorithm-update-spam

Warzel, C (2017) [accessed 30 October 2017] How People Inside Facebook Are Reacting to the Company's Election Crisis [Online] https://www.buzzfeed.com/charliewarzel/how-people-inside-facebook-are-reacting-to-the-companys

Information ethics and data governance

09

What will we cover in this chapter?

In this chapter we explore in more detail the relationship between information ethics and data governance. By the end of this chapter you will:

- Understand the role of data governance in the E2IM framework.
- Understand how data governance supports ethics, with reference to the 'fake news' scandals that have plagued social media.
- Be able to explain models of data governance with reference to classic forms of governance in other spheres.
- Be able to explain how the model of governance adopted can affect ethical decisions and outcomes.
- Be able to explain how the ethic of the individual is supported in the E2IM framework by effective, principles-led data governance.
- Be able to explain information stewardship as an ethical concept in the context of a principles-based data governance framework.
- Understand the relationship between maturity of data governance practices and the maturity of your information ethics.

Introduction

In Chapter 5 we introduced some background concepts of data governance in our discussion of fundamental data management disciplines in the context of the DAMA DMBOK. In this chapter you will get a more detailed insight into how effective data governance structures in your organization enable, and are enabled by, effective information ethics practices. At the heart of this interaction is the fact that core principles for the handling of information form the bedrock of effective data governance. Without clearly defined principles for what constitutes acceptable or unacceptable practices in the handling of information in the organization, and without appropriate controls and oversight frameworks to ensure the right things are being done, it is inevitable that ethical issues and associated legal liabilities will arise for organizations.

Effective data governance spans the strategic and structural layers of the strategic information model the E2IM framework builds from. It must include business strategy and governance, business planning, technology strategy and governance, and technology architecture and planning. Above all, it must focus on the appropriate governance of the information assets of the organization, to ensure that the required information and process outcomes are consistently delivered, which is something we measure through the quality systems approaches to information management discussed in Chapter 8. Figure 9.1 highlights how data governance spans the strategic and structural/tactical levels of the E2IM framework and encompasses elements of business strategy, information strategy, technology strategy, and the design of the operational structures that support the execution of these strategies.

How data governance supports ethics

As we discussed in the introductory chapter to this book, the innovator's dilemma in information management often arises in contexts where codified laws or standards do not yet exist. In these contexts, one of the key functions of an effective data governance framework is the codification of the rules about 'how to decide how to decide' (The Data Governance Institute, n.d.). While this is important even in the context of scenarios where there are regulatory requirements or guidelines in place, when the organization is 'boldly going where no one has gone before' it becomes even more important to have predefined methods and practices for making critical data decisions and documenting the organization's rationale for those decisions.

An ethically based framework for data governance decisions, particularly in scenarios where codified standards or laws lag behind the technological capabilities available, supports a wider ethics-based approach to information management as it enables and coordinates the definition and communication of ethical values in setting and enforcing data-related policies, standards and

Figure 9.1 Data governance in the E2IM framework

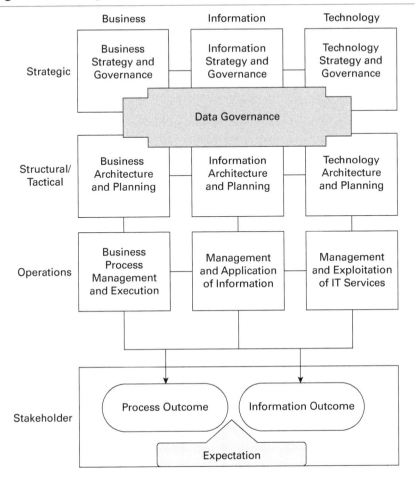

processes. It will ensure a clear escalation and remediation path to raise any ethical issues regarding data access, quality, ownership, standards, security, usage and management.

A well-defined data governance framework interacts with civil or criminal governance functions of external regulators or enforcement agencies in the context of regulatory compliance. It helps to maintain the organization's ability to meet compliance standards set by external regulatory bodies by supporting a proactive approach to risk identification and mitigation. This is particularly important when the organization is operating in an area that is applying information technology or data-processing capabilities in a novel way, or where the proposed technology or processing represents a significant change in the state of the art. An ethically aligned approach to data governance ensures an ethical alignment of all the other data management disciplines that may be brought to bear in any project or process. It ensures that there is evidence of debate while defining the processing activity. Furthermore, it creates an environment in which ethical issues can be identified in a timely manner and escalated for decision and resolution.

If we consider the Facebook example in Chapter 8, a clear data governance and stewardship failing arose in the context of 'fake news' when a Facebook engineer identified something unusual in the data, a preponderance of extreme content aggregators and publishers in the top 25 sources of shared content (Warzel, 2017). Warzel reports that the engineer in question raised the issue in an internal discussion forum. The response to the issue was a discussion that 'was brief – and uneventful'. In Warzel's article a red flag for governance issues stands out as he reports that the engineer in question described the response they received as being 'a general sense of "Yeah, this is pretty crazy, but what do you want us to do about it?"'

This would suggest a lack of appropriate, and appropriately formalized, systems of governance over information that might have helped Facebook get ahead of the ethical issues raised by 'fake news' and the filter bubble. It would seem there was no agreed-upon models of how to decide what to decide, and no defined principles against which an issue like this could be assessed and prioritized. Tellingly, there seems to have been no formal escalation path to raise the issue and track it to a resolution.

It is not entirely one-way traffic between governance and ethics. A strong ethical culture supports and enables effective data governance in organizations in several key areas. Ultimately, governance of any kind includes a strong ethics component. This manifests in the style and method of governance, and the ethos applied to communicating and promoting governance in the organization. This ethic of the organization is an essential part of effective data governance, and part of that ethic may be the need to formally recognize that information is something that needs to be governed. It also manifests itself in how the organization handles conflicts of ethical values and priorities between the ethic of the organization and the ethic of society – as well as between the ethic of the individual in the organization, in how they execute their duties and tasks for handling data.

Principles and modes of governance

One of the fundamental principles of governance, whether data governance, organization governance or governance in general, is that you are always doing some form of governance and it is a *conscious choice* for you and your organization to make as to what mode of governance you apply. There tend to be four distinct approaches to governance in organizations, and society in general. These are set out in Table 9.1.

For example, we have worked with organizations who embraced the philosophies of Agile development or Agile management. The executive teams in these organizations usually espoused a belief that they were not doing governance. However, they had taken a conscious choice to apply a specific mode of governance in their projects (in this case Democracy as all stakeholders had a say in the Backlog prioritization exercises). If you have ever run a Scrum session or managed a Kanban board in an Agile development project you will know that there can be a *lot* of operational governance in using Agile methods (if you are doing them right).

From an information ethics perspective, each of these generic modes of governance can have strengths and weaknesses (see Table 9.2).

Another key principle of governance is that the motivation for why data governance is being introduced in your organization must be clearly

Table 9.1 General modes of governance

Governance Mode	General Description
Anarchy	Individual process owners or end users have decision rights and there are no formal mechanisms for exercising decision rights, with decisions made locally on an ad hoc basis (Weill and Woodham, 2002)
Dictatorship/Feudal	Single decision maker at the most senior level in the organization or business unit. The dictator/monarch may delegate decision rights to direct reports. (Often results in people working around the dictator.)
Oligarchy/Federal	Governance rights are shared by a combination of senior executives across the organization in a leadership forum. Decision rights are federated out based on defined and agreed models such as service level agreements (SLAs) (based on Weill and Woodham, 2002)
Democracy	Direct engagement with frontline staff and/or external stakeholders. In a traditional 'government' model, it is the importance of the voice of the citizen being recognized in the execution of governance decisions. In an information management context, it reflects the need to consider the 'voice of the customer' in critical decisions

Table 9.2 Modes of governance with ethics considerations

Governance Mode	Potential Strengths (from Ethics Perspective)	Potential Weaknesses (from Ethics Perspective)
Anarchy	• Potential for faster response to front-line issues	• Inconsistent approaches • Decisions taken by individuals who may not be fully aware of all facts/implications • Potentially more likely to be prone to individual bias
Dictatorship/Feudal	• Clear articulation of single vision of ethics and values • Clear escalation point for issues	• Potentially prone to individual bias. • May lead to a 'groupthink' risk where strong personality dominates ethical discussion
Oligarchy/Federal	• Collaborative leadership model • Supports cross-organization alignment	• May lead to slower decisions • Groupthink may still be an issue
Democracy	• Open and engaged • Inclusive of disparate opinions	• Minority opinions may be drowned out • Will lead to slower decision-making processes

communicated. This choice taken in this context sets the 'tone at the top' within which governance decisions and risk assessments will be taken. We discussed the importance of 'tone at the top' back in Chapter 3 and it has recurred as a theme in Chapter 6. This 'tone at the top' needs to find its expression in guiding principles that can be readily cascaded and communicated throughout the organization.

The DAMA DMBOK (DAMA International, 2017: 76) tells us that 'guiding principles are the foundation of DG policy'. Of course, it is not enough to declare your organization's mission is 'Don't be Evil'; clearly articulated precepts of what 'Evil' is and how it might best be avoided are essential to avoid falling afoul of ethical issues in information management (Wikipedia, 2017). Likewise, in the context of an organizational 'tone at the top' that demands that staff 'move fast and break things', or that emphasizes the stability of the technical infrastructure (the 'Technology' vertical in the E2IM framework model in

Figure 9.1), should we be surprised when the organization struggles to consistently apply or meet ethical standards in how it governs data (Murphy, 2014)?

Data governance consultant John Ladley has described the importance of principles in data governance as follows (Ladley, 2012): 'Principles are statements of philosophy. Think of them as a bill of rights – core beliefs that form the anchor for all policies and behaviours around information asset management (IAM). They are beliefs to be applied every day as guidance for procedures and decision-making efforts.'

While organizations can begin to develop policy-absent formal principles, data governance initiatives that are not grounded on articulated statements of information philosophy invariably end up being very narrowly focused and reactive, which leads to challenges in sustaining the governance disciplines. This is compounded further when the 'tone at the top' decides to declare 'mission accomplished' on a data governance initiative. Data governance initiatives that are underpinned by a clear set of principles are more likely to achieve sustainable change.

Defining principles

The DAMA DMBOK defines a number of principles for data governance. Some of these are directly applicable to the discussion of information ethics. Their application is constrained somewhat by their focus on the financial perspective of information governance such as data valuation. However, they can be mapped to the requirements of an information ethics initiative and provide a starting point for the development of ethical principles. Yet we should not forget that fundamental ethical principles themselves can be restated as data management principles, and that governance principles need to be underpinned by a guiding business strategy or philosophy.

This means that in defining your principles for ethical information governance you will need to consider what normative theory of business ethics your organization is aspiring to and what business objectives you are seeking to support in an ethically appropriate manner. This is an essential aspect of ensuring an alignment of your 'tone at the top' with the 'action in the middle' to ensure you consistently deliver the right 'outcomes on the ground'. This process will require sincere engagement from senior management to be effective and it is important, in Ladley's words, 'to spend time with the implications and ramifications of the principles' as you will need to be able to explain the rationale and understand the implications of that rationale for the policies and procedures that will flow from your principles. Table 9.3 sets out some principles drawn from the DAMA DMBOK and explores their ethical perspective.

Table 9.3 DMBOK data governance principles through ethics lens

Generic DG Principle	Description	Ethical Perspective
Accountability Principle	An organization must identify individuals who are ultimately accountable for data and content of all types.	Accountability is a function of the consequentialist ethical principle. If the required standards are not met, there must be mechanisms for holding the organization and leadership to account. This is an explicit principle in the EU's GDPR (Data Privacy) legislation.
Asset Principle	Data and content of all types are assets and have characteristics of other assets. They should be managed, secured and accounted for as other material or financial assets.	From an ethical perspective, it is important to know where the data you are processing is stored, how it is managed and how it is secured.
Due Diligence Principle	If a risk is known, it must be reported. If a risk is possible, it must be confirmed. Data risks include risks related to poor data management practices.	Ethically, this is the principle of avoiding maleficence in the processing or management of information.
Going Concern Principle	Data and content are critical to successful, ongoing business operations and management (ie they are not viewed as temporary means to achieve results or merely as a business by-product).	Ethically, this principle comes close to the Kantian formulation of 'Treat people as ends in themselves', but falls short. However, the emphasis on 'going concern' implies a longer-term planning and governance window, potentially aligning with stakeholder theory model of ethics.
Liability Principle	There is a financial liability connected to data or content based on regulatory and ethical misuse or mismanagement.	This is a consequentialist restatement of the accountability principle. However, it expresses the consequence from the perspective of the organization only.
Quality Principle	The meaning, accuracy and life cycle of data and content can affect the financial status of the organization.	Again, the ethical component that is missing is the motivation other than financial impact to the organization.
Risk Principle	There is risk associated with data and content. This risk must be formally recognized, either as a liability or through incurring costs to manage and reduce the inherent risk.	This is a utilitarian/consequentialist ethical principle at work. We have a thing that creates risk, therefore we need to formally manage that risk and mitigate it (or accept consequences).

SOURCE adapted from DAMA DMBOK

In addition to these generally applicable principles for data governance programmes, Robert Seiner, another independent data governance consultant, highlights four other core principles (shown in Table 9.4) that should be considered when developing a data governance initiative (Seiner, 2014).

Robert Seiner tells us that 'the simpler we stay with our concepts around data governance, the easier it is for people in our organizations to understand what data governance is all about' (Seiner, 2014). This is true. But a review of the example principles outlined above reveals precious little about the ethical principles that the organization applies to the processing and management of information. These kinds of principles are needed, in conjunction with the many other excellent principles for information management, to provide a properly rounded and holistic statement of principles for the ethical governance of information in the organization.

What might these additional ethical principles be? On one hand, organizations might choose to translate some of the core ethical principles that we

Table 9.4 Core data governance principles (Seiner)

Principle	Description	Ethical Perspective
Recognize data as a valued and strategic asset	The organization must shift perspective from 'my data' to 'our data'	From ethical perspective, this principle would need to articulate the value of outcomes arising from the processing or use of data
Assign clearly defined accountability	The organization must define data governance as everyone's responsibility	This is an articulation of a consequentialist frame for ethics and is a restatement of the accountability principle outlined above
Manage data to follow internal and external rules and regulations	Data must be governed to avoid risk and compliance issues	This is essentially a statement of a shareholder theory minimalist approach to ethics that risks setting the bar low for ethics
Consistently define and manage data quality across the data life cycle	Right first time, every time	This quality systems principle could be supportive of information ethics if 'right first time' was defined with reference to the dimensions of ethical information quality defined in this book

SOURCE adapted from Seiner

have discussed in earlier chapters into their own body of principles. This is a good starting point, but increasingly the approaches that organizations take to managing and governing the ethical implications of how they manage data are a source of competitive advantage in the market. As such, your ethical principles for information management should be aligned with the core brand values of your organization.

CASE STUDY   Ethical principles driving data decisions at Lego

Lego is a good example of how ethical principles have informed their strategies, practices and processes for how they handle the data of their most valued customers – the 50 million children who play in their online universes (Hasselbach and Tranberg, 2016).

Lego has determined that the children who use their platform are the ends that their platform serves, supporting their creativity and enabling communication in a safe and secure manner. According to Hasselbach and Tranberg, Lego opted not to use social media connect buttons – despite many children already being on social media platforms – because they could not get assurances as to what data would be gathered from their sites.

In this way, Lego affirmed an information-centric variation on an existing core principle of corporate responsibility in the organization – that they are accountable for the social and environmental behaviour of their physical suppliers.

Another key ethical principle Lego has applied is that they want to remain in control of what happens to the data about their customers. As a result of this, Lego hosts all its data in Denmark (except for data that must be stored in Russia for compliance with Russian data localization laws); they don't use free third-party analytics tools; they encourage children to use pseudonyms to protect their identities; and they comply with age verification and parental consent rules under COPPA and the GDPR.

In the context of the E2IM model, this also shows that Lego has taken the time to identify and define who their stakeholders are. While parents might be the purchasers of Lego kits, the ultimate customer is the child (or child-at-heart) who plays with the Lego kits and interacts with the Lego online universes.

Case study questions

1 How might the ethical principles underpinning Lego's information strategy in this context be expressed?

2 What situational modifiers might arise in Lego to discourage the use of technologies that track identifiable users of their universe?

3 How does the E2IM model help explain the relationship between Lego's business ethics and strategy, their information ethics and strategy, and the implementation of specific technology services and functionality in their online environments?

CASE STUDY Ethical information governance at Apple

Apple also have well-defined ethical principles for information management. Speaking at the CPDP conference in Brussels in early 2017, Jane Horvath, Senior Director of Global Privacy at Apple, outlined some of the core principles they apply in the development of their products and services. You can watch a video of her presentation online at: https://www.youtube.com/watch?v=nK_T6KLc6l0.

The ethical principles espoused by Apple include:

- Right and wrong is determined from the perspective of their customers.

- Technology should enable individuals to control their data.

- Data is processed on devices.

- Where server-side responses are required, the data is collected with an identifier that is not tied to any other identifier.

- Data is the customer's, not Apple's.

- Privacy is strategically and deliberately designed into products.

These principles are key cornerstones that Apple has developed their product strategy around, avoiding the rush to monetize their customer's data directly but instead seeking to develop capabilities in their devices that allow advanced functionality to be deployed with minimal server-side processing of data that would identify an individual user of an Apple device or service.

Mapping them to the E2IM model, you can see a very strong alignment of principles. Apple defines 'ethical' from the perspective of their customer, just as the E2IM framework requires organizations to consider the ethical expectations of their customers in the context of the information and process outcomes that are delivered. It also influences the architectural choices that Apple make in the design of their services. Data that is gathered has to be processed on the device rather than being processed in Apple's data centres at an individual or identifiable level. Data that has to be processed on the server-side has a pseudonymous identifier associated with it. These are conscious design choices that inevitably reduce the granularity of data that Apple gathers about its customers.

By having a clearly articulated set of ethical principles for information, Apple is able to implement appropriate governance and controls to ensure that the information and process outcomes experienced by their customers meet their ethical expectations.

Case study questions

1 What might Apple be losing by adopting these kind of ethical information principles?

2 What differences do you see between the approach Apple is adopting and the approaches adopted by Facebook or Google or other companies in the information industry?

3 What ethical framework (reference Chapter 1 and Chapter 2) best describes Apple's approach?

Looking at these two case studies, and considering the various ethical frameworks we discussed in earlier chapters, we can start to formulate some candidate ethical principles for data governance (Table 9.5). Note that these are candidate principles. You will need to define and develop principles that are appropriate to your organization. Ideally, you should align these information ethics principles with existing statements of business ethics and business values in the organization.

A key point about these principles when you define them for your own organization is they must be simple for people to understand, and the rationale, benefits and implications of the principles must be communicable and must be capable of being translated into policies, procedures and governance controls. This hierarchy of governance is an important concept, particularly in the context of ethical information management. It is through this cascading of values that your organization brings the ethic of society and the ethic of the organization into alignment.

Ultimately, the more understandable the core ethical principles that are applied to your organization's information management practices are, the more likely it is that individuals will interpret and apply policies and procedures correctly. Equally importantly, where there is a gap in the defined

Table 9.5 Example ethical principles for data governance

Ethical Principle	Description
People are an end in and of themselves, not a means to an end	The processing of data about people in the organization is done in a way that respects them and their privacy
The arbiter of our ethics is the customer, through the outcomes they experience	The information and process outcomes that our stakeholders experience, and the degree to which those experiences match expectations, is the benchmark for our ethical standards
The customer owns their data. We use it on trust	Data that is obtained from or about our customers is their data. We use it on trust and must ensure we are transparent and truthful about what we will do with that information
The only mode of expression for ethics is action	It is not enough to talk about information ethics, we must design our information handling processes in an ethical manner, and design ethics in
The processing of data should be designed to serve mankind	We need to design our processes for acquiring, analysing and using data in a way that serves mankind, delivering utility, equality and supporting dignity, while avoiding unnecessary invasion of privacy or infringement of other fundamental rights
First, do no harm	When engaging in any processing of information, we must aim to avoid information or process outcomes that cause harm or loss to people
Accountability follows the data life cycle	Everyone in the organization is accountable for how they obtain and use data, and have an obligation to ensure the effective stewardship of information to ensure the appropriate information and process outcomes are consistently delivered

policies and procedures, clearly defined ethical principles should encourage and support individuals to make appropriate choices to deliver 'fit for purpose' information and process outcomes (Figure 9.2).

Figure 9.2 The hierarchy of principles to outcomes

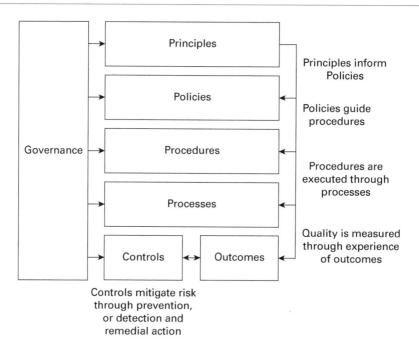

Information stewardship and the ethic of the individual

One of the ethical principles we identified in the last part of this chapter was the principle of accountability throughout the life cycle of the information. We expressed this accountability in the terms of stewardship, which is a term we encountered first back in Chapter 5 where we introduced the DAMA DMBOK and some of its core management disciplines. In the context of ethical information management, effective information stewardship in the context of a formally defined and designed information governance framework is essential.

To recap, information stewardship is usually defined along these lines: 'An approach to information/data governance that formalizes accountability for managing information resources on behalf of others and for the best interests of the organization' (McGilvray, 2008).

From an information ethics perspective, though, you need to consider expanding this definition. As it is defined usually, information stewardship is strongly linked to the ethic of the organization as it focuses on the 'best interests of the organization' and does not explicitly consider the interests of those who are outside the organization, the stakeholders in wider society.

As such, the current definitions of information stewardship risk falling into a shareholder theory normative model of ethics. However, this is actually not consistent with the fundamental concept of stewardship, which is generally recognized as 'the acceptance or assignment of responsibility to shepherd and safeguard the valuables of others' (Wikipedia, 2017). We might also want to consider the definition of stewardship in ISO20121:2012, the standard for environmentally sustainable event management, which defines the concept as the 'responsibility for sustainable development shared by all those whose actions affect environmental performance, economic activity and social progress, reflected as both a value and a practice by individuals, organizations, communities and competent authorities' (International Organization for Standardization, 2012).

From an ethical perspective, this definition of stewardship creates a broader set of principles and values and also reflects a broader perspective on who the stakeholders are in the information and process outcomes you are trying to deliver through your management and processing of information. It also highlights the importance of the *practice* of stewardship. In this context, we would define ethical information stewardship as follows:

> Ethical information stewardship is an approach to information/data governance that formalizes responsibility and accountability for sustainable information management shared by all those whose actions affect the information and process outcomes experienced by stakeholders, inside the organization and in wider society, expressed as both a value and a practice by individuals, organization communities and competent authorities.

This definition of information stewardship from an ethical perspective reflects a number of key aspects of ethics and governance. Among these is the idea of *sustainable* information management. By this we mean that the processing and management of information is sustainable from both the perspective of the organization and other stakeholders. This is consistent with a stakeholder theory normative ethical framework. Furthermore, the definition incorporates a reference to the 'sole medium of expression' for ethics – action.

The definition above also highlights the various data governance structures that organizations tend to put in place. The DAMA DMBOK (DAMA International, 2017) identifies the generic structures listed below. Your organization may choose to call them by different names, and not all levels are implemented in every organization. We have also expanded on the DAMA definitions slightly for this text. Figure 5.2 illustrates these concepts and how they relate in the context of the DMBOK view of data governance:

- **Data Governance Steering Committee:** the primary and highest authority organization for data governance in your organization. Operating as a cross-functional group of senior executives, it is responsible for oversight, support and funding of data governance activities. Consists of a cross-functional group of executives. They may be aligned with other top-level steering committees in the organization such as risk or audit committees. They are the competent authority for final decisions on information/data management policies, strategies, principles and definitions.

- **Data Governance Council:** an executive-level line-of-business-level co-ordinating council responsible for managing and overseeing the execution of data governance initiatives and acting as a first level of escalation for issues. They are the competent authority for second-line escalation of data governance issues in the organization.

- **Data Governance Office:** responsible for day-to-day management and co-ordination of data standards and definitions across the organization and across all data management disciplines in the organization. Consists of co-ordinating roles such as data stewards or data owners. They are the competent authority for the co-ordination and management of definitions and standards in the organization.

- **Data Stewardship Teams:** communities of interest focused on one or more specific subject areas or projects. They consist of business and technical data stewards and collaborate on defining data definitions and standards in the organization. They are also the 'eyes and ears' of the data governance function. Data stewardship teams are an organization community addressing data issues. They are sometimes referred to as 'communities of practice' or 'stewardship forums'.

These governance structures serve to support different levels of information/data stewardship in the organization. These structures are, in effect, the lines that link the different boxes in the E2IM framework. They are the formal, and semi-formal, lines of communication that ensure alignment between business, information and technology verticals in the organization, and ensure alignment across the different levels in the organization.

As you learnt in Chapter 5, there are different data stewardship roles that can be defined at the different operating levels of the organization (see Figure 9.3). It is important, particularly in the context of transversal issues such as ethics, that you avoid defining stewardship roles rigidly based on the concepts of 'business' or 'IT' stewards. The people performing these roles do so due to their relationship with data and information in the organization.

Figure 9.3   The Castlebridge 3DC stewardship model

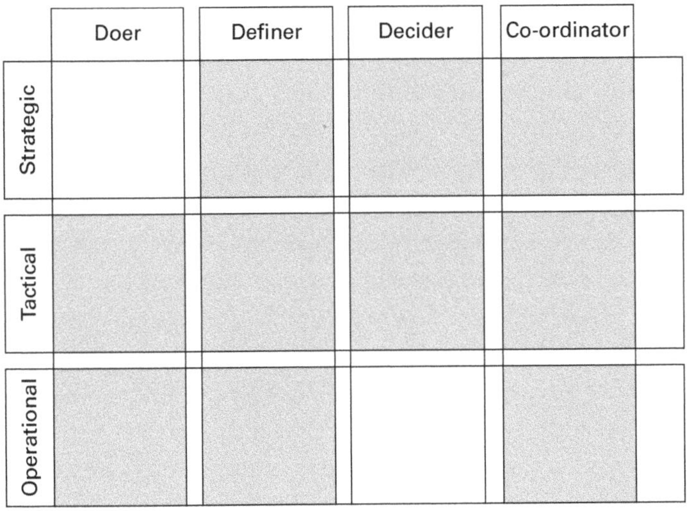

	Doer	Definer	Decider	Co-ordinator
Strategic				
Tactical				
Operational				

Ideally, they are 'self-selecting' and the structures you implement in your data governance framework will recognize their efforts and enable them to be more successful and to contribute more. Even where they are appointed, the structures that are put in place for data governance in your organization should work to support effective alignment around common standards, both in the context of technical standards and definitions but also in the context of ethical standards and values in the organization. The E2IM model we introduced in Chapter 7 (see Figure 7.4) illustrates the alignment challenge that needs to be addressed and provides a basis for establishing the various roles and responsibilities that need to be filled, and establishes a basis for alignment of the ethic of the organization with the ethic of society in the context of information management.

This brings us to an important point. As with many things in life and business, ethical information management, and the associated data governance activities, are ultimately about ensuring alignment of people towards a common vision, a common cause and a common way of working. How this is implemented, and how successful that implementation will be, is a factor of the ethic of the individual. The ethic of the individual represents the bundle of beliefs, perceptions and values that we each bring to the organization and constitutes the lens through which we view and interpret the ethic of the organization and the various policies, standards and guidance that might exist in relation to ensuring the consistent delivery of appropriate information and process outcomes. The disconnects and conflicting priorities that this can give rise to are issues that need to be managed through effective governance and a clear 'tone from the top'.

Steven Feldman (Feldman, 2007), a noted author in the field of business ethics, describes the 'split personality' problem that faces business managers: 'On one hand, they can develop a single-minded pursuit of profit that sometimes has difficulty even bridling itself at the boundaries of the law; on the other hand, business managers are socialized in communities where virtues of honesty, fairness and trustworthiness are held in high regard.'

The challenge in your organization is to define and communicate ethical values for information management that people can align with the ethic of the individual that they bring to work. Some of your colleagues may instinctively get the importance of ethical information management and may readily adopt and adapt to a stakeholder theory or social justice model of ethics. Others may default to a 'do the minimum necessary to tick a box and move on' approach that aligns more with a shareholder-theory normative model. You may find you have some hard-core utilitarian consequentialists in your organization. The opportunity that is presented through effective stewardship roles and supporting data governance structures in the organization is that formalized stewardship roles and responsibilities for the promotion of ethics and ethical principles can help support and sustain necessary changes in the ethic of the organization.

For example, Apple's stewardship around data privacy involves the engagement of data privacy experts within product development teams early in the design and development processes in the organization. This is a formal stewardship function as part of the ethic of the organization that serves to support, and is supported by, the ethics of the individual. However, in other organizations you will often see conflict between the ethic of the individual and the ethic of the organization, and even the ethic of society. This conflict needs to be managed through agreed-upon models for decision making. Handled well, conflicts of this kind can improve the alignment between the ethic of the organization and the ethic of society – after all, the individuals in your organization are also members of society. Handled badly, this may result in the development of groupthink in the organization, in which individual concerns are not given due consideration. In such cases, your organization may find itself facing whistleblowing, brand damage or other impacts.

The Facebook 'fake news' example discussed in Chapter 8 (Warzel, 2017) is a good example of where the ethic of the individual can run into problems with the ethic of the organization. In that case, an individual engineer identified something that looked unusual in the data about content sharing. This was raised through a discussion forum. But in the absence of agreed-upon models and methods for escalating issues like this (such as agreed models for root cause analysis and upwards reporting for guidance or action), the signal that there was a potential problem in the news feeds was missed. The ethic of the organization was driven by quantifiable numbers, but did not stretch to looking behind those numbers to perform a qualitative analysis – the 'Study' part of the Deming/Shewhart PDSA cycle we have discussed elsewhere.

This is consistent with research into organizational and individual ethical decision making, which highlights the importance of the dominant ethic of the organization when individuals are making ethical decisions (Elango et al, 2010). The researchers found (unsurprisingly) that 'managers come to ethical decision making with their own experiences and values, but they also are influenced by the ethical standards and practices they observe in the workplace' (Elango et al, 2010). This is something we would understand intuitively, but it is starkly laid out in the academic research. Other research in this area also highlights the importance of planned change in this context, including the importance of providing information and training (Sullivan, 2004). In Sullivan's research the statistical data indicated that accounting students' use of professional judgement increased after being given four hours of training on the relevant professional code of conduct, and demonstrates the positive impact that ethics instruction can have in the organization.

But, as to the question of why good people sometimes allow bad things to happen, the work of Linda Trevino (Trevino, 1986) provides a model to represent and explain this (see Figure 9.4). This model will also look very familiar in the context of an organizational model for data governance. Trevino presents an interactionist model for the relationship between the ethics of the individual and the ethical context of the organization, which work together to produce ethical or unethical behaviours.

In Trevino's model, ethical dilemmas are first filtered through the individual's own moral filters (the ethic of the individual). Trevino builds on the work of Kohlberg (Kohlberg and Kramer, 1969) in this area to identify three key stages of moral development:

- Preconventional – the individual is concerned with personal impacts to them, including punishment or rewards, and they tend to stick to rules for the sake of penalty avoidance. This mirrors closely at the individual level the ethos of shareholder theory that we see at the organizational level.

Figure 9.4 The ethic of the individual in E2IM

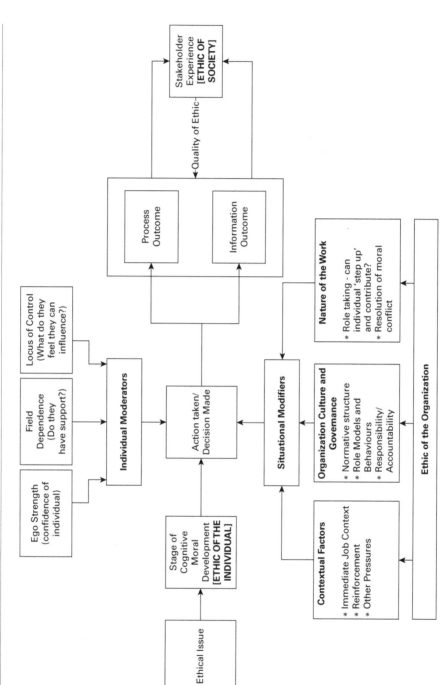

SOURCE adapted from Trevino's interactionalist model for ethical decision making in organizations

- Conventional – at this level the individual displays stereotypical 'good' behaviour and does what is expected of them by people close to them. At this stage, individuals seek to fulfil obligations they have entered into with others and to meet expectations. As individuals mature at this level, they increasingly focus on contributions to society or to the group. In many respects, this echoes stakeholder theory as a normative ethical model at the organization level.

- Principled – at this level the individual is focused on the 'social contract' and social justice and supporting individual rights. They are aware that different groups may hold different values and they seek to find balance where possible. At the most 'mature', the individual follows self-chosen ethical principles that guide their actions.

Trevino identifies a few other individual factors that will affect the ultimate outcome of an ethical decision. If the person has good impulse control and follows their convictions they will tend to make more consistent ethical decisions. If they are dependent on external referents and validation, they may be more likely to carry out an unethical act if asked to by a superior, or if they are unaware of or are shielded from consequences stemming from that act. Finally, the 'locus of control' that the person feels they have over events in their lives. People who have an internal locus of control believe their efforts deliver outcomes and take a great deal of personal responsibility for their actions. People with an external locus of control are less likely to take personal responsibility for the ethical outcomes of their actions.

In the context of the organizational influences, Trevino identified several factors that can influence the ethical development of individuals. Among these is the influence of 'role taking', the ability to be centrally involved in the communications and decision making of the group, especially when placed in democratic leadership roles. This sounds an awful lot like the co-ordinator role of a data steward, where the individual needs to exercise 'soft power' to guide and develop standards and practices in the organization. The organization culture around stewardship therefore is a key influencer of how individuals in the organization will evolve their ethical frameworks. Organization culture sets behavioural norms, and the collective norms about what is or is not appropriate behaviour will influence the actions of the individual. These norms not only guide the individual's decisions about what is 'right' in the context of the organization, but they also define who the individual (and by extension the organization) perceives as being responsible for remedying the issues.

Aligning Trevino's model with the E2IM framework, we establish that the ethic of the individual is a factor of their personal cognitive moral development. However, in an organizational context, even the most ethical person can suffer as a result of individual moderators that affect or impair their ability to act or decide in congruence with their personal moral code. For this to be counterbalanced, there needs to be effective situational modifiers that support ethical conduct through the ethic of the organization. These situational modifiers need to support individuals in acting ethically, and should clearly set out what 'ethical' is in the context of the organization. The interplay between the ethic of the individual and the ethic of the organization in the context of an action or a decision that is being taken about or with information results in a series of outcomes that the ethic of society then judges to be either acceptable or not.

Appropriate structures and frameworks are therefore needed, and must be *planned for* to ensure appropriate alignment of the ethic of the individual with the ethic of the organization, and ultimately with the ethic of society. Research (Schwarz, 1968; McLagan, 1983) has shown that an awareness of the consequences of actions on others, and an ascription of responsibility to oneself, are necessary conditions for the activation of the ethic of the individual in an organization context. Where the culture diffuses responsibility for actions or ethical outcomes to others, this can lead to people claiming they were 'acting under orders' or seeking some other entity to remedy the situation (such as Facebook staff looking to governments to regulate the 'fake news' issues).

In designing your information stewardship model for ethics, it is essential therefore that:

- Individuals are given a chance to engage and be involved in role taking as democratic leaders.

- Supports should be in place to give people a normative structure for discussing ethical issues in information management.

- Ethics should be made relevant and relatable to the immediate context of the individual's job.

- There should be clear mechanisms for consequences to be identified and understood, both in terms of consequences for the external stakeholders affected by actions, but also in the context of consequences within the overall governance structure of the organization.

Information ethics and the separation of duties

Another key aspect of effective data governance is the development of an effective separation of duties between oversight and execution in the context of information management processes. This is, in and of itself, an ethical value relating to the governance and execution of processes. According to the American Institute of Certified Public Accountants: 'The principle of SOD is based on shared responsibilities of a key process that disperses the critical functions of that process to more than one person or department' (AICPA, n.d.).

While generally considered an accounting concept, segregation of duties is also a prudent risk-management concept. In the context of information management, it means that no part of the organization should be defining what 'right' is in relation to the required information and process outcomes as well as being accountable for the management of data to achieve goals. We see this in action in the field of software quality, where it is not good practice to allow a developer to test their own code before production release. We also see it in the EU's General Data Protection Regulation, which explicitly requires that data protection officers are independent of influence in the performance of their oversight and monitoring tasks.

Ultimately, segregation of duties is a backstop control against the ethic of the individual to ensure that, at a minimum, people in the organization execute their functions in a way that helps avoid conflicts between different ethical perspectives. In the context of Trevino's model discussed earlier in this chapter, segregation of duties gives you a normative culture, a defined mechanism for addressing moral conflict, and a mechanism for ensuring awareness of consequences of actions. Therefore, when defining and developing your frameworks for ethical information governance it is important to consider how you would implement an equivalent separation of duties for ethical decisions about information management, as you would for the governance of the financial accounting or procurement functions of your organization.

Information ethics and risk perception

A key function of data governance is to ensure that information-related risks are managed appropriately. Risk is defined in ISO 31000 (ISO, 2009) as 'the effect of uncertainty on objectives'. Traditionally, organizations assess risk from the perspective of risk to the organization or the organization's objectives. This is a very strong cultural norm in most organizations and can form part of the ethic of the organization. However, this internal focus can constrain the perspective of the organization and may result in unethical decisions being taken.

In Chapter 3 and subsequent chapters we introduced the Volkswagen emissions scandal as a reference example. In this case, the organization sought to manage the risk of failing emissions tests by designing their engine management system so that it would pass the tests. From an internal perspective, the stated objective to pass emissions tests appears to have been interpreted as a requirement to pass the tests at all costs. However, the ethic of society was that people wanted to be able to rely on the data provided regarding vehicle emissions, as did governments who used that data for wider social policy planning around issues such as healthcare (fewer emissions means fewer people with chronic respiratory conditions) and climate change (reduced greenhouse gas emissions means targets in climate change agreements might be met).

This highlights a very critical aspect of risk management and governance in the context of information ethics. It is essential that the organization's risk management and governance approach for information and data consider the impacts on external stakeholders as a result of the information and process outcomes that are delivered. This is actually an explicit feature of legislation such as the EU's General Data Protection Regulation (GDPR), which requires the risk to the data privacy of individuals and the risks to the rights and freedoms enabled by data privacy rights to be considered when conducting or designing any information-processing activity.

From a normative ethics perspective this represents a shift from a shareholder-theory model, where the prime emphasis is placed on protecting the bottom line of the organization, to a stakeholder-theory model, where there needs to be a broader identification of stakeholders and a balancing of competing interests and objectives. This means risks to both the individual and the organization need to be considered, and formal structures and processes are required to ensure that those decisions are taken objectively and are recorded.

Information ethics and data governance maturity

In the discussion of stewardship and the ethic of the individual we mentioned the idea that individuals tend to evolve their cognitive model of ethics over time as they age and mature. The hope is that, as you grow and experience life, your frame of reference for ethics evolves and you have the potential to become more principled, which Kohlberg aligned with concepts we find in social-justice ethical models rather than the more utilitarian or consequentialist models. Of course, not everyone evolves and matures at the same pace. Indeed, it is a constant challenge of the human condition that some people do not mature their cognitive model of ethics beyond a cause-and-effect consequentialist frame of thinking.

Similarly, data management practices in organizations evolve and mature. Data-management-capability maturity models are defined in terms of a progression through a number of stages, with each stage representing a certain desired set of process characteristics or capabilities. Just as people ideally mature in their ethical capability, organizations should also, ideally, mature in their information management capabilities. Unfortunately, just as people sometimes get stuck at a particular level, organizations can also struggle to break through to the next level of maturity in their management practices for information.

According to the DAMA DMBOK (DAMA International, 2017), common labels applied to different levels of information management capability include:

- Level 0 – Absence of Capability.
- Level 1 – Initial or ad hoc: success depends on the competence of individuals.
- Level 2 – Repeatable: minimum process discipline is in place.
- Level 3 – Defined: standards are set and used.
- Level 4 – Managed: processes are quantified and controlled.
- Level 5 – Optimized: process improvement goals are quantified.

To find out more about the theory and practice of data-management maturity models, and to learn about some of the more common frameworks that exist, we would recommend you look at the relevant section of the DAMA DMBOK as a detailed discussion of the topic is outside the scope of this chapter. For our purposes, it is enough for you to understand that at each level of maturity in an organization the formalization of processes, controls and governance increases and the emphasis shifts from firefighting of issues to management of processes and, ultimately, to continuous improvement of processes. Improved processes in turn lead to improved certainty of process and information outcomes.

If you consider data management maturity from the perspective of information ethics, the increased formalization, consistency and scalability of your organization's information management practices bring with it a number of factors that contribute to better ethical decision making by individuals and promote better alignment of the ethic of the individual with the ethic of the organization and, ultimately, with the ethic of society (Table 9.6).

Table 9.6 Information management maturity and ethical maturity

Maturity Level	Data Management Characteristics	Ethical Dimension
Level 0	• No organized data management practices • No formal processes	• Limited situational moderators • No referent models for behaviour • No formalized consequences
Level 1	• General-purpose data management, with no formal governance • Reliance on a few key experts • Roles and responsibilities are managed within silos • Data quality issues are pervasive but not addressed	• No normative structures • No clearly defined authority • Referent models rely on a few core people • Limited role taking • Ethics/governance are not linked to job context
Level 2	• Consistent tools and role definitions exist to support process execution • Some roles and responsibilities defined • Roles are not dependent solely on specific experts • Organizational awareness of data quality and other issues and concepts	• Increasingly structured normative systems • Authority for decision making is increasingly defined • Role taking increases through increased opportunities • Clearer linking of ethics and governance to job context
Level 3	• Scalable data management processes institutionalized across the organization • Co-ordinated policy definition • Formal process definition and centralized design processes	• Normative structures are more widely standardized across the organization • Governance and ethics are increasingly embedded in job context • Formalized structures for accountability and consequences
Level 4	• Institutional knowledge enables prediction of results and improves risk management • A well-formed centralized planning and governance structure • Data management includes performance metrics	• Strong normative structures exist and are centralized • Referent models are available against which ethical standards can be evaluated • Structures exist for resolution of ethical/moral issues
Level 5	• Processes and outcomes are highly predictable • Focus is on continuous improvement	• Strong role taking by staff in improvement processes • Referent models based on prior learning exist

As your organization's information management maturity increases, the range of situational modifiers identified in Trevino's model likewise increase. This increases the likelihood that individuals will act in accordance with the ethic of the organization. However, in the absence of an effective data governance culture that focuses on the information and process outcomes that are expected by society, you may still struggle to be seen as an organization that is managing information ethically. For that reason it is important to have effective feedback loops in place to ensure that feedback from society is identified and acted upon.

Building a governance framework for information ethics

It is important for you to realize that implementing a governance framework for information ethics does not require your organization to pursue a strategy based on YABGE (Yet Another Building Governance Effort).[1] What it requires is the design of a data governance framework that explicitly recognizes the role of and need for ethics and ethical oversight of information management processes and practices. It is equally important to formally recognize ethical information management as a component of your overall data governance framework. In designing your data governance organization, you should also ensure that it is flexible enough to support the evolution of data management in the organization and can scale to the challenges and opportunities in an increasingly complex information management and information ethics landscape.

You need to consider several key factors as you architect the structures for your governance model.

- **Cultural norms (about data)**: are there potential barriers or cultural obstacles to implementing or improving governance structures and processes in the organization?

- **Cultural norms (about ethics)**: what is the dominant ethical culture or bias in the organization? What is the ethic of the organization?

- **Data governance practices**: how and by whom are decisions about data made currently in your organization? What are the rules for deciding how to decide?

- **How is work organized and executed:** what is the relationship between governance and project/operational execution? What committee structures or forums are in place to manage the oversight and execution of ethical principles?

- **How are reporting structures organized:** is your organization structured around centralized, decentralized, hierarchical or flat reporting models? What is the potential for role taking in your current governance models? How do your current reporting models support or impede alignment of data governance and ethical principles with the individual's perception of their role and the context of their job function? How will you align your data governance and ethics function with the existing organizational hierarchy of your organization?

- **Skill levels:** what are the skill levels among staff in relation to data management, data governance and ethics? What level of skills are needed?

A key aspect of data governance for ethical information management is the need to formally create a structure within the organization where ethical issues and principles can be discussed and debated as part of the policy formulation and governance function. This needs to be formally convened and should ideally sit parallel to the data governance function within the organization. However, it may share resources and representation. Another approach would be to formally include the discussion of ethics and ethical issues as a formal item on the agenda of the Data Governance Council.

A significant risk is that the ethics forum in your organization could become a 'talking shop' for ethical topics. It is essential that the charter and operating model for your ethics forum links it to formal policy and practice issues that are overseen by the data governance function and the execution of information management processes and functions in the organization. As with all data governance frameworks, its effectiveness is only measurable through the actions taken and the outcomes achieved.

The model outlined in Figure 9.5 is one possible approach to integrating your ethics forum into your data governance framework. It ensures that your ethics discussions are linked to real business problems and challenges, and ensures a centralized control of oversight of the execution of information management processes in line with those ethical principles. By engaging your information stewardship model as part of the design of your overall governance framework you can create the normative structures and role-taking opportunities for your data stewards.

Ethical information management does not happen by accident. Your data governance structures are an essential component of the architecture for ethics in your organization that is essential to ensure alignment between the ethic of the organization and the ethic of society, while at the same time ensuring you are able to support individuals in your organization to make consistently ethical decisions.

Figure 9.5 An example governance framework for ethics and data governance

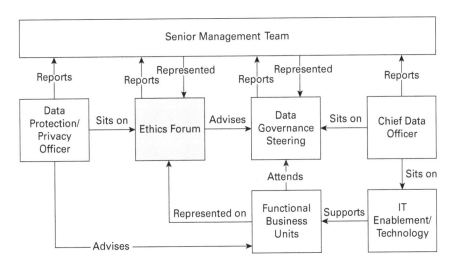

Chapter summary

In this chapter you have learnt:

- The role of data governance in the E2IM framework.

- The critical role of defined data governance structures when faced with ethical issues. You have learnt that the absence of defined protocols for addressing ethical issues can result in significant problems not being addressed in a timely or appropriate manner.

- How to describe your current data governance models with reference to classic governance frameworks. Coupled with a basic understanding of maturity models, you understand more how to identify the ethical goals for your data governance initiatives.

- You understand how the ethic of the individual is supported in the E2IM framework by effective, principles-led data governance and how effective, transparent and accessible data governance frameworks are essential to ensuring that the ethic of the individual, the ethic of society and the ethic of the organization are aligned.

- To be able to explain information stewardship as an ethical concept in the context of a principles-based data governance framework.

- You have learnt how two leading companies use simple ethical principles to guide their decisions on information management and information exploitation at the design stage of their activities.

- You have learnt of the importance of consciously designing your data governance framework for information ethics to ensure you have the right resources, skills, structures and practices in place.

- You have learnt that your data governance framework needs to be underpinned by robust and communicable statements of principles and values. In an ethical information management context, these principles should be aligned with clear statements of ethical values and should be placed in the context of a clear normative structure for ethical decision making. These principles should be supported by clear roles, responsibilities and accountabilities for decisions about ethics in information.

Questions

1 Is it possible to implement ethical information management without effective data governance systems?

2 What ethical information management principles would you like to see the organization you work for adopt?

3 What ethical information management principles would attract you to an organization, as a customer or as an employee? Why?

Note

1 The original draft of this did not say 'building' but Katherine made Daragh clean up the language…

Further reading

DAMA International (2017) DAMA DMBOK, *DAMA DMBOK – Data Management Body of Knowledge*, Technics Publications, New Jersey

Floridi, L (2016) *The Fourth Revolution: How the infosphere is reshaping human reality*, Oxford University Press, Oxford

Ladley, J (2012) *Data Governance: How to design, deploy, and sustain an effective data governance program*, Morgan Kaufmann, Waltham, MA

Seiner, R (2014) *Non-Invasive Data Governance: The path of least resistance and greatest success*, Technics Publications, LLC, New Jersey

References

AICPA (n.d.) [accessed 17 August 2017] Segregation of Duties [Online] https://www.aicpa.org/InterestAreas/InformationTechnology/Resources/Auditing/InternalControl/Pages/value-strategy-through-segregation-of-duties.aspx

DAMA International (2017) [accessed 17 August 2017] DAMA DMBOK, *DAMA DMBOK – Data Management Body of Knowledge*, Technics Publications, New Jersey

Elango, B, Paul, K, Kundu, S and Paudel, SK (2010) Organizational ethics, individual ethics, and ethical intentions in international decision-making, *Journal of Business Ethics*, **97**, pp 543–61

Feldman, SP (2007) Moral business cultures: the keys to creating and maintaining them, *Organizational Dynamics*, 36 (2), pp 156–70

Hasselbach, G and Tranberg, P (2016) *Data Ethics: The new competitive advantage*, PubliShare

International Organization for Standardization (2012) [accessed 20 October 2017] ISO20121:2012 Event Sustainability Management Systems – Requirements With Guidance For Use [Online] https://www.iso.org/obp/ui#iso:std:iso:20121:ed-1:v1:en

ISO (2009) ISO 31000:2009, *Risk Management – Principles and Guidelines*, International Organization for Standardization, Geneva

Kohlberg, L and Kramer, R (1969) Continuities and discontinuities in childhood and adult moral development, *Human Development*, 12, pp 93–120

Ladley, J (2012) *Data Governance: How to design, deploy, and sustain an effective data governance program*, Morgan Kaufmann, Waltham, MA

McGilvray, D (2008) *Executing Data Quality Projects: Ten steps to quality data and trusted information*, Morgan Kauffman, Boston

McLagan, P (1983) The concept of responsibility: some implications for organisational behaviour and development, *Journal of Management Studies*, 20, pp 411–23

Murphy, S (2014) [accessed 28 October 2017] Facebook Changes Its 'Move Fast and Break Things' Motto [Online] http://mashable.com/2014/04/30/facebooks-new-mantra-move-fast-with-stability

Schwarz, S (1968) Words, deeds, and the perception of consequences and responsibility in action situations, *Journal of Personality and Social Psychology*, 10, pp 232–42

Seiner, R (2014) *Non-Invasive Data Governance: The path of least resistance and greatest success*, Technics Publications, LLC, New Jersey

Sullivan, GR (2004) [accessed 20 October 2017] Enhancing Public Trust in the Accounting Profession Using Professional Judgment Rather than Personal Judgement in Resolving Accounting Ethics Dilemmas [Online] http://digitalcommons.liberty.edu/cgi/viewcontent.cgi?article=1038&context=fac_dis

The Data Governance Institute (n.d.) [accessed 20 September 2017] Data Governance Basics [Online] http://www.datagovernance.com/adg_data_governance_basics/

Trevino, LK (1986) Ethical decision making in organizations: a person–situation interactionist model, *The Academy of Management Review*, 11 (3), pp 601–17

Warzel, C (2017) [accessed 27 October 2017] How People Inside Facebook Are Reacting To The Company's Election Crisis [Online] https://www.buzzfeed.com/charliewarzel/how-people-inside-facebook-are-reacting-to-the-companys

Weill, P and Woodham, R (2002) [accessed 25 October 2017] Don't Just Lead, Govern: Implementing Effective IT Governance [Online] http://dspace.mit.edu/bitstream/handle/1721.1/1846/4237-02.pdf?sequence=2

Wikipedia (2017) [accessed 25 October 2017] Don't Be Evil [Online] https://en.wikipedia.org/wiki/Don%27t_be_evil

Wikipedia (2017) [accessed 25 October 2017] Stewardship [Online] https://en.wikipedia.org/wiki/Stewardship

Information ethics and risk

10

The rise of the Ethical Impact Assessment

What will we cover in this chapter?

This chapter will discuss the concept of assessing ethical risks and impacts through the comparable and more familiar concept of a privacy impact analysis. Examples of key questions you should be asking and answering in this planning process include:

- What are the potential real-world impacts of your information process?
- Does your new idea for a product, service or other process create a win-win situation or is it potentially predatory or harmful?
- Are you overlooking a potentially easily solvable issue that, if not addressed, could cost a great deal in terms of reputational damage or reactive efforts to fix?

You will learn about the concepts of Ethical Impact Assessments in the context of a quality systems-based approach to ethical information management. By the end of this chapter you will have a deeper understanding of the relationship between planning for quality, risk management and ethical information management practices.

Introduction

Effective risk management is a key component of any management system. In Chapter 8 we discussed the concept of ethical information management as a quality system. This is an important conceptual connection in the design of the E2IM framework for ethical information management. Your objective in the ethical management of information is to ensure that the information and process outcomes that are delivered to your stakeholders in society meet the ethical expectations of your stakeholders, such as supporting rights to privacy or enabling the support of or improvement of human dignity or freedom of expression. Indeed, Tom Peters describes management as 'the arrangement and animation of human affairs in pursuit of desired outcomes' (Peters, 2015).

As we introduced in Chapter 8 and discussed further in Chapter 9, if you consider ethical information management as quality system, you can begin to seek out principles and practices from other domains of management and information management to help you build ethics into information management. By adopting and adapting proven methods to support the arrangement and animation of your information management affairs, you can consistently delight your stakeholders with outcomes that are aligned with the ethic of society or exceed the positive expectations of society as to what good information management practices and ethics can be.

You have also seen how information management is on the brink of a crisis of confidence as the ethical risks and pitfalls of new technologies we are adopting are becoming more apparent in the mainstream. In many respects, we are facing a crisis, just as manufacturing faced a quality crisis in the 1980s (see Table 10.1). One of the subtexts of the E2IM framework and the approach we have taken to this book is that there are patterns, principles and practices in history that we can learn from. In Table 10.1 we have taken some statements from a paper presented to the American Society for Quality (ASQ) in 1986 (Juran, 1986). You can see some interesting parallels with the challenges we face today.

In Juran's 1986 paper he introduced a fundamental concept of quality management that has become known as the Juran Quality Trilogy (Figure 10.1). The underlying concept of the Juran Quality Trilogy is that managing for quality consists of three basic quality-oriented processes:

- quality planning;
- quality control;
- quality improvement.

Table 10.1 Mapping Juran's quality crisis to information ethics challenges

Joseph Juran Statements (paraphrased for brevity)	Ethical Information Management Equivalent
There is a crisis in quality. The most obvious outward evidence is the loss of sales to foreign competition and the huge costs of poor quality	There is a crisis in information ethics. The most obvious evidence is the concerns about algorithmic bias and the potential for misuse of big-data technologies and the huge risks of abuse
The crisis will not go away in the foreseeable future. Competition in quality will go on and on. So will the impact of poor quality on society	The crisis will not go away in the foreseeable future. Technological evolution will go on and on. So will the impact of poor consideration of ethical issues on society
Our traditional ways are not adequate to deal with the quality crisis. Our adherence to those traditional ways has helped to create the crisis	Our traditional approaches to IT project management are not adequate to deal with the ethical crisis. In a sense our adherence to those traditional ways has helped create the crisis
Charting a new course requires that we create a universal new way of thinking about quality – a way applicable to all functions and to all levels in the hierarchy	Charting a new course requires that we create a universal way of thinking about ethics in information management – a way applicable to all functions and all levels in the hierarchy
An essential element in meeting the quality crisis is to arm upper managers with experience and training in how to manage for quality, and to do so with a sense of urgency	An essential element in meeting the information ethics crisis is to arm upper managers with experience and training in how to ethically manage information, and to do so with a sense of urgency
Charting a new course also requires that we design a basis for management of quality that can readily be implanted into the company's strategic business planning and has minimal risk of rejection by the company's immune system	Charting a new course also requires that we design a basis for management of information ethics that can readily be implanted into the company's strategic business planning and has minimal risk of rejection by the company's immune system

Juran viewed these as being universal processes that exist across a range of activities, but he explicitly called out quality planning as the starting point for all things quality. As he put it (Juran, 1986):

Figure 10.1   The Juran Quality Trilogy

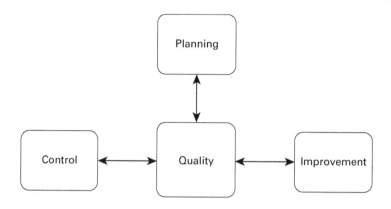

The starting point is quality planning – creating a process that will be able to meet established goals and do so under operating conditions. The subject matter of the planning can be anything.

This is precisely what we are seeking to achieve from the perspective of ethical information management, the creation of a process (or set of processes) that will be able to meet established ethical goals and do so under operating conditions. Our subject matter is data and information, which might be directly about people or might indirectly relate to them, or which may lead to outcomes that are positive or negative for individuals or society. What is required is a planning process where the uncertainties around the alignment of business, information and technology domains are addressed to ensure the consistent delivery of information and/or process outcomes that are ethically acceptable to society.

As with any other potential product or project, it is worthwhile for you to conduct an assessment to identify potential issues affecting your proposed processing activities as early as possible in the life cycle of a process or initiative. This should then inform your planning for how to address the ethical issues or considerations that may arise.

Looking for parallel models

Juran drew parallels between his Quality Trilogy and the trilogy of processes that exist in the financial management function of the organization (budgeting, cost control and cost reduction). When discussing his Quality Trilogy in 1986, he described how he would 'look sideways' at how finance is managed, to call out the parallels. In the spirit of Juran, you need to look sideways at other models of quality management for information to identify approaches and methodologies that might bring forth parallels that your ethical information-planning process can be modelled on.

This is an important consideration given the sentiments expressed by Juran in Table 10.1 in relation to the need for a speed of implementation of skills and training in quality management, and the need to do it in a way that does not meet with excessive resistance from the organization:

- You need to be able to train management quickly in how to do these types of assessments and to understand how to manage for ethical information and process outcomes.

- You need to be able to introduce processes for ethical information planning into the organization in a manner that will have 'minimal risk of rejection by the company's immune system' (Juran, 1986).

Thankfully, by taking a quality systems approach to ethical information management, you can readily identify parallels with the planning principles of information quality management and data governance. However, a closer parallel can be found in the disciplines of Privacy by Design and Privacy Engineering.

Privacy by Design

Privacy by Design is an approach to designing and developing information management and processing systems that requires privacy and human values to be taken into account throughout the entire life cycle of the design, build and operation of the system. The concept of Privacy by Design has been popularized by Dr Ann Cavoukian when she was serving as the Information and Privacy Commissioner for the Province of Ontario in Canada (Cavoukian, 2011).

Privacy by Design is characterized by seven foundational principles that map to fundamental principles of quality management, as set out in Table 10.2.

Note that these are essentially statements of ethical principles relating to privacy and security applied to the design of information processes. It should be no surprise therefore that Dr Cavoukian has recently published an updated set of principles specifically for the development of AI Ethics by Design (Cavoukian, 2017).

Table 10.2 Privacy by Design principles

1	Proactive not reactive; preventative not remedial
2	Privacy as the default setting
3	Privacy embedded into design
4	Full functionality – positive-sum, not zero-sum
5	End-to-end security – full life-cycle protection
6	Visibility and transparency – keep it open
7	Respect for user privacy – keep it user-centric

Privacy Engineering

Where Privacy by Design, and its cousin AI Ethics by Design, are concerned with defining design principles for privacy and AI ethics, Privacy Engineering is concerned with getting things built with privacy baked in and improving the function. Privacy Engineering takes methodologies and practices from software engineering, information management and business process engineering, amongst other disciplines, to enable you to implement the development of systems and technologies that support Privacy by Design principles. The underlying concepts of Privacy Engineering are best explained in books by Michelle Dennedy (Dennedy, Finneran and Fox, 2014) and Ian Oliver (Oliver, 2014). It is outside the scope of this chapter to dive deeply into the detail on those topics.

What we will focus on, however, is the model that Dennedy describes for the Privacy Engineering process. This process encompasses the three elements of the Juran Quality Trilogy and provides a model we can adapt to represent the process for engineering ethics into information processes (Figure 10.2; Table 10.3).

One of the key tools used in the planning and quality assurance phases of Privacy Engineering is a Privacy Impact Assessment (Dennedy, Finneran and Fox, 2014). Privacy Impact Assessments (PIAs) are a process that can help you identify, prioritize and mitigate privacy-related risks during the design and development of systems and processes. They help you implement Privacy by Design principles as an ethos in the development life cycle. As a governance tool, Privacy Impact Assessments ensure regulatory compliance and adherence to standards by making sure the rules are defined and applied to your proposed processing activities.

Figure 10.2 The Privacy Engineering development process

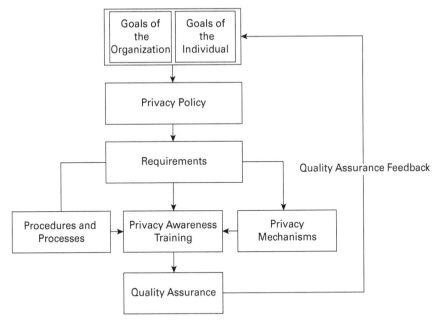

SOURCE adapted from Dennedy (2014)

Table 10.3 Mapping Privacy Engineering to Juran's Quality Trilogy

Juran Quality Trilogy Component	Privacy Engineering Development Step
Planning	• Understanding goals of organization and individuals • Privacy policy • Requirements
Control	• Procedures and processes • Privacy awareness training • Quality mechanisms
Improvement	• Quality assurance • Quality assurance feedback

In some situations, and locations, Privacy Impact Assessments may be a statutory or contractual requirement. In many jurisdictions, they are a requirement for public-sector bodies or bodies receiving public funds. Under the EU General Data Protection Regulation, 'Data Protection Impact Assessments' are required in many cases. Impact assessments may also be required as part of contractual terms of a project. The EU's Article 29

Working Party (or the European Data Protection Board as they will be known after 25 May 2018) also explicitly references the need to conduct PIAs as an iterative process where individual steps may need to be repeated as 'the development process progresses because the selection of certain technical or organizational measures may affect the severity or likelihood of the risks posed by the processing' (Article 29 Working Party, 2017).

Other reasons why organizations would consider carrying out a Privacy Impact Assessment include:

- **Risk management** – in addition to data privacy risks other risks such as ethical risks can be identified. The organization can also identify risks associated with the internal culture and ways of thinking about data. A PIA requires you to make formal decisions about what you will do about those risks.

- **Organizational learning** – this goes to Juran's point about needing to develop management competence in these areas. PIAs can help the organization learn about and better understand data privacy risks, the nature of their data flows, and the perspectives of their stakeholders and customers on data issues.

It is good practice to conduct your PIAs iteratively and review at different stages in the development and implementation of a project. This allows for iterative elaboration of detail and refinement of your plan. It also allows the PIA process to be used as a quality control and validation process to make sure that the things you had identified as needing to be done are actually done.

Reflecting the concerns of individuals and society

One key element of the regulatory guidance on Privacy Impact Assessments globally, in particular in the European Union, is the clear focus on the need for the assessments to reflect privacy concerns of individuals and society. In this context, the PIA requires the organization to assess the 'privacy risk appetite' of society to ensure that the developed solutions and processes meet the expectations and needs of society. This is explicitly referenced in Dennedy's recognition of the need to address both the goals of the organization as well as the goals and requirements of the individuals affected by your proposed use of data.

Towards ethical information engineering?

This requirement in Privacy Impact Assessments to consider the external stakeholder's concerns and expectations is entirely consistent with the stakeholder expectation component of the E2IM framework. After all, the objective of ethical enterprise information management is to ensure that the right outcomes are being delivered to the stakeholders in society. In that context, we can reimagine the E2IM framework as a variation on Dennedy's Privacy Engineering process. Just like Dennedy's model, the various stages in this process map to Juran's Quality Trilogy (Figure 10.3).

Just like the discipline of Privacy Engineering, the planning process requires you to conduct some form of assessment to enable you to determine questions of policy and requirements for implementation of your processes, training and controls. That assessment will also provide a quality assurance function by enabling you to check if the things you determined needed to be done actually were done. In short: effective ethical information engineering requires an Ethical Impact Assessment.

The E2IM Ethical Impact Assessment model

Because you are not reinventing the wheel when it comes to conducting your Ethical Impact Assessment (EIA), at this point you should be able to

Figure 10.3   The ethical information engineering process

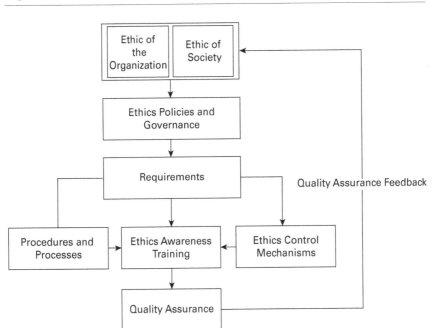

identify methods and processes from Privacy Impact Assessments or other risk-assessment processes in your organization that you can adopt and adapt. If not, the rest of this chapter provides an overview of a model approach you can use.

Principles

Privacy by Design provides a strong core set of design principles that can guide a Privacy Impact Assessment. But where can you look to find equivalent principles for ethics? By drawing on and distilling the ethical principles and models we discussed in the first half of this book, we have codified five basic interrogative rules to help formulate your starting position for analysis.

These interrogatives seek a positive outcome as a determiner of ethical action. Where the positive contribution to the social good is not the priority, it balances the priorities against the social ethic of the necessity of preserving human rights. An action with an outcome that violates these rights may be expected to come into conflict with the societal ethic that regards human rights as a fundamental priority. As modern information management capabilities may process, combine or link, and make available vast amounts of information, it is important to consider the outcomes resulting from data processing that are not the focus or intended outcome. This test will need to consider not just the intended outcome but other anticipated possible outcomes.

We explored these questions in Chapter 7 with some worked example scenarios. You will recall that these questions can often be straightforward to answer, but can, and should, provoke debate, particularly where the data that is proposed to be processed is particularly sensitive or the potential impacts on individuals are significantly far-reaching. For example, in the context of individuals with diminished or diminishing capacity to make informed choices about how their information is processed, what ethical issues might arise? We will use this scenario as a reference in the rest of this chapter.

Scenario: applications of life-logging technology for Alzheimer's patients

An organization is developing advanced life-logging capabilities to aid people suffering from conditions affecting their memory and cognitive processes. Day-to-day actions and events are recorded to serve as a reviewable record of events, acting, in effect, as a prosthetic memory.

Question 1: Does it preserve human dignity? Does it enhance human dignity?

As this application of technological advancements might possibly do a great deal to ease the distress of a person suffering from conditions such as Alzheimer's disease, it could very much enhance the dignity of the person.

Question 2: Does it preserve the autonomy of the human?
The planned capabilities of the technology would help to preserve the autonomy of the device-wearer. However, the life-logging technology would by its nature record the interactions of the device-wearer with other people, capturing their personal data as well. Controls would need to be implemented to take their autonomy into account, including the possibility of choosing not to have their data processed.

Question 3: Is it necessary and proportionate?
In the context of the device-wearer, the processing would likely be necessary and proportionate. However, the question of necessary and proportional processing also arises in the context of the other people the device-wearer comes into contact with. Measures should be taken to ensure that processing of the personal information of these people is minimized, particularly if there are no measures in place to ensure free and informed consent.

Question 4: Does it uphold the common good?
This application of technology is primarily focused on the enhancement of individuals' dignity, but it could also be argued that its availability would also be of more general benefit to communities as a whole. Family and friends of a person affected by Alzheimer's disease might also benefit from its use. Developments in care to aid members of a community are likely to improve the community as a whole.

Good governance requires decision-making processes to be recorded. If you are to ensure the alignment of the ethic of the organization with the ethic of society, and if you are to properly recognize controls and other situational modifiers for the ethic of the individual (Trevino, 1986), a more formal analysis of the ethical issues and risks in the proposed processing activity is required. This is especially the case if you want to be able to audit your processing later, or if you want to support the development of effective organizational learning about ethics and their application in information management.

To that end, you need a process!

Process

In our consulting work, we like to find models and methods that we can use over and over again to simplify the execution of processes for clients. In our experience, if you are trying to get management in an organization to adopt a new way of doing something, it should be as simple as possible. Ideally, it should also be a process that can be applied to different aspects of the organization.

Our impact assessment framework is an adaptation of Danette McGilvray's '10 Steps to Trusted Information process' (McGilvray, 2008). This process works well as it is a simple, structured method that follows a clear and logical flow. In our consulting work, we use this methodology for Privacy Impact Assessments (PIAs) and Ethical Impact Assessments (EIAs). As it is grounded in quality management principles and methods, it is a perfect fit for the quality systems-based approach to ethical information management that you will be applying through the E2IM framework. In addition, it provides a relatively standardized way of working for management and staff who may already be looking at information quality problems and opportunities in your organization. Finally, this framework allows for iterative loops and refinement of the proposed processing activities, depending on the ethical or privacy issues that are identified (Figure 10.4).

This methodology also supports a clear separation of duties between the assessment phase and the remediation/implementation phase of the process. This is in line with good practice in data governance (Figure 10.5).

This approach to structuring an EIA allows for a common set of process steps to be conducted regardless of the scale of the PIA or the range of jurisdictional variants on recommended PIA process steps that a project may require. It also allows for iterative review through the assessment phase if additional detail is required to identify root causes, inform improvement plans, or understand the impacts of proposed processing on individuals.

The inputs and outputs of the process

In this section, we outline the key process steps for the EIA. Note that the Impact Assessment phase of this method, set out below, extends to Step 6: 'develop improvement plans'. The actual implementation of recommendations and requirements from an Impact Assessment is the responsibility of the teams in your organization who are developing and implementing the proposed processing activities or information management systems. The objective of the assessment is to identify requirements for processes and

Figure 10.4 Castlebridge Ethical Impact Assessment methodology

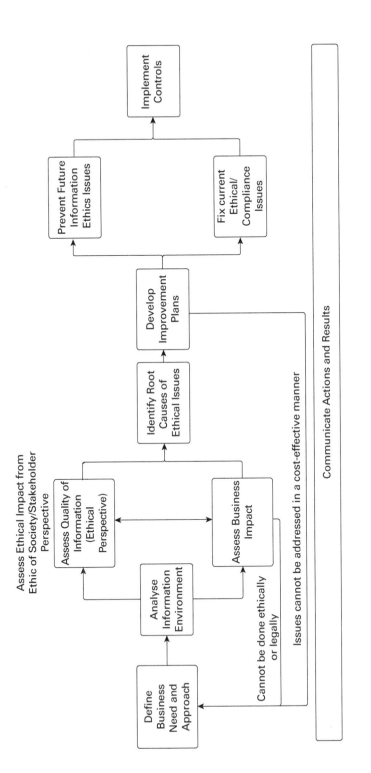

Figure 10.5 Castlebridge Ethical Impact Assessment method – phases highlighted

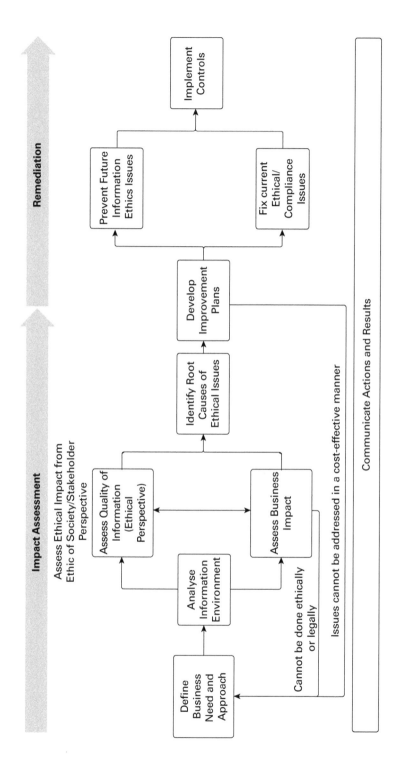

procedures, training or other control mechanisms for ethical outcomes that need to be designed in to avoid or mitigate ethical risks.

Step 1: define business need and approach

Clarity on the goal is an essential part of quality management. You need to think about what the desired information and process outcomes are that you are aiming to deliver. Without that clarity, there is a risk of misunderstanding, miscommunication or failure to identify critical risks.

This process begins with a requirement for a clear statement of the business need and approach for the proposed processing. This is an important first step in the methodology as it supports the following key functions:

- ✔ Determination of what kind of assessment is required. Are you going to constrain your analysis to just the privacy and privacy-derived outcomes in a Privacy Impact Assessment, or are you conducting a broader Ethical Impact Assessment?

- ✔ Defining the purpose of the proposed processing. What is the objective? What are the information and process outcomes you are trying to achieve?

- ✔ Identifying if there are multiple purposes and outcomes potentially to be achieved within the proposed processing, and identifying if there might be conflicts between those goals.

- ✔ Identifying the proposed benefits from the proposed processing of information.

- ✔ Identifying the relevant stakeholders and beneficiaries of the proposed processing.

- ✔ Define processing activities that are not in scope for the impact assessment.

This definition of your need and approach will be an important reference throughout the rest of the assessment, and indeed will be an important reference point for data governance and other control activities after the proposed information processing and management capability is deployed.

You can derive your business need and approach from the project charter or scope documents for a given project. For an Ethical Information Assessment, the focus in this instance is on the proposed processing of information, and information and process outcomes that your organization is looking to deliver as a result. It is important in the definition of the business need and approach that attention be paid to the needs of and benefits to individuals as stakeholders.

This is an essential requirement to ensure that you are considering what the expectation of the ethic of society would be in the context of your processing activities, and who that society is made up of. It is critical at this point to ensure this is done to ensure that an appropriate stakeholder theory normative approach to ethics can be applied. As a principle, it is one we find articulated in legal concepts such as the 'Neighbour Principle' in Tort law.[1] This principle holds that 'one must take reasonable care to avoid acts or omissions that could reasonably be foreseen as likely to injure one's neighbour'. Your 'neighbour' in turn is defined as 'someone who was so closely and directly affected by the act that one ought to have them in contemplation as being so affected when directing one's mind to the acts or omissions in question' (Oxford Reference, 2017).

In the context of Data Privacy Impact Assessments, the Article 29 Working Party also explicitly references the need to conduct assessments as an iterative process where individual steps may need to be repeated as 'the development process progresses because the selection of certain technical or organizational measures may affect the severity or likelihood of the risks posed by the processing' (Article 29 Working Party, 2017). The same is true of Ethical Impact Assessments. As more information is learnt about the nature and purpose of processing and the potential complexities or social issues that might arise, it is likely that the process will need to be revisited to reassess decisions taken.

In such a context, it is important to refer back to the original statement of business need and approach, determine if the ethical risks identified in relation to the proposed processing are appropriate in the context of the business need, and update the statement of business need and approach or your assessment of risk, as appropriate. As such, it is very important to define and capture the initial statement of business need and approach in a structured format (Table 10.4).

In our example of the life-logging application for people suffering from memory loss or other cognitive impairment, the statement of business need and approach would look something like in Table 10.5.

Step 2: analyse information environment

In this phase of the framework we gather, compile and analyse information about the current situation and information environment, as well as the proposed processing. The goal of this phase is to develop an understanding of the landscape the proposed processing will take place in. The objective is to identify the components of the business, information and technology

Table 10.4 Business need and approach template

We want to	Describe the information-processing activity that is the subject of the Ethical Impact Assessment. This should be sufficiently detailed to help you and your colleagues assess and identify potential ethical challenges
So that we can	Describe the organization capability that the processing is intended to provide or the social problem that the information processing is intended to address
Which will deliver the following benefits	Describe the intended benefits to the organization and to stakeholders. Focus should be on the outcomes in terms of information and process outcomes and the impact of those outcomes
To the following stakeholders	Describe the stakeholders, both internal and external, who it is intended will benefit from the proposed processing activity or whose data will be processed as part of this activity

Table 10.5 Example statement of business need and approach

We want to	Provide a 24/7 recording capability through audio and video recording using wearable and smartphone applications. We will use machine-learning processes to categorize and tag 'memories' with relevant metadata and provide a web-based or app-based search portal for users
So that we can	Provide a prosthetic memory by delivering a searchable repository of interactions and events that the user will have been party to
Which will deliver the following benefits	This will allow people with a cognitive or memory impairment to operate and live more independently through the provision of memory prompts or confirmation evidence for events they may misremember or forget entirely
To the following stakeholders	The persons with cognitive impairment, their families and friends, third parties who may have their image or other data recorded or stored, medical practitioners, carers

environment that will need to be aligned, and also to identify the driving ethic of the organization and relevant ethic of society that will need to be matched to ensure the information and process outcomes meet expectations.

In conducting this analysis, it is useful to consider the environment from four distinct perspectives or 'compass points' (see Figure 10.6):

- Social (putting the processing in the context of society and the organization culture).

- Technical (considering the technical architecture and design).

- Legal (considering the legal issues that might affect the processing).

- Moral (considering the ethical and moral dimensions of the proposed processing).

Figure 10.6   The four compass points for Ethical Impact Assessment

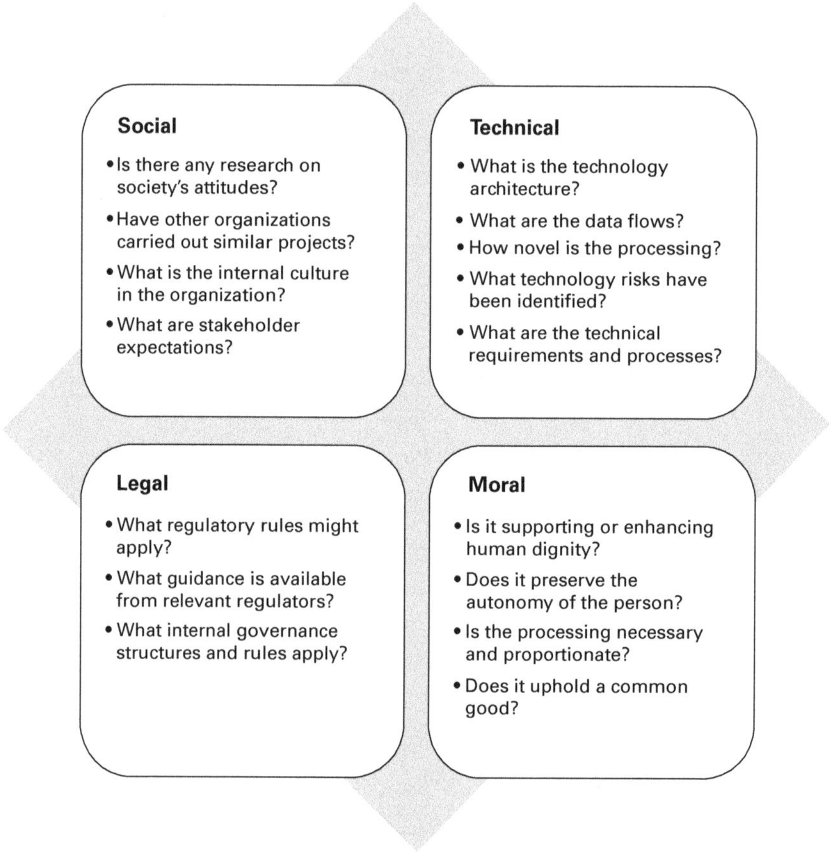

Social
- Is there any research on society's attitudes?
- Have other organizations carried out similar projects?
- What is the internal culture in the organization?
- What are stakeholder expectations?

Technical
- What is the technology architecture?
- What are the data flows?
- How novel is the processing?
- What technology risks have been identified?
- What are the technical requirements and processes?

Legal
- What regulatory rules might apply?
- What guidance is available from relevant regulators?
- What internal governance structures and rules apply?

Moral
- Is it supporting or enhancing human dignity?
- Does it preserve the autonomy of the person?
- Is the processing necessary and proportionate?
- Does it uphold a common good?

It is important to be clear about how you are engaging the ethic of society and seeking to understand their expectations. Key questions you need to answer at the 'Social' compass point include:

- What are the attitudes of people in society to the type of processing proposed?
- What are the attitudes of people in society to the proposed benefits?
- Are the proposed benefits credible to society?
- Have you engaged with people to find out this information? Have you used surveys, commissioned research, sought out existing research etc?
- What experiences exist in other jurisdictions for similar things?

In the context of the 'Moral' compass point, you need to have a structured method to tap into the views of the people in your organization, and potentially representatives of your external stakeholders. Surveys and facilitated brainstorming can be very effective techniques to elicit information. One method that we use with clients is a form of silent brainstorming that poses the ethical question in a structured way.

The utility/invasiveness matrix The method for this is actually quite simple. In a facilitated workshop, you present the statement of business need and approach to the group. On a post-it note, or using an electronic voting process, each participant ranks the proposed processing on a scale of 1 to 10 (low to high) along two axes:

- **Utility** ranks the degree to which the proposed processing and its associated information and/or process outcomes will do good in society or will promote happiness.
- **Invasiveness** is the measure of the level of intrusion into the personal life, relationships, correspondence or communications of the individual or a group of individuals as a result of the processing activity or the information outcome or process outcome that is delivered.

Participants are then asked to record their 'margin for error' on that ranking scale. This is the level of 'wriggle room' that they think might exist in the application of trade-offs and balancing rights and obligations. It is essential, however, that this part of the process is done SILENTLY after a discussion of the proposed business need and approach. This is to help avoid group-think and to allow for individuals to have an opportunity for role taking and to avoid the ranking being dominated by the views of a single dominant or persuasive voice.

The facilitator should collect the scores and the margins for error and plot these on the four-box matrix in Figure 10.7. Each respondent's co-ordinates map out a box indicating their personal 'moral space' for the proposed processing. Overlaying each respondent's 'moral space' on top of each other, the facilitator can quickly identify the zone of consensus. This zone is what the group who have been taking part indicate is their 'ethical risk appetite' for the proposed processing.

This area of 'ethical risk appetite' will sit somewhere in the four quadrants of the utility/invasiveness grid:

- High utility–low invasive initiatives are relative no-brainers. The ethical risks are potentially far outweighed by the benefits to individuals or society.

- High utility–highly invasive initiatives need to have additional controls, checks and balances, or other factors considered to reduce the level of invasiveness or at least provide some level of redress and balance.

- Low utility–highly invasive initiatives need to be reconsidered to see how the invasiveness can be reduced or the utility increased.

- Low utility–low invasiveness initiatives are not adding any value to society but are unlikely to be causing any great harm.

In the context of our life-logging example, the processing would likely be rated quite invasive but also of high utility and supportive of human dignity.

Figure 10.7 The utility versus invasiveness matrix

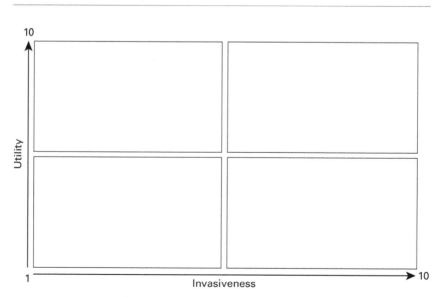

Therefore, it is important to understand how critical the impact might be on the ability to implement.

Steps 3 and 4: assess information privacy quality and business impact

The next steps in the process occur in parallel. These relate to the assessment of the 'quality of information privacy' in the proposed processing activity. The objective here is to begin the process of risk assessment and evaluation by identifying critical issues that will prevent the proposed initiative proceeding as initially scoped. Examples of these showstoppers could include:

- lack of a legal basis for conducting the processing;
- the proposed scope and scale of processing not meeting the necessity or proportionality requirements under GDPR;
- the proposed processing being highly invasive and of limited utility.

In the first instance, our methodology proposes a review of the defined business need and approach to determine if the identified issues can be remedied through a refinement of or clarification of either the need or the approach to be taken. The strategy here is to seek to increase utility or reduce invasiveness or restructure the proposed processing to address any blatant illegality (Figure 10.8).

Figure 10.8 Reviewing business need and approach – the utility/invasiveness goals

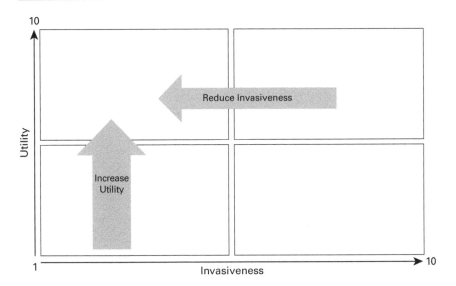

Once the business need and approach has been reviewed to determine if it can be amended, the organization should conduct a second review of the information environment and assess quality of information privacy again, particularly if the remediation/mitigation resulted in a change to their proposed information architecture or environment, to determine if findings of that review still hold or if new issues or risks are identified.

For our life-logging scenario, we will assume that there is no critical showstopper. There is no legal issue that is terminal to the execution of the processing, but there are a range of root causes that need to be identified and mitigated to reduce the invasiveness of the proposed processing and maximize its utility. For example, is it possible to reduce the level of recording or increase the awareness of third parties that there is recording taking place?

Step 5: identify root causes

For ethical issues that have been identified that are not terminal to the proposed project, it is necessary to identify the root causes of the issues and gaps identified. This is important as it ensures that the correct remediation is applied to address the correct problem. It also allows for identification and determination of interim measures that might be applied.

The root-cause identification should be conducted through a facilitated workshop. This may be conducted as an onsite workshop or as an offsite review and voting cycle.

This phase is grounded on several key assumptions derived from quality management principles:

- Any issue identified may have multiple potential root causes.

- Addressing one or more issues will reduce the inherent risk, but will leave residual risks to be considered, particularly where lower-priority root causes are not addressed.

- The focus should be on identifying what the root causes are for any individual failure mode (in this case, a privacy-impacting issue).

- To determine the appropriate solution, we need to identify the relevant root cause.

In the context of conducting the assessment, it is important to consider the probability and impact of an issue or risk from the perspective of the data subject as well. Likewise, the probability of detection should be addressed from both the internal (existence of an internal detective control) perspective and from the customer/data subject perspective (how easy would it be for them to demonstrate that the failure mode and root cause existed and impacted on their fundamental rights?).

Quality management techniques for root-cause analysis should be used here, such as 'five whys' analysis and fishbone diagrams. 'Five whys' analysis is as uncomplicated as it sounds. It requires you to ask 'why' five times about a particular problem or issue until you have identified what the precipitating root cause is. A fishbone diagram is a tool for clustering those root causes based on common factors such as people, process, management and technology factors.

Five whys analysis

The five whys analysis method is relatively straightforward. You define your problem statement (in our case, the ethical dilemma we are faced with) and then you ask 'Why?' a number of times to get to the real root cause and the solution that addresses that most appropriately in light of any constraints that may exist (eg budget). For example, if the problem you are facing is birds leaving droppings on your car if it is parked outside your house for a while, you might proceed as follows:

- Q: Why are birds leaving droppings on my car? A: Because it is parked outside and because birds are well fed.
- Q: Why are birds well fed? A: We have fruit trees in the back garden, as do our neighbours.
- Q: Why can't we get rid of the fruit trees? A: Our neighbours like them, as do we.
- Q: Why are bird droppings landing on my car? A: It is parked outside with no cover.
- Q: Why don't I buy a car cover or build a garage? A: No space or money to build a garage.
- Why don't I buy a car cover?

Fishbone diagrams

A fishbone diagram (Figure 10.9) is a quality management tool used to cluster common root causes together to help identify the critical areas of a problem leading to an issue. You write your problem statement at the 'head' of the fish and you identify the contributing areas as the 'ribs', with each root cause you identify being an offshoot of one of the 'ribs' of the fish.

Figure 10.9 An example of a fishbone diagram

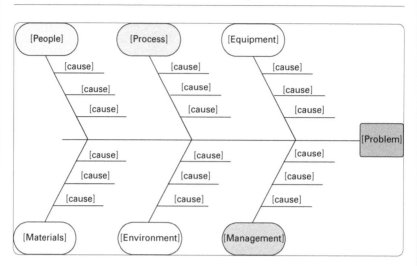

Fishbone diagrams are often called 'Ishikawa diagrams' because their first use is credited to Kaoru Ishikawa.

For our life-logging example, one potential root cause is the issues arising from the automated processing of people's data for the generation of the metadata to support search. It might also be the case that there are concerns about the retention of identifiable data in the form of video. Therefore, the improvement plans might need to focus on security, disclosure of processing purposes, and potentially the provision of technology to support redaction of faces in videos.

Step 6: develop improvement plans

Once you have identified the root causes for the ethical issues in your information management processes, you need to make your plans to do something about it. At this point in the process you are aiming to define requirements for:

- processes, procedures and controls;
- training and awareness;
- ethics mechanisms.

A key requirement of this phase in the process is that the remedial action proposed should be mapped directly to one or more identified root causes. You should then conduct a business-case analysis on the proposed remedial actions and may choose not to implement one or more of the proposed actions. Likewise, if the cost of implementing remedial actions of any kind is prohibitive, it should trigger an immediate review of the originally proposed business need and approach, or your senior management team need to sign off on the fact that they are choosing to engage in a form of processing that has been assessed to be unethical, and potentially unlawful.

Even where you fund all possible remediation actions, there will always be a level of risk that the ethic of society and the expectations of individuals in society will not be aligned with the ethic of the organization and that your information and process outcomes will not deliver the desired results. This can happen where the public perception and awareness of the impacts on utility, invasiveness, beneficence and the other ethical characteristics we identified in Chapter 8 differ from the perception of those values held by the organization and the individuals in the organization. This is similar to the perception of quality in manufactured goods or information when the customer expects something different to what the manufacturer has produced. To put it another way, when people become aware of the impacts that can arise due to misuse or abuse of a technology, it may change the risk calculation for your ethical balancing act.

You should also be clear about who is responsible for delivering the mitigating actions and by when. This is an important audit and verification control for post-implementation review of the PIA process to ensure that all things that were to be done have been done. Controls should be designed and defined at this point as they are part of the improvement process. You might not execute or implement these controls until the end of the remediation phase, but the earlier you consciously begin designing, the earlier you can pilot and test these controls for effectiveness.

In this context, controls can include (non-exhaustive list):

- Organizational:
  - training;
  - implementing governance controls;
  - revised policies and procedures.
- Technological:
  - implement user access controls;
  - detection and logging of access to data;
  - data masking or anonymization/pseudonymization technologies.

- Customer/user facing:
  - changes to data privacy statements/notices;
  - changes to how information is presented and communicated about data-processing activities;
  - provision of controls for data subjects regarding the exercise of their rights.
- Society facing:
  - lobbying for legislative change;
  - educating mass market on benefits (utility) of processing.

Step 10: communicate

We skip straight to Step 10 at this point because assessment is not concerned with remediation, although this step is common to both high-level phases. This step is a key supporting activity across the entire life cycle of the Ethical Impact Assessment process. It relates to the need to document key findings and outputs during the activity. It is not an 'end of project' activity but is rather an ongoing regular process. It is important to be clear about who the stakeholders are, who you are communicating with and what their role will be. Are you seeking feedback? Are you seeking direct input? Will you be conducting ongoing testing of assumptions? Are you just letting people know that you are still in existence?

Communication is a key element internally for driving ethical changes in information management, aligning the ethic of the individual with the ethic of society. It is also a critical process for ensuring alignment between the ethic of the organization and the ethic of society. These communication processes will not happen by accident and need to be properly designed and managed in order to be effective.

Supporting and extending the methodology

The European Union has funded research into Ethical Impact Assessments. The aim of the project was to develop a common EU-wide framework for the ethical assessment of research and innovation. Over four years the project looked at a range of issues and perspectives on the question of Ethical Impact Assessments. Their outputs provide a useful resource for individuals and organizations looking to develop their own in-house Ethical Impact Assessment methodology. Among the issues that the Satori project (Satori Project, 2017) has examined are:

- the different types of assessment you might perform;
- what types of ethical values, issues and principles might arise in different types of assessment;
- understanding the trade-offs that might arise as a result of decisions made in Ethical Impact Assessments.

It is outside the scope of this chapter, and indeed this book, to review and summarize the entirety of the Satori project's outputs, but it is a valuable reference resource.

Chapter summary

In this chapter we have:

- Set out a methodology for conducting Ethical Impact Assessments in an information management context.
- This methodology is grounded in proven quality management principles and an established information quality management framework.

Questions

1 What is the value in adopting a structured and standardized approach to Ethical Impact Assessments?

2 What other tools, techniques or methods from quality management might be applicable in this context?

3 There is a strong conceptual link between quality management, information quality management, data privacy and ethical information management. What are the differences that exist and why are they important?

4 What would you identify as the critical components of a methodology for running Ethical Impact Assessments in your organization?

Note

1 Tort law is the law of civil wrongs. It is the field of law you litigate in if you have slipped on the wet floor in a shopping mall. Is it ethical for a shopping mall not to provide adequate notice of the wet floor and appropriate barriers? If you ignore the barriers and notices, is it ethical that the shopping mall would need to pay for your injuries?

Further reading

Article 29 Working Party [accessed 5 February 2018] Guidelines on Data Protection Impact Assessment (DPIA) and Determining Whether Processing is 'likely to result in a high risk' For the Purposes of Regulation 2016/679 [Online] http://ec.europa.eu/newsroom/document.cfm?doc_id=47711

Brey, PAE (2012) Anticipating ethical issues in emerging IT, *Ethics and Information Technology*, **14** (4), pp 305–17

BSR (Business for Social Responsibility) (2017) [accessed 20 October 2017] Case Study: Telia Company: Human Rights Impact Assessments [Online] https://bsr.org/en/our-insights/case-study-view/telia-company-human-rights-impact-assessments

Burgess, J. Peter et al (2018) [accessed 5 February 2018] EDPS Ethics Advisory Group Report 2018 [Online] https://edps.europa.eu/sites/edp/files/publication/18-01-25_eag_report_en.pdf

De Hert, P, Kloza, D and Wright, D, eds (2012) [accessed 5 February 2018] Recommendations For a Privacy Impact Assessment Framework for the European Union; Brussels – London, November [Online] http://www.piafproject.eu/ref/PIAF_D3_final.pdf

Moor, JH (2005) Why we need better ethics for emerging technologies, *Ethics and Information Technology*, 7 (3), 111–19

Nissenbaum, H (2009) *Privacy in Context: Technology, policy, and the integrity of social life*, Stanford University Press, Stanford

Pasquale, F (2016) *The Black Box Society: The secret algorithms that control money and information*, Harvard University Press, Cambridge, MA

Satori Project (2017) [Online] http://satoriproject.eu/

Telia (2017) [accessed 20 October 2017] Human Rights Impact Assessment – Telia Sweden [Online] http://www.teliacompany.com/globalassets/telia-company/documents/sustainability/hria/human-rights-impact-assessment-telia-sweden.pdf

Vallor, S (2016) *Technology and the Virtues: A philosophical guide to a future worth wanting*, New York, Oxford University Press

Wright, D (2011) A framework for the ethical impact assessment of information technology, *Ethics and Information Technology*, **13** (3), 199–226

References

Article 29 Working Party (2017) [accessed 20 October 2017] Guidelines on Data
Protection Impact Assessment (DPIA) and Determining Whether Processing is
'likely to result in a high risk' for the Purposes of Regulation 2016/679 [Online]
http://ec.europa.eu/newsroom/document.cfm?doc_id=44137

Cavoukian, DA (2011) [accessed 20 October 2017] Privacy by Design: The 7
Foundational Principles [Online] https://www.ipc.on.ca/wp-content/uploads/
Resources/7foundationalprinciples.pdf

Cavoukian, DA (2017) [accessed 20 October 2017] AI Ethics by Design [Online]
http://www.ryerson.ca/content/dam/pbdce/papers/AI_Ethics_by_Design.docx

Dennedy, M, Finneran, TR and Fox, J (2014) *The Privacy Engineer's Manifesto:
Getting from policy to code to QA to value*, Apress, Berkeley, CA

Holmberg, I, Ahlberg, M and Romberg, A (2017) [accessed 20 October 2017]
Telia Company – Paving the Way for Responsible Business [Online] https://
www.hhs.se/contentassets/6932d66acb534542aa0f4acc48fe83f3/rt-telia-final-
october-9-2017.pdf

Juran, J (1986) [accessed 20 October 2017] The Quality Trilogy: A Universal
Approach to Managing for Quality [Online] http://pages.stern.nyu.edu/~djuran/
trilogy1.doc

McGilvray, D (2008) *Executing Data Quality Projects: 10 steps to quality data and
trusted information*, Morgan Kaufmann, Boston

Oliver, I (2014) [accessed 20 October 2017] *Privacy Engineering: A data flow and
ontological approach*, CreateSpace Independent Publishing Platform

Oxford Reference (2017) [accessed 20 October 2017] Neighbour
Principle [Online] http://www.oxfordreference.com/view/10.1093/oi/
authority.20110803100227619

Peters, T (2015) [accessed 20 October 2017] Management... the Arrangement and
Animation of Human Affairs in Pursuit of Desired Outcomes [Online] http://
tompeters.com/wp-content/uploads/2016/08/Management_collective_behavior_
032215A-1.pdf

Satori Project (2017) [accessed 20 October 2017] Satori [Online] http://
satoriproject.eu/

Trevino, LK (1986) Ethical decision making in organizations: a person-situation
interactionist model, *The Academy of Management Review*, **11** (3), pp 601–17

Making the ethical information management change

11

What will we cover in this chapter?

Throughout this book we have discussed ethics, governance, architecture and quality in the context of information management. One of the common elements of the topics you have read about thus far is that, when it comes to implementing them in your organization, you will need to manage a change in the way in which the organization and the people in it think about information.

In this chapter we will:

- Discuss some of the tools and techniques you will need to deploy to make the change happen and to get the transition to stick.
- Introduce the basic principles of change management.
- Discuss how storytelling and fairy tales have been used throughout the ages to guide the development of ethics.

Our discussion of storytelling and fairy tales in many respects closes the circle in this book, as we began in Chapter 1 with the story of Plato bemoaning the impact that the technology of writing would have on the ability of people to recall, understand and use information.

The key challenge for you is to recognize that the change you are executing is as much a change of organization culture (the ethic of the organization) as it is a change of technology capability. Indeed, the culture change, supported by appropriate governance structures and metrics, is a significant proportion of the effort you will have to make to ensure that your information management technologies can consistently deliver ethically appropriate outcomes.

What is change management (and why does it often go wrong)?

In Chapter 5 we introduced you to John Zachman and the concepts of his enterprise ontology. We also introduced you to the fact that 'the history of all the known disciplines that deal with complex objects (things) reveals that change starts with the engineering descriptions of the things' (Zachman, 1996). Change management can be described as the process of defining the descriptions of the things that need to be changed, the ways in which they will be changed, and then overseeing and governing the evolution and roll-out of that change so that the desired results are delivered.

To give a more formal definition, it is the collective term for all approaches to preparing and supporting individuals, teams and organizations in making organizational change, including methods and practices to support the redirection or reallocation of resources, or the realignment of values and cultural norms within the organization. It entails the development of reward structures, development of metrics to measure the effectiveness of the change, and needs to realistically address a time period of one to three years.

In the context of ethical information management, change management is the process that the organization must implement and work through to adapt and align the ethic of the organization with the ethic of society. This may be an internal change within the organization, implementing new methods, processes and practices, such as Ethical Impact Assessments and data governance functions for ethics. Alternatively, it could be an externally facing change where the organization is seeking to influence the ethic of society. For the purposes of this chapter we will focus on the issues raised by the internal change, but many of the same issues, principles and approaches are applicable to both scenarios.

Change does not happen overnight and it is also notoriously difficult to do, with failure rates in change management initiatives reaching up to 70 per cent. It is critical that it is managed and co-ordinated so as to avoid dead-end initiatives, loss of trust, and damage to the credibility of the E2IM function and its leadership. As part of the planning for effective change, it is important to understand:

- why change fails;
- the triggers for effective change;
- the barriers to change.

Change physics – the immutable laws of change

Every high-school student learns that there are fundamental laws of physics that affect the way the universe around us works. By understanding those principles, we are able to make things happen in the world. Whether it is billiard balls rolling across a table to spacecraft breaking free of the bounds of earth, there are fundamental forces at work. Organizations are no different.

One of the most important laws of change is that organizations are made up of people. Therefore, to effect change in the ethic of the organization, you will need to effect change in the ethic of the individual. Merely announcing you are adopting an ethical approach to information management does not magically mean that the following day in the office there will be no data skullduggery or misalignment with the ethic of society. Buying a technology does not introduce change to the organization. Organizational change takes place when people behave differently because they see the value in doing so, both to the organization and to them, and sometimes to society as a whole.

Another fundamental is that the resistance to change that is often experienced by change leaders is usually not a resistance to change, but rather a resistance to *being changed*. Peter Senge describes this in his seminal book *The Fifth Discipline* (Senge, 1990) and it is a challenge in change management that is often overlooked. People will not accept a change that is imposed upon them. They will also resist change that affects any aspect of their role that has become part of their self-identity. You might be telling them that the process outcome or method is wrong and needs to be changed, but they are hearing that they are wrong and need to be changed. People are more likely to engage with change if they have had the opportunity to contribute to the change and if they can understand the vision and values behind the change. This is similar to Trevino's work on individual ethical decision making in organizations, which we discussed in Chapter 9. When your colleagues have had an opportunity to engage in role taking in the change process they are more likely to be engaged with the process.

One of the common pitfalls that change initiatives fall into is the quagmire of blaming, or appearing to blame, for the current problem state. Things are the way they are because that's the way they are. Even if you are a hard-core utilitarian consequentialist in your outlook on things, it does not serve your change agenda to be seen to be taking names and settling scores. Understanding root causes for the current situation is important, but you must make sure to address the situation, not the actors in the situation.

Finally, unless there is some driver or direction requiring the change, no change will happen. This is one of the reasons that you were advised in Chapter 9 on information ethics and data governance to ensure your ethics forum is linked into the execution of your data governance processes and practices. If it remains a disconnected talking shop, nothing will improve.

Managing transition, not change

Another common mistake that people make is not realizing that they are managing a transition, not a change. Different people in the organization will embrace and adapt to the change at different paces. Change management expert William Bridges defines transition as the psychological process that people go through to come to terms with the new situation. While many people think of change solely in terms of a new beginning, Bridges recognizes that change involves moving through three distinct phases, starting with the ending of the existing state (Table 11.1).

Endings are difficult because people need to let go of existing conditions. People then enter the neutral zone, in which the existing state has not quite ended and the new state has not quite begun. Change is complete when the new state is established. Of these three, the neutral zone is the least predictable and most confusing, because it is a mix of old and new. If the people in the organization do not transition through the neutral zone, then the organization is at risk of slipping back into old habits and failing to sustain the change.

According to Bridges, the single biggest reason that organizational changes fail is that people driving change rarely think about endings and therefore do not manage the impact of endings on people. He describes the problem like this: 'Most organizations try to start with a beginning, rather than finishing with it. They pay no attention to endings. They do not acknowledge the existence of the neutral zone, and then wonder why people have so much difficulty with change' (Bridges, 2009).

When experiencing a change, all individuals go through all three phases. But they go at different speeds, depending on factors such as past experience, personal preferred style, the degree of involvement in recognizing the problem and developing possible solutions, and the extent to which they feel pushed towards a change rather than moving towards it voluntarily.

Table 11.1 Bridges' transition model

Transition Phase	Description	Ethical Change Implications
The Ending	• When we acknowledge that there are things we need to let go of • When we recognize that we have lost something • Example: changing jobs – even when an individual chooses to change jobs, there are still losses such as losing close working friends	Changing ethical behaviour can be challenging as it requires people to accept that the things they have been doing may be wrong, or even unlawful. This is particularly the case where the organization relies on the ethic of the individual
The Neutral Zone	• When the old way has finished but the new way isn't here yet • When everything is in flux and it feels like no one knows what they should be doing • When things are confusing and disorderly • Example: moving house – the first few days or even months after moving, the new house is not home yet and things are quite probably in turmoil	The problem that can arise in this context in quality systems change or ethical change is that the old way is sometimes perceived as the 'easy way' or the 'better way', particularly where there is a lack of clarity around the end-goals. Individuals may fall back on the old ethic of the organization or may rely on their personal ethics (ethic of the individual) when unsure what to do
The New Beginning	• When the new way feels comfortable, right and the only way • Example: moving to a new home – after a few months in the neutral zone of turmoil, you come to a stage when you have settled into your new environment (and have perhaps found your new favourite coffee shop)	Individuals will reach this phase at different paces. Much will be influenced by their ethic of the individual and personal moral development, but the effectiveness of the situational modifiers that are implemented as part of ethical change in the organization will be essential to embedding the desired behaviours in the organization

Bridges makes it clear that while the first task of the change manager is to understand the destination (vision) and how to get there, the role of the transition management is to convince people that they need to start the journey and to keep them on the right track. When managing change and transition, the role of the change agent, and of any manager or leader in the process, is to help people recognize the process and the stages of a transition as something that is perfectly natural. The following checklist summarizes the key points that managers should be aware of as they help people transition:

Checklist for managing transition

- The ending:
- ✔ Help everyone to understand the current problems and why the change is necessary.
- ✔ Identify who is likely to lose what. Remember that loss of friends and close working colleagues is just as important to some as status and power is to others.
- ✔ Losses are subjective. The things one person may grieve about may mean nothing to someone else. Accept the importance of subjective losses. Don't argue with others about how they perceive the loss and don't be surprised at what you may consider to be an 'overreaction'.
- ✔ Expect and accept signs of grieving and acknowledge those losses openly and sympathetically.
- ✔ Define what is over and what isn't. People must make the break at some time and trying to cling on to old ways prolongs difficulties.
- ✔ Treat the past with respect. People have probably worked extremely hard in what may have been very difficult conditions. Recognize that and show that it is valued.
- ✔ Show how ending something ensures the things that matter to people are continued and improved.
- ✔ Give people information and do it again and again and again in a variety of ways. Give people written information to go away and read, as well as the opportunity to talk and ask questions.
- ✔ Use an internal stakeholder analysis to map out how best to approach different individuals – understand how their perspectives might need to be engaged to initiate the change and what the likely points of resistance might be.

- The neutral zone:
  - ✔ Recognize this as a difficult time that everyone goes through.
  - ✔ Get people involved and working together and give them time and space to experiment and test new ideas.
  - ✔ Help people to feel that they are still valued.
  - ✔ Particularly praise someone who had a good idea even if it didn't work as expected. The Plan-Do-Study-Act (PDSA) model encourages trying things out and learning from each cycle.
  - ✔ Give people information and do it again and again and again in a variety of ways.
  - ✔ Provide feedback about the results of the ideas being tested and decisions made.

- The new beginning:
  - ✔ Do not force a beginning before its time in the ethic of the individual.
  - ✔ Ensure people know what part they are to play in the new system.
  - ✔ Make sure that policies, procedure, and priorities are clear; do not send mixed messages.
  - ✔ Plan to celebrate the new beginning and give the credit to those who have made the change.
  - ✔ Give people information and do it again and again in a variety of ways.

If you think back to our various discussions of Facebook and the reactions of Facebookers to the various algorithmic scandals that have embraced the company from 2016 through to 2017, we can see the beginning of an ending in which individuals are struggling to understand what the problem is and what the destination needs to be for their new beginning.

Bridges is not the only one to point out some of the key reasons why change management initiatives often fail. In *Leading Change*, John P Kotter, one of the most respected researchers in the field of change management, outlines eight reasons why organizations fail to execute change (Kotter, 2012). These are particularly pertinent in the context of information and data management. The eight common mistakes provide perspective on issues that commonly arise in information management projects:

Error #1: allowing too much complacency

According to Kotter, the biggest mistake people make when trying to change organizations is plunging ahead without first establishing a high-enough sense of urgency among their peers and superiors. Kotter's analysis provides valuable pointers for change managers looking to avoid the errors of others.

Change agents often:

- overestimate their ability to force big changes on the organization;
- underestimate how difficult it can be to shift people out of their comfort zones;
- don't see how their actions and approach might reinforce the status quo by driving up defensiveness;
- rush in where angels fear to tread – kicking off change activities without sufficient communication of what change is required or why change is required (the vision);
- confuse urgency with anxiety, which in turn leads to fear and resistance as stakeholders retrench (often quite literally) in their silos.

While it is tempting to think that in the face of organizational crisis complacency would not be a problem, often the opposite is the case. Stakeholders often cling to the status quo in the face of too many (often conflicting) demands for change (which are often processed as 'if everything is important, then nothing is important'). Again, if we look at the response of Facebook staff to the criticisms of the company, they are faced with demands for change from a number of perspectives ('fake news', abuse of data privacy, potential competition-law issues in the EU and elsewhere). Therefore, there is a resistance to change.

Error #2: failing to create a sufficiently powerful 'guiding coalition'

Kotter identifies that change requires leadership commitment. Major change is almost impossible without active support from the head of the organization and without a coalition of other leaders coming together to guide the change. Leadership engagement is especially important in data governance efforts, as these require significant behavioural change. Without commitment from top leaders, short-term self-interest will outweigh the argument for the long-term benefits of better governance.

A 'guiding coalition' is a powerful and enthusiastic team of volunteers from across the organization that helps to put new strategies into effect and transform the organization.

Error #3: underestimating the power of vision

Urgency and a strong guiding team are useless without a clear, sensible vision of the change.

The vision provides the context of the change effort. It helps people understand the meaning of any individual component of the change. A well-defined and communicated vision can help drive the level of energy required to properly implement the change. Without a public statement of vision to guide decision making, every choice risks becoming a debate and any action could derail the change initiative or undermine it.

Vision is not the same thing as planning or programme management. The vision is not the project plan or project charter or a detailed breakdown of all the components of the change.

A vision must be a clear and compelling statement of where the change is leading

You need to have a clear and compelling vision. This is sometimes called the 'elevator pitch', but that is the wrong approach. Your vision needs to be sufficiently thought through that you can articulate the key next steps to get there and it needs to be compelling enough that people will: 1) want to go there with you; and 2) that some of them might want to take the lead through broad-based action.

The vision must also be communicable – capable of being shared, in an intact manner, by your co-workers in a way that engenders a positive and engaged response.

Communicating vision means connecting with people. For ethical information management initiatives, the vision must articulate the challenges with existing data management practices, the benefits of improvement, and the path to get to a better future state.

Error #4: undercommunicating the vision by a factor of 10, 100 or 1,000

Even if everyone agrees that the current situation is unsatisfactory, people will still not change unless they perceive the benefits of change as a significant improvement over the status quo. Consistent, effective communication of the vision, followed by action, is critical to successful change management. Kotter advises that communication comes in both words and deeds. Congruence between the two are critical for success, as 'Do as I say, not as I do' is the quickest way to kill a change effort. To an extent, the guiding coalition should assist with developing, communicating and refining the communication of the vision. It is important to measure how well the change vision is branded and communicated.

Error #5: permitting obstacles to block the vision

New initiatives fail when people feel disempowered by huge obstacles in their path, even when they fully embrace the need for and direction of the proposed change. As part of its transformation, the organization must identify:

- How roadblocks that exist in people's heads can be overcome (are they fear-based, stemming from lack of knowledge, or some other cause?).

- What roadblocks exist due to organizational structures – such as narrow job categories or performance appraisal systems – that force people to choose between the vision or their own self-interest?

- What roadblocks exist due to people who refuse to adapt to the new set of circumstances and who make demands that are inconsistent with the transformation? If key members of the organization make the right noises about the change vision but fail to alter their behaviours or reward the required behaviours, or continue to operate in incompatible ways, the execution of the vision will falter and could fail.

Kotter calls on 'smart people' in organizations to confront these obstacles. If they do not, others will feel disempowered and change will be undermined.

Error #6: failing to create short-term wins

Real change takes time. Anyone who has ever embarked on a fitness regime or a weight-loss plan knows that the secret to keeping going is to have regular milestone targets that keep up momentum and motivation. Anything that involves a long-term commitment and investment of effort and resources requires some element of early and regular feedback of success.

Complex change efforts require short-term goals in support of long-term objectives. Meeting these goals allows the team to celebrate and maintain momentum. The key thing is to *create* the short-term win rather than merely hoping for it. In successful transformations, managers actively establish early goals, achieve these goals and reward the team. Without systematic efforts to guarantee success, change is likely to fail.

Error #7: declaring victory too soon

All too often in change projects, particularly ones stretching over several years, there is a temptation to declare success at the first major performance improvement. Quick wins and early wins are powerful tools to keep up momentum and morale. However, any suggestion that the job is done is usually a mistake. Until the changes are embedded in the culture of the organization, new approaches are fragile and old habits and practices can reassert themselves. Kotter suggests that changing an entire company can take three to ten years.

Error # 8: neglecting to anchor changes firmly in the corporate culture

Until new behaviours are embedded into the social norms and shared values of an organization they are subject to decay and degradation as soon as the focus of the change effort is removed. This is the equivalent of Bridges' 'neutral zone'. Kotter is clear: you ignore culture at your peril when engaging in any change activity.

To combat these common errors, Kotter proposes an eight-step model for major change (Figure 11.1). Kotter's model provides a framework within which each of these issues can be addressed in a way that supports sustainable long-term change. Each step is associated with one of the fundamental errors that undermine transformation efforts.

The first four steps of the model soften entrenched status-quo positions. As Kotter says, this effort is only needed because change is not easy. The next three steps (steps 5 to 7) introduce new practices and ways of working. The last step locks the changes in place and provides the platform for future gains and improvement. Kotter advises that there is no shortcut in following these steps. While it might seem appropriate to focus on 'doing the change', you need to ensure a solid foundation for sustaining the change, hence the precursor steps are essential.

In the context of ethical information management, we suggest you approach this model for change as a continuous improvement process. As

Figure 11.1 Kotter's change model as a wheel

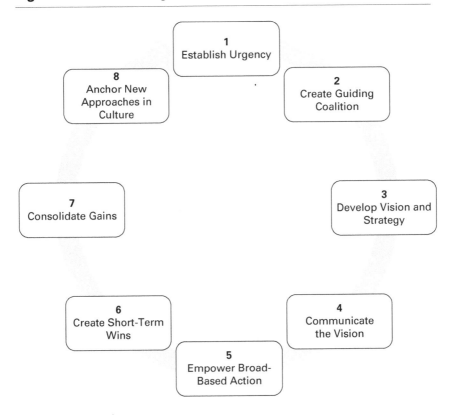

the organization develops its maturity in ethical information management, it is likely that the ethic of the organization will go through the same stages of moral evolution as the ethic of the individual. Therefore, constant management is needed to ensure that the gains you have attained are secured and sustained while at the same time ensuring that you are alert to changes in the ethic of society that might need you to further evolve your ethical information-management culture.

Culture and stories

As organizations grow and company cultures develop, as language is used, meanings of words change – and they generally change in different ways in different language-use communities. So, what do folklore and fairy tales have to do with ethics and information management? Scholars define 'folk' as 'any group of people who share one common factor' and have developed some common traditions (Bauman, 1971). Common factors could be anything from ethnicity, language, religion or occupation to a shared hobby. Members of a college or people who play World of Warcraft are a folk community by this definition. (In fact, folklore studies on World of Warcraft players have been published.) Folklore and folk narratives, the traditions we have and the stories we tell each other, are ways in which we communicate our identity, values and collective character with each other. This is still true in micro-cultures, like for instance company or organizational cultures.

Stories and storytelling are one of the most important ways we have to teach and share our culture. Think back to how you learnt some of your first lessons or explored some of your first questions about morals and ethics. Globally, cultures give different emphasis and prestige to the place of stories in their culture, whether they are seen as a part of 'non-essential' entertainment, as is often the case in the way contemporary US culture may deprioritize it, or as sacred, vital and essential to cultural identity, history and understanding of the universe, as in Indigenous Australian culture. In all cases, though, storytelling is universally a way in which our cultures and values are transmitted.

Before Katherine, co-author of this book, came to work at Castlebridge she taught children's literature to university students. The most popular text on the course syllabus was *Harry Potter and the Philosopher's Stone*, because the students were of an age that they grew up with Harry Potter. Revisiting the book for analysis as well as enjoyment was a revelation to them, as they now saw the techniques J K Rowling used in creating the story they loved so much. As young adults they could observe metaphors for fascism and prejudice, and parallels to real-world situations that they had not noticed as young children. But while they had not explicitly noticed the literary devices – the metaphors, parallels and archetypes that J K Rowling used in her fantasy series – the children who read the books had a framework to talk about the things they saw in their lives and as they got older and learnt to read a text with more sophistication. The stories they read had influenced them and taught them to consider moral and ethical questions, and to empathize with people not like them. What Katherine observed about her students in class has been the subject of studies. Researchers found that, in groups of different ages, reading *Harry Potter* resulted in measurable improvements in empathy and attitudes towards people of stigmatized 'out-groups' such as immigrants, refugees and LGBT people (although the effect was much less prominent in readers who identified with the character of Voldemort rather than Harry Potter). Discussions in the focus groups suggested that this influence came both from relating to the character of Harry, who befriends and defends various characters from fictional stigmatized groups, and also from identifying with the values of the protagonist and wanting to distance themselves from the values of the villain (Vezzali et al, 2015). Essentially, values are transmitted on multiple levels in the story.

The stories we know, their images and archetypes, give us concrete images to anchor abstract concepts and values. Storytelling can stretch our imaginative and empathetic powers, and we use it to frame possible ethical problems that we have not personally encountered in concrete ways. We can use extended metaphors to approach difficult issues in slightly different ways. Science-fiction authors have tangled with the implications of some of the questions we are now facing in reality. We have borrowed new concepts from these imaginary futures that examined the author's present. The word 'Robot' comes from a 1920 play by Czech writer Karel Capek, *R.U.R.* (Rossum's Universal Robots). Isaac Asimov took the ideas and possible threat of Capek's robot revolt and created hypothetical 'Laws of Robotics' that might prevent a 'robot' uprising. Now, even though we are not facing the question of a self-aware autonomous artificial being, we are facing immediate problems of what types of ethical or moral 'laws' we need to encode in our creations. This can be a powerful tool for shaping common understanding of what we envision of our values and standards.

Storytelling, Deming and Denning

Deming's 14 points for transformation, which we discussed in Chapter 8 (see Table 8.1 for a refresher on these principles), begin by advising organizations to adopt a 'new philosophy' and to ensure a 'constancy of purpose'. The adoption of a 'new philosophy' of ethical information management requires the organization to package and communicate specific messages about the ethical values and standards that are expected of individuals in the organization. What does the expected behaviour look like? How will we know we have achieved it?

Stephen Denning (2000, 2011) has identified a number of common narrative objectives or goals for culture change in an organization. In doing so, he suggests several different categories or types of story, each serving a distinct purpose (see Table 11.2). For example, a 'springboard story' is a narrative pattern used to spark action and gather support for broad-based action to achieve an objective. Another narrative pattern is the 'transmitting values' pattern, which often takes the form of a fable or a parable and includes details of desired behaviours in the ethic of the organization. Increasingly, change managers are turning to old established and well-trodden principles

Table 11.2 Denning's narrative patterns and the ethical context

Your Objective	Key Element of Story	Relevance to Ethics Change
To spark action	Describe how successful change was implemented in the past, but allow audience to apply it	Necessary to engage thoughts of colleagues on the nature of the ethical problem. Set a vision of how this change, or a similar one, was implemented in the past or by others
Communicating who you are	Provide some audience-engaging drama and reveal a strength or vulnerability from your past (objective is to build rapport)	Necessary if you are seeking to engage people in the ethical vision. Also useful to communicate your ethic of the individual
Transmitting values	The story must feel familiar to the audience and prompt discussion about the issues raised by the value being promoted	Essential for supporting the ethic of society, ethic of the individual, and ethic of the organization. Historically, fairy tales have been crafted to serve this purpose
Communicating organization brand	The story is usually told by the product or service, through customer word of mouth or a credible third party	Establishes the ethic of the organization. How are you perceived by your customers and stakeholders? What is the story that is being told about you?
Fostering collaboration	Movingly recounts a situation that listeners have also experienced and prompts sharing of their own stories	This is a useful narrative type when you want to get a group to collaborate to define new shared values
Taming grapevine	Highlights an aspect of a rumour, often with humour, that reveals it to be untrue or unreasonable	Essential to the alignment of the ethic of the organization with the ethic of society and to tame rogue ethic of individual influences that might arise. A critical element of change management, particularly during the transition phase of change

(*continued*)

Table 11.2 (*Continued*)

Your Objective	Key Element of Story	Relevance to Ethics Change
Sharing knowledge	Focuses on problems and shows, in some detail, how they were corrected, with an explanation of why the solution worked	Useful for sharing the outputs of projects, the lessons learnt on Ethical Impact Assessments, etc. Also useful for finding existing approaches that can be repurposed to reduce the risk of rejection by the organizational immune system
Leading people into the future	Evokes the future you want to create without providing excessive details that will only turn out to be wrong	Essential to the establishment of the new ethical culture in the organization. Needs to be matched with appropriate conduct and alignment of governance and rewards in the organization or it will fall flat

and practices of storytelling to communicate the meaning, objective and vision for changes to the ethic of the organization.

When using stories and narrative in this way, it is important that you understand the fundamentals of crafting your narrative. To engender a broad-based action, your story will need to be communicable, relatable and, above all else, true to the vision you have for the future ethic of the organization and how it will align with the ethic of society.

What is your quest?

Your vision of the change you are trying to make is your quest, and it is the quest you want your colleagues and co-workers to join you on. Therefore, you need to make it compelling for them. Within the narratives you craft you also need to ensure that there is an objective, a mission or a goal. Otherwise there is little to retain peoples' attention.

It is important to keep your goal or 'happy ending' in mind, and craft your story to fit your message. Consider the type of story you are telling, whether it is a comedy or tragedy (both work to engage and keep peoples' interest), and whether you are showing lessons learnt or setting out a description of the ethical values you want the organization to begin to adopt.

Think about your favourite fairy tale (or the Disney reimagining of it). What was the moral of the tale? What was the lesson about ethics or values that the protagonists had to learn?

What is the plot?

When you craft your story, keep in mind that a story needs a structured plot. Plot is not just a sequence of events, it is cause and effect. Look for the actions and events that cause something else to happen. Other sequences of events in a story can add colour and depth, but to control the narrative you need to know the plot. At the most basic, this means your story should have a beginning, middle and end. Aristotle identified this requirement for structure in the context of ancient Greek tragedies, requiring what he called 'unity' of action. Gustav Freytag (1970) broke down further this beginning, middle and end into a focus on how you use and maintain tension in a plot. You can visualize this as a pyramid, or a mountain structure, as shown in Figure 11.2.

The plot of a story, whether a simple tale or a novel, begins with **Exposition,** which sets your scene. This can be as simple as 'Once upon a time in a kingdom...' or far more detailed and elaborate, but it anchors your story. The action of the plot begins with an **Inciting Incident,** which begins the action or sets up a conflict that drives the tension of the story and makes people care what happens. The action continues and tension rises with the

Figure 11.2 Freytag's pyramid

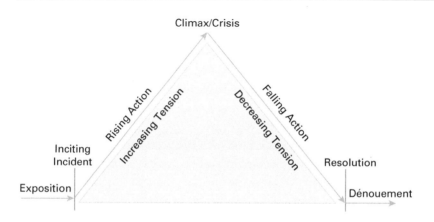

Rising Action, leading to the **Climax** of the story, which Freytag saw as the point of greatest tension. Your climax may be a crisis or a decision point. The events resulting from the action taken at the Climax are the **Falling Action**, which ends in a **Resolution** of the conflict or action, bringing the story to a close. Finally, the story concludes in a *Dénouement*, which ties up any loose ends or engages with the overall thematic questions or future possibilities of the story (Freytag, 1970).

There are different possible structures to your plot, but to keep a tight focus you should make sure that events you relate happen as a result of actions you describe. You can think of this as setting up a domino effect. If a movement or action does not cause something else to happen, your story can stall somewhere around the middle, and the result or resolution may be less convincing. A plot is not 'this happened, and then that happened, and then this happened', but 'This happened, which caused that, and as a result this happened.'

Character and relatability

Character is another essential element of a story. Who is your protagonist? This should be a person, or people, not an abstract concept like an organization. Figure out who you want your listeners to relate to, what qualities they have, and how you want people to make a connection to that character. Whether you are telling a personal story about something you learnt, or how your experiences influenced you, or telling the story of how a problem got solved or the effects of a change on stakeholders, the characters in the story are essential to getting your listeners to connect with your story.

In many cases, oral storytelling will not provide the luxury of creating fully fleshed characters with internal motivations, or an in-depth psychological portrait. In that case, draw your characters with broad brushstrokes and use archetypes. Some incredibly popular and enduring characters in literature are not particularly developed, full fleshed or three dimensional. Creating relatable characters often involves working with convention and recognizable archetypes as a type of shorthand. While these types of characters may lack in-depth verisimilitude and full psychological realism, we as audiences respond to them, either because we are culturally attuned to the pattern of story type or motif they feature in (David and Goliath), or because we all know that one person. Cartoonists such as Scott Adams use broadly drawn stock-character archetypes for comedic effect, and it works because people recognize that type of character in their experience of the quirks of corporate life.

However, the use of archetypes can run into the danger of stereotyping. To avoid this, you need to consider the balance necessary for the story you are crafting. When you use types or stock characters, you work with patterns and cultural expectations external to your story. You may play on these expectations as assumptions that need to be confronted, or work with them to reduce barriers to acceptance or engagement.

Using fairy tales and techniques from folklore and oral traditions

Storytelling is a universal in human cultures. As humans, we have always told stories. However, in contemporary Western cultures with a strong emphasis on text-based communication and literacy, we have de-emphasized the art of oral storytelling. It is a very different skill set to being able to write a compelling novel or craft a solid grant proposal. When you tell a story, you are engaging in an act of performance and connecting with your listeners. These kinds of stories all have certain things in common that are different from more modern entertainment. When you tell a story, you are taking part in a centuries-old tradition that has developed certain techniques. Storytelling tradition is both linked to and separate from the literary tradition. It is a different skill set. The reason we have emphasized the difference between 'folk tales' and 'fairy tales' here, is that there will be a difference in the folklore and stories current in your organizational culture and the 'fairy tales' that you may want to adapt from them to help guide the values. Oral storytelling is not fixed, and the storyteller crafts their performance in a way that is sensitive to the response of their audience. When you tell a story to people, you need to consider this difference. Unlike other narrative entertainments you may be more familiar with such as literature (or fairy tales), TV, movies or playing videogames, the storyteller directly engages with their listeners. Your listeners are, in a sense, part of your story as you create it. You have the ability to adapt your story as you tell it, paying attention to the reactions and interest of your listeners. There are several techniques you will often find in oral storytelling traditions that you can add to your toolkit:

1 Keep it simple. Don't give too much detail

One difficulty you will probably have in crafting your story is remembering not to give all the granular data you have to prove your argument. Think about fairy tales here. The time setting for a fairy tale is 'Once upon a time' – not 'It is this day 348 years, 6 months and 19 days since the good people of Paris were awakened by a grand peal from all the bells in the three districts of the city.' There's a reason for that. As with the difference between an elevator pitch and a fully fleshed roadmap, what may be wonderful exposition for a realist novel simply does not work when telling a story face-to-face. When you have all the data to create the granular detail to give the depth of a realist novel, it may be tempting to put it in. But in most cases, less is more. Have the data to back up your story, but don't feel the need to put it all into your narrative. Think about the wall of text, for example, in a bad PowerPoint presentation.

2 If you can, anchor your narrative with a strong image or metaphor
Stories, images and archetypes give us concrete images to anchor abstract concepts and values. Among other things, this also aids memory and increases accuracy in transmission of knowledge. In a low-literacy society, this was incredibly important. Plato in teaching his philosophies often used a nearly dramatic form of dialogues that told stories of people having conversations with each other. But his most famous and memorable teachings are his 'Trial of Socrates', and his 'Allegory of the Cave', which uses a strong image as an extended metaphor.

In Christian traditions, teachings are similarly transmitted through stories, whether narratives of the lives of various important figures or through Jesus' own parables. Many of these stories have impact far beyond religious practice and have entered the cultural shorthand of cultural references and archetypes.

3 Repetition and the 'rule of three'
If you listen to a compelling public speaker, you will probably notice that they use patterns of three quite often. In oratory, this can be traced at least back to Cicero. It is a cadence of speech and pattern that we respond to at a subconscious and symbolic level. Three is a number just large enough to build a pattern of repetition and to break that pattern for effect. It is often very culturally significant as well: 'The third time is the charm.' We expect things to come in threes, and fulfilling that pattern is often deeply satisfying.

One usage of the repetition of threes that you will often come across in fairy tales is that of two failures and a success. This may be the third (and youngest) son who succeeds where his brothers failed, or the 'Three Little Pigs', the 'Three Billy Goats Gruff', 'Goldilocks and the Three Bears'. If you are familiar with these stories you may have noticed that a lot of them have 'bad path' and 'good path' stories built into them. This technique can be used to show 'what went wrong' and 'how we fixed it', or it can illustrate the importance of proper governance.

Listen to the stories people are telling and use them to help set the tone

Fairy tales are a very interesting form of storytelling that we have used for centuries to transmit values. What we know of as 'fairy tales' are mostly a hybrid literary form. They are written short stories crafted by an artist that use and adapt the oral folktales of a culture (Zipes, 2000). While they are crafted as fixed texts for publication, they tend to keep or emulate some characteristics of folklore and oral culture. Many fairy tales borrow plot and narrative from folk stories that have been told for centuries, transmitted orally down through generations of cultures throughout the world. These stories have such staying power that the earliest recorded variants of the basic story we popularly know by the name 'Cinderella' are described by the Greek historian Strabo in the first century BCE as 'Rhodopis', and published in ninth century China as '叶限' ('Yè Xiàn'). If you look at the different versions of this basic story motif, told through many cultures over centuries, you will find that the different versions reflect the values of the cultures they are told in and are also used to try to teach those values. Each recorded version of a folk tale will have the unique interpretation of the person who recorded or edited it as well. What you see in fairy tales is a mix of 'top-down' and 'bottom-up' transmission of culture and values. From Strabo to the authors of the Contes des Fées of the French salons, to the Grimm Brothers to Disney, the authors of fairy tales took the stories they heard from the tellers of tales in the oral tradition, recorded them and, in so doing, edited and shaped them to fit their values.

This hybrid of top-down and bottom-up in creating stories is a useful consideration for organizational culture change. To get value out of storytelling in an organizational setting and for culture change, make use of both aspects. To use storytelling as a tool for leadership and to guide the values of the organization, you will be making use of stories as a tool to help set the tone from the top – to create and shape a vision, or goal, to communicate a sense of common identity or values, or for other specific purposes. However, setting the tone from the top will not succeed if it does not resonate with the stories being told from the bottom up. Communities of data professionals are a folk community. Your more immediate work community is another folk community with its own set of shared factors. Your organization will have its culture and stories already, and if your story is at odds with organizational culture it will be much more difficult to use your stories to generate change. Listen for those folk narratives. You often have one or a few unofficial keeper(s) of knowledge of the company culture, who know the stories of the organization. These stories are valuable. They will tell you a great deal about the values of the organization as understood by the people facing the day-to-day problems. These stories can help tell you where the pain points are and what pitfalls to avoid.

The stories being told from the 'bottom up' will help you to understand the ethic of the organization as *is*, which may be very different from the ethic of the organization as envisioned. Your goal in generating cultural change is to close the gap between these two, and to present a compelling story that gets people to respond to the vision of the ethic of the organization as *envisioned*. You will need to be aware of how large the gap is, and how compelling any competing narratives might be.

Does it ring true? Is your story consistent with reality?

The stories told from the bottom up will tell you about what people in your organization perceive to be true about your organization. When you tell a story, you create a narrative model of reality. Like any data model, it needs to clearly describe a structure that works and that fits the requirements of the organization and takes into account constraints. Your story needs to work. You need to be able to take into account different levels of abstraction, and the level at which you are telling your story. You do not necessarily need to include all the data, but your story must be *true*.

Your story needs to take into account the needs of the organization. But above all, it must be true and consistent with reality. A true story is not just a story that lacks inaccuracies. You can mislead using facts and statistics, just as well as you can tell the truth using fiction. People may not immediately detect the lack of consistency with reality or a greater context, but perceived deception will result in a loss of trust. Even subtle misinformation in factual headlines can have ongoing effects. Researchers have studied the effects of misleading newspaper headlines. Even when misconceptions are corrected by correct representation in the full article, this can still lead to 'misperceptions and misinformed behavioral intentions' (Ecker et al, 2014). The recognized tendency for many newspapers to use misleading headlines has directly impacted people's willingness to trust the Fourth Estate, and this lack of trust has been weaponized with a direct impact on society. If you tell factually correct stories that go against a greater emotional truth or the spirit of ethical engagement, you risk losing trust and engagement. It is the equivalent of a process that while technically compliant violates the ethical outcome characteristic of verity/non-deceptiveness.

It is important to remember, though, that while these culturally transmitted ideas have power and help shape our understanding of things, they can also result in misunderstanding of reality. In our fiction we create models of the world in varying relations to reality. In doing so, we create assumptions about the world, about humanity, and consequences of actions. These can be wonderful tools for teaching, and incredibly useful tools for teasing out complexities of ethical issues and their possible impacts. But no fiction or model can completely match the complexity of reality, and our models will also carry with them assumptions and blind spots.

Tell me a story...

When we are teaching courses to prospective data protection officers, our advanced class ends with an activity where we ask the learners to tell us the story of why data privacy is important. First they have to tell us why it is important to them personally and then they have to tell us the story of why it is important to the organization. When teaching classes on information ethics, we sometimes do the same.

Daragh's go-to story about why he became interested in and passionate about information quality and the ethics of information is simple. There are approximately 11 different ways to spell the name Daragh. In most languages it appears as a gender-neutral name. So, having spent his childhood getting upset because people did not spell his name right, or thought he was a girl, Daragh understood the power of poor data management to impact on human dignity. While this is a somewhat light-hearted introduction to the topic, it opens up discussions with the learners on our courses. What is your 'story of you' that you might tell people to get them interested in the issues of ethical information management?

Of course, a personal story can be a powerful trigger. Equally powerful can be stories about ethical failings in organizations, arising from poor information management, or poor information management that arises from ethical failures. It pays to look behind the news stories to find parables that you can use to tell cautionary tales, or to highlight how ethical information management is not an impossible goal for organizations. Throughout this book we have given examples from news stories that are topical at the time of writing. Your homework is to gather your own stories and see where in them you can find either the example of a strong ethical or information management principle or practice, or the red flag indicating a failure of ethics or information management practices.

The value proposition for ethical information management?

It is difficult to put the value of ethics on the bottom line. How your organization's brand is perceived by society is usually reflected in your balance sheet by accountants as an intangible asset – goodwill. The perception of your organization's ethical position can be linked to this class of intangible asset. Indeed, many of the business-case benefits for doing ethical management of any kind are often attributed to other processes or factors in the organization. But, once upon a time, there was a man who thought very deeply about the importance of quality and ethics in his organization. He was a pioneer in the field of quality management and was a highly respected visionary in his own country and his own industry. When thinking about the role of ethics in quality management, Kaoru Ishikawa (1985) wrote: 'In management, the first concern of the company is the happiness of people who are connected with it. If the people do not feel happy and cannot be made happy, that company does not deserve to exist.'

That is the value proposition for handling information in an ethical and respectful manner.

Chapter summary

In this chapter we introduced some fundamental concepts in change management and also of storytelling. While Plato may have warned of the rise of writing as the end of knowledge in the story we shared back in Chapter 1, the irony is that the spoken word – and crafted narrative – remains one of the most important, and effective, tools of organization change.

You learnt about:

- Common causes for failure in change management.
- Approaches to addressing failure in change management.
- The differences between change management and 'transition management'.
- The importance of managing the change in a planned and co-ordinated manner.

- The use of fairy tales and stories through the ages to impact knowledge, values and ethics.
- The importance of a clear, compelling and, above all, **communicable** vision for your ethical information management change.

Questions

1 What are some errors in culture change management that you have observed in your organization?

2 What stories have deeply influenced your values or the way you frame or think about things? Can you think of stories that you have used to understand the world or people's actions?

3 Consider a change in behaviour or an action that you want to convince people in your organization to undertake. What kind of story would be appropriate to influence that change?

Further reading

Bridges, W (2009) *Managing Transitions: Making the most of change*, 3rd edn, Nicholas Brealey Publishing, London

Denning, S (2011) *The Leader's Guide to Storytelling: Mastering the art and discipline of business narrative*, Jossey-Bass, San Francisco, CA

Kearney, R (2009) *On Stories*, Routledge, London

Kohn, A (1995) *Punished by Rewards: The trouble with gold stars, incentive plans, A's, praise and other bribes*, Houghton Mifflin, Boston

Kotter, JP (2012) *Leading Change*, Harvard Business Review Press, Boston

Saunders, G and Lockridge, TM (2010) Ethics and culture: is there a relationship?, *The International Business & Economics Research Journal*, **9** (1), p 111

Senge, P (2006) *The Fifth Discipline: The art and practice of the learning organization*, 2nd edn, Random House, London

Travis, M (2016) Teaching professional ethics through popular culture, *The Law Teacher*, **50**, pp 147–59

References

Aristotle (2016) *Poetics*, WW Norton, London

Bauman, R (1971) Differential identity and the social base of folklore, *The Journal of American Folklore*, 84 (331), pp 31–41

Bennison, G (1971) Repetition in oral literature, *The Journal of American Folklore*, 84 (333), pp 289–303

Bridges, W (2009) *Managing Transitions: Making the most of change*, 3rd edn, Nicholas Brealey, London

Denning, S (2000) *The Springboard: How storytelling ignites action in knowledge-era organizations*, KMCI Press, Boston

Denning, S (2011) *The Leader's Guide to Storytelling: Mastering the art and discipline of business narrative*, Jossey-Bass, San Francisco, CA

Ecker, UKH, Lewandowsky, S, Chang, EP and Pillai, R (2014) The effects of subtle misinformation in news headlines, *Journal of Experimental Psychology: Applied*, 20 (4), pp 323–35

Freytag, G (1970) *Technique of the Drama: An exposition of dramatic composition and art*, Scholarly Press, Michigan

Ishikawa, K (1985) *What is Total Quality Control? The Japanese Way*, Prentice-Hall, New Jersey

Kotter, JP (2012) *Leading Change*, Harvard Business Review Press, Boston, MA

Ong, W (1982) *Orality and Literacy: The technologizing of the word*, Methuen, London

Senge, P (1990) *The Fifth Discipline*, Doubleday, New York

Vezzali, L, Stathi, S, Giovannini, D, Capozza, D and Trifiletti, E (2015) The greatest magic of Harry Potter: reducing prejudice, *Journal of Applied Social Psychology*, 45, pp 105–21

Zachman, JA (1996) [accessed 5 August 2017] Enterprise Architecture: The Issue of the Century [Online] https://enterprisearchitecture.dk/links/files/EA_The_Issue_of_the_Century.pdf

Zachman, JA (2016) [accessed 5 August 2017] The Issue is THE ENTERPRISE [Online] https://www.zachman.com/resources/zblog/item/the-issue-is-the-enterprise

Zipes, J, ed. (2000) Introduction: towards the definition of the literary fairy tale, *The Oxford Companion to Fairy Tales*, Oxford University Press, Oxford

And in conclusion...

Technology and information have always been ethically neutral, and ethical questions and challenges about the use of new technologies have been with us since time immemorial. However, never before in human history have we faced a technological capability to capture and process information at such a scale, which creates challenges for us in identifying and addressing ethical issues in a timely manner so that impacts on people can be avoided or mitigated.

At a macro level, 2017 has seen a litany of issues come to the mainstream about how data is being processed by social media companies, and there is a growing concern about the potential impacts on people of the privacy-infringing technologies that have been developed to catalogue and index the minutiae of our daily lives. But on the other hand, the same core technologies can be applied in different ways and deliver benefit to people and society through the delivery of capabilities such as crop management, as we discussed in the Introduction to this book.

Elsewhere, organizations are facing potential brand impacts and regulatory penalties over their use of data. Global data privacy legislation is accelerating, and more countries are formally recognizing a right to privacy that their legal systems will uphold in response to unethical practices by companies or unforeseen unethical outcomes from government projects.

Data ethics is increasingly seen as a basis for competitive advantage by organizations and by consumers alike. This is happening to the extent that we are beginning to see companies 'ethics washing' their practices by making public pronouncements on ethics that may not always be met by internal capability, rigour or desire to do so. However, there is still (to our view) a dearth of training or education for the information management workforce on the fundamentals of ethics and how to put ethical principles into practice in your organization.

What is a data geek to do?

We have been here before, and we will be here again. Rather than considering data ethics to be a radically new concept, you need to learn the lessons of the data-quality and data-governance communities. There are fundamental concepts and principles that we can apply to framing and addressing these problems, in the same way as information quality stood on the shoulders of manufacturing quality, and data governance stands on the shoulders of frameworks and practices for governing other asset classes in the organization, you need to understand ethical concepts and principles and understand how to translate them into actionable values and operative models in your organization.

This book was conceived and written with a view to helping you to do that. Ethical enterprise information management will not happen by accident but must be designed into the organization structures. Unless you have defined mechanisms to ensure the ethic of your organization can be aligned with a potentially changing ethic of society, your organization will be left behind as the expectation of society changes in response to the identified problems in analytics, big data and AI.

With great power comes great responsibility. It is time to adopt a new philosophy!

CASE STUDY Telia

While not directly related to the issues of ethical information management, this case study from Swedish telecommunications company Telia highlights, in relation to their overall ethical management of human rights issues, the value of rigorous and structured assessments of ethical impacts in the organization.

Between 2011 and 2013, the Swedish mobile telecommunications company faced crisis and scandal with accusations of corruption and accepting bribery in Uzbekistan, and of tacitly facilitating human-rights abuses in countries with totalitarian regimes where Telia subsidiaries had a major telecommunications presence. In tandem with government-led investigations, Telia commissioned an independent investigation into their own practices and committed to transparency with the results. The independent investigation called out a lack of risk mitigations and controls to ensure that corruption and bribery had not taken place.

Their business need and approach was to ensure that the organization and its suppliers were not engaged in unethical business practices in the countries that they operated in. Their approach was to conduct an independent review and to commit to transparency. This was a clear statement of a set of core ethical principles.

In the aftermath, the CEO resigned and the board was substantially replaced and a new chair appointed. Further investigation taken under the new CEO revealed 'a pattern of unethical, possibly unlawful business transactions' (Holmberg, Ahlberg and Romberg, 2017) and, as a result, several high-level leaders were replaced. Since then, Telia has taken major steps to improve corporate and social responsibility, transparency and ethical conduct group-wide, including instituting a new Chief Ethics and Compliance Officer, communicating clear codes for conduct, and implementing Human Rights Impact Assessments (HRIAs).

This highlights the implementation of improvement plans (changes to processes, procedures and governance) and the remediation of legacy issues (the replacement of staff who had failed to execute their roles in line with ethical standards). This is not possible without a robust analysis of the root causes and a clearly defined remediation plan. Without a rigorous analysis of their ethical environment and the root causes of their historic ethical failures, Telia might simply have dismissed staff and declared 'mission accomplished' without addressing the underlying root causes arising from a lack of appropriate governance structures. This echoes the importance of situational modifiers, which we discussed in Chapter 9 in our examination of data governance as a tool for ethical information management.

In 2013, Telia commissioned the Danish Institute for Human Rights to conduct a group-wide HRIA based on the UN Guiding Principles on Business and Human Rights, and has been conducting country-specific HRIAs with the non-profit organization Business for Social Responsibility (BSR).

This approach by Telia highlights the importance of a holistic, standards-based approach and the importance of considering the entire ethical environment or information environment to ensure that there is the appropriate identification of all ethical risks. This allowed Telia to conduct a transparent and benchmarked ethical quality assessment, which informed decisions on root causes and remediation. Telia did not simply refer the matter to legal, in the same way as ethical information management should not be a simple tick-box compliance activity.

Telia instituted an ethics and compliance model based on '10 cornerstones' with a strong focus on 'tone from the top' (Holmberg, Ahlberg and Romberg, 2017) and instituting preventative, detective and remediating controls, with a strong emphasis on risk mitigation, governance, culture change and communication. The model adopted by Telia is strongly grounded in the quality-control concepts we discussed earlier in this book. Creating consistency of purpose has been a large part of ensuring a group-wide culture that was part of the root-cause analysis.

The root-cause analysis in Telia identified problems in 'tone from the top' about ethical behaviours, and identified the need for appropriate governance controls and culture change, led from the senior management team down. This is consistent with what we have discussed about best practices in data governance in Chapter 5 and Chapter 9 and the importance of 'tone at the top' that we discussed at the beginning of this book.

In 2015, Telia decided to reduce its presence in Azerbaijan, Georgia, Kazakhstan, Moldova, Tajikistan and Uzbekistan and commissioned BSR to conduct an HRIA on its divestment plans. This indicates that Telia has recognized the importance of congruence in action on ethical issues and has also recognized the value of a repeatable process for Ethical Impact Assessments.

Telia and BSR have reported a number of lessons learnt from the HRIAs that they conducted. The results of the HRIAs gave leaders in Telia insight into significant issues, with useful and real information to base their decisions on. They found that increased transparency regarding their approach to freedom of expression and privacy resulted not just in greater understanding and trust in the organization, but in useful tools for human-rights advocates. They found a very strong link between ethics and human rights, with the most vulnerable populations often the victims of the outcomes of ethics or human-rights violations (Business for Social Responsibility, 2017). The results of the impact assessments materially benefited both the organization internally and the society externally.

This maps very closely to the concepts of the ethic of the organization and the ethic of society that we have discussed throughout this book. Telia was addressing the macro issues of business ethics. However, at the level of information management strategy and execution the same focus on fact-based decision making – based on an assessment of the social attitudes to proposed processing and with clearly defined and implemented governance and feedback mechanisms to ensure alignment between the ethic of society and the ethic of the organization – is at the heart of the E2IM framework and the assessment methodology outlined in this chapter.

In conducting their HRIAs, Telia and BSR learnt that it was necessary to understand the specific contexts of the organization internally, and the external contexts of the industry specifically, and of the cultures and societies the organization interacted with. This reflects the importance of continued attention to the alignment of the ethic of society and the ethic of the organization. It echoes our discussion of the motivation and location verticals in the Zachman framework set out in Chapter 6.

The telecommunications industry has its own unique ethical challenges and industry-specific questions. In conducting any Ethical Impact Assessment in the context of telecoms, it will be necessary to consider the ethics-related impacts of the internet of things, locational data processing, freedom of expression and privacy (Business for Social Responsibility, 2017).

For the Eurasian divestment HRIA, BSR and Telia had the following main focuses:

- Minimization of human-rights risks from the announced divestment.
- What to look for in potential buyers to minimize risk to human rights.
- What to do during the sale to help the future buyer act with respect for human rights.

Some of the human rights they focused on were: privacy, freedom of expression, security, non-discrimination, labour rights, children's rights and land rights. Telia implemented results of the HRIA for the Eurasia region as part of due diligence of potential buyers, and has shared their HRIAs with buyers. Ongoing implementation of recommendations and progress is being tracked (Telia, 2017).

While not yet a definitive practice, we would expect to see similar approaches to ethical information management assessments for suppliers or potential acquirers of businesses in the future as part of standard due diligence. This is particularly the case in light of the focus on accountability for information-related outcomes that is a cornerstone of legislation such as the EU's General Data Protection Regulation. Organizations that prepare now will have a potentially significant competitive advantage in years to come.

Case study questions

1 What parallels can you draw from Telia's reaction to ethical issues in their business with the recent resignations or sackings of senior executives in companies arising from data security breaches? What are the key differences? What does that suggest about the ethical information management cultures in those organizations?

2 Telia's remediation of their organizational ethical challenges required changes in governance. From what you have read about data governance and the E2IM framework approach in this book, what changes do you think your organization needs to make to meet the challenge of the Ethical Information Age?

References

BSR (Business for Social Responsibility) (2017) [accessed 20 October 2017] Case Study: Telia Company: Human Rights Impact Assessments [Online] https://bsr.org/en/our-insights/case-study-view/telia-company-human-rights-impact-assessments

Holmberg, I, Ahlberg, M and Romberg, A (2017) [accessed 22 October 2017] Telia Company – Paving the Way for Responsible Business [Online] https://www.hhs.se/contentassets/6932d66acb534542aa0f4acc48fe83f3/rt-telia-final-october-9-2017.pdf

Telia (2017) [accessed 20 October 2017] Human Rights Impact Assessment – Telia Sweden [Online] http://www.teliacompany.com/globalassets/telia-company/documents/sustainability/hria/human-rights-impact-assessment-telia-sweden.pdf

INDEX

Note: Acronyms are filed as presented; numbers within headings and 'Mc' are filed as spelt out. Page locators in *italics* denote information contained within a Figure or Table.

Lightning Source UK Ltd.
Milton Keynes UK
UKHW050335230222
399050UK00002B/8